Accounting Techni

CW00410504

INTERMEDIATE STAGE
NVQ/SVQ 3

Unit 7

Preparing Reports and Returns

TEXTBOOK

FOULKS LYNCH
PUBLICATIONS

British Library Cataloguing-in-Publication Data

A catalogue record for this book is available from the British Library.

Published by:

Foulks Lynch Ltd
4, The Griffin Centre
Staines Road
Feltham
Middlesex
TW14 0HS

ISBN 0 7483 5950 8

© Foulks Lynch Ltd, 2003

Printed and bound in Great Britain.

Acknowledgements

We are grateful to the Association of Accounting Technicians for permission to reproduce extracts from the Standards of Competence for Accounting.

CONTENTS

FOULKS LYNCH
PUBLICATIONS

INTRODUCTION

This is the new edition of the AAT NVQ Textbook for Unit 7 – *Preparing Reports and Returns*.

Tailored to the new Standards of Competence, this Textbook has been written specifically for AAT students in a clear and comprehensive style.

This book takes a very practical approach, with the inclusion of numerous examples and activities to help you practise what you have learnt. Self test questions and key terms at the end of each chapter reinforce your knowledge.

STANDARDS OF COMPETENCE

A unit of competence (for example, Unit 7 *Preparing Reports and Returns*) is made up of **elements** which contain all the essential information to define the standard and how it can be achieved. These elements consist of **performance criteria**, **range statements** and **knowledge and understanding**.

Performance criteria: These are the tasks you need to do to complete each element.

Range statements: These are the methods to use to complete the performance criteria.

Knowledge and understanding: These statements are the underpinning requirements to be able to complete the tasks.

Listed below are the elements, performance criteria, knowledge and understanding and range statements. These have been referenced to the chapters in the book where they are covered.

Unit 7:   Preparing Reports and Returns

Unit commentary

This unit relates to the preparation of reports and returns from information obtained from all relevant sources. The candidate is required to calculate ratios and performance indicators and present the information according to the appropriate conventions and definitions to either management or outside agencies, including the VAT office. The unit is also concerned with the communication responsibilities of the candidate which include obtaining authorisation before despatching reports, seeking guidance from the VAT Office and presenting reports and returns in the appropriate manner.

Elements contained within this unit are:

Element 7.1   Prepare and present periodic performance reports

Element 7.2   Prepare reports and returns for outside agencies

Element 7.3   Prepare VAT returns

Knowledge and understanding

To perform this unit effectively you will need to know and understand:

	The business environment	*Chapter*
1	Main sources of relevant government statistics (Elements 7.1 & 7.2)	1
2	Awareness of relevant performance and quality measures (Element 7.1)	1, 10
3	Main types of outside organisations requiring reports and returns: regulatory; grant awarding; information collecting; trade associations (Element 7.2)	1, 10
4	Basic law and practice relating to all issues covered in the range statement and referred to in the performance criteria. Specific issues include: the classification of types of supply; registration requirements; the form of VAT invoices; tax points (Element 7.3)	11, 12
5	Sources of information on VAT: Customs and Excise Guide (Element 7.3)	11
6	Administration of VAT: enforcement (Element 7.3)	12
7	Special schemes: annual accounting; cash accounting; bad debt relief (Element 7.3)	14

Accounting techniques

The organisation

Element 7.1 Prepare and present periodic performance reports

Performance criteria

Range statement

Performance in this element relates to the following contexts:

Information:

Ratios:

Performance indicators:

Methods of presenting information:

Element 7.2 Prepare reports and returns for outside agencies

Performance criteria

In order to perform this element successfully you need to:

Range statement

Ratios

Reports and returns

Element 7.3 Prepare VAT returns

Performance criteria

In order to perform this element successfully you need to:

Range statement

Recording systems:

Inputs and outputs:

ASSESSMENT

Unit 7 is assessed by means of **Skills Testing.**

Skills testing when your approved assessment centre (AAC) is a workplace

You may be observed carrying out your accounting activities as part of your normal work routine. You need to collect documentary evidence of the work you have done in an accounting portfolio.

Skills testing when your AAC is a college

This will use a combination of:

- documentary evidence of activities carried out at work, collected in a portfolio
- realistic simulations of workplace activities
- projects and assignments.

Skills testing when you don't work in accountancy

Don't worry – you can prove your competence using one of AAT's simulations, or from case studies, projects and assignments.

Portfolio building

Your portfolio is where you will keep all of your **evidence** to show your competence. It should contain different types of evidence from a range of sources.

Rules of evidence

Evidence must be:

- Valid – clearly related to the standards being assessed
- Authentic – must be your own work
- Current – make sure it is as recent as possible
- Sufficient – all performance criteria need to be met

Sources of evidence

- Prior achievement
- Performance in the workplace
- Performance in specially set activities
- Questioning: oral, written or by computer

Portfolio contents

For Unit 7, ensure your portfolio contains the following:

- Title page (your name, contact details and what you are studying)

- Your CV

- Information about your organisation (name and address, type of business, staff numbers, organisation chart if you have one)

- Job description

- Summary of your previous and current work experience (if appropriate)

- Witness statements from supervisors at work listing performance criteria and details of the job undertaken (these need to be on headed paper, be signed by your supervisor and have their job title on it)

- Manual and computerised evidence of preparing and processing documents, posting entries, making adjustments, balancing, calculating, analysing information etc.

- Evidence that you possess the underpinning knowledge and understanding (this could be written answers to questions set in class or a statement from your tutor outlining the oral questioning you received)

- Any simulations and classroom work set that covers some of the performance criteria or knowledge and understanding.

- Evidence grid (from the AAT's student record)

- Index to evidence

Chapter 1

SOURCES OF INFORMATION FOR REPORTS AND RETURNS

The purpose of this chapter is to discuss the need for reports and returns, and look at the sources from which data or information can be obtained for producing reports and returns.

CONTENTS

1   The nature of reports and returns

2   Outside organisations asking for information

3   Internal reporting

4   Sources of relevant government statistics

KNOWLEDGE AND UNDERSTANDING

		Reference
1	Main sources of relevant government statistics	Item 1
2	Relevant performance and quality measures	Item 2
3	Main types of outside organisations requiring reports and returns: regulatory; grant awarding; information collecting; trade associations	Item 3
4	How the accounting systems of an organisation are affected by its organisational structure, its administrative systems and procedures and the nature of its business transactions	Item 15
5	The purpose and structure of reporting systems within the organisation	Item 16
6	Background understanding that a variety of outside agencies may require reports and returns from organisations and that these requirements must be built into administrative and accounting systems and procedures	Item 17
7	Background understanding that recording and accounting practices may vary between organisations and different parts of organisations	Item 18

LEARNING OUTCOMES

At the end of this chapter, you should be able to:

- explain why outside organisations might ask for or demand reports or returns

- explain the nature of the information that outside organisations might ask for

- describe in broad terms how the requirement to prepare reports and returns for outside organisations can be built into accounting and administrative procedures

- explain why reports are prepared internally within an organisation

- describe the sources of the data or information for producing reports and returns

- describe in broad terms how recording and accounting practices might vary between organisations and different parts of organisations.

1 THE NATURE OF REPORTS AND RETURNS

Reports and returns are used to provide information. Information might be supplied both to external organisations and to managers within the organisation.

- Information to external organisations is often supplied on standard forms or **returns**, which an organisation completes and submits.

- Information to internal management is often provided in the form of **reports**. Reports are often in a standard format and produced regularly as a matter of routine. However, special 'one off' reports might also be produced.

Reports and returns should have a purpose; otherwise, there is no point in having them. An external organisation requesting information on a return will know what it wants to do with the information. Similarly, managers asking for a report will look at the report, and act on anything of significance they read in it.

2 OUTSIDE ORGANISATIONS ASKING FOR INFORMATION

Authorisation of reports

When an outside organisation asks for information, it either has a right to demand the information or it would like the information to be provided on a voluntary basis.

Certain government departments and agencies have a right to demand information from organisations and individuals. Here are just a few examples.

- The **Inland Revenue** can demand information from businesses and individuals relating to their tax affairs, and obtain this information on tax returns that the individual or business has to complete and submit.

- Similarly, **HM Customs and Excise** can demand information from businesses that are registered for Value Added Tax (VAT). These businesses are required to submit regular VAT returns stating their liability to pay VAT.

- Companies are required by law to provide certain information to **Companies House** (the Registrar of Companies). This includes an annual report and set of financial statements (the 'annual report and accounts'), providing information about the financial performance of the company during the financial year just ended, and its position as at the end of that year.

Governments are able to make the requirement to provide information a legal obligation. Some statistical reports are collected by the government and published as industry averages. Typically companies are required to provide this information so that the government can calculate gross national product and similar statistics.

Government organisations or bodies with the power to **award grants** might ask applicants to provide a report or return to support their application for a grant of funds. Government grants might be available at any time from a department of the UK government (local or national), or from the European Community or perhaps from a specially appointed government body. Grant-awarding schemes vary over time. An example of a government body providing grants is the European Social Fund (ESF).

Some other outside organisations ask for information on a voluntary basis. For example, a company might belong to a **trade association**, which is a voluntary association of businesses in the same industry or trade. The trade association might ask its members to submit information about their business, so that it can consolidate all the information into a single report about the industry as a whole. For example, an Association of British Widget Makers might ask its members to provide information each year about their sales volumes, so that it can produce a report for all its members about the volume of the growth or decline in sales in the industry during the year.

Some trade associations offer an **interfirm comparison** service. Member businesses submit an annual return giving certain details about their financial performance and financial position. The trade association then publishes financial data for the industry as a whole, so that participating businesses can compare their individual performance against the industry average.

Occasionally, an outside organisation might ask for information from businesses on an entirely voluntary basis.

A feature of information provided to an outside organisation is that it is usually in a standard format, on a return or form. You might be given the task of completing a return using data that is available to you. The task is then to transfer the data on to the form, following the instructions for completion that ought to be printed on the form itself or in accompanying guidelines.

2.1 ADAPTING ADMINISTRATIVE AND ACCOUNTING SYSTEMS

When an organisation knows that it has to (or wants to) provide information on a regular basis on returns, it will improve efficiency if:

- the accounting systems are designed in such a way as to produce any relevant information as a matter of routine, or on request

- one individual or work section is given specific responsibility for completing and submitting the return.

Whatever type of report is being produced, it should always be necessary to follow an organisation's authorisation procedures. No document should be despatched before having been authorised by the appropriate person.

3 INTERNAL REPORTING

Most reports produced by organisations are for internal use. Managers might ask for reports about:

- the performance of the business in the past

- the expected future performance of the business.

Reports help managers to assess whether performance has been good or bad, or good in some aspects but bad in others. They can be used to identify areas of weakness or strength in performance. Managers can then use the information to decide what needs to be done, if anything, to improve performance or sustain performance in the future.

Much of the information provided to management in internal reports is financial in character and is sourced from data in the accounting system. One of the major functions of accountants in business is therefore to provide management information.

3.1 PERFORMANCE MEASURES

Many aspects of performance can be measured. It might be helpful, however, to identify four broad aspects of performance that will be of continuing interest to management.

- **Effectiveness**. Measures of effectiveness show what an organisation has achieved. For example, a business should want to know what its sales volume has been in a given period and what profit or loss it has made in the period. Measures of achievement can be compared with planned targets, to assess how well or badly actual results have turned out, and so how effective the business has been in reaching its targets.

- **Efficiency**. Businesses are often concerned with their efficiency. Performing well is not just a matter of achieving targets for sales volume or production volume or activity level. It is also important that results are achieved in the most efficient way possible, avoiding excessive waste of materials or cash, and with an efficient work force. (Work force 'productivity' is often a major management concern.)

- **Economy**. Management should always try to deal with wasteful spending when it occurs. 'Economy' refers to spending wisely and avoiding unnecessary expense that provides no benefit. Performance can be assessed in terms of whether certain items of expenditure are necessary at all, and if they are, what is a sensible and realistic price to pay. There have been many stories in the past, for example, of government departments ordering stores and supplies, and paying far more than they should by agreeing to excessive prices from their suppliers.

- **Quality**. Managers need to know not only about what operations are costing and what profits they are making; they should also want to know about the quality of the goods or services the organisation has provided. Better quality is often achieved only at a higher cost. However, if customers do not like the quality of the goods or services provided by an organisation, they will take their business somewhere else.

Performance is often measured by **comparing results**. The results in one period can be compared with:

- the results in a previous period (for example, the current year's results can be compared with those of the previous year)

- the planned or target results

- the results achieved by other firms in the same industry (where a scheme of interfirm comparison operates).

You might well be required to prepare a report in which the results of one period have to be compared with a previous period.

3.2 SYSTEMS FOR MEASURING PERFORMANCE

All businesses above the smallest size prepare reports for managers. When the quantity of routine reports is large, there could be teams of staff whose job it is to ensure that the information is extracted and reported. For example, a large part of the work of the accounting department is concerned with extracting reports from the accounting system.

Not all business are the same, and the way in which they gather and report information to management will vary according to the structure of the organisation.

You need to be aware that organisations are different, and that you might need to be careful that the information you collect is relevant and correct in the given situation. The example below attempts to illustrate just one example of such differences.

Example

Company X consists of two departments, Y and Z. Each department is treated as a profit centre, which means that its performance is measured by the amount of profit it earns. The two departments are entirely independent of each other, and have no dealings with each other.

Sales and costs of each department for the past three months are as follows.

	Department Y	Department Z
	£	£
Sales	300,000	400,000
Costs	240,000	325,000
Profit	60,000	75,000

Another company, company R, has two departments P and Q. Each department is treated as a profit centre. However, department P produces some output for the external market, but supplies exactly one half of its output, at full market price, to department Q. Department Q then does further processing on the output from department P and then sells it all in the external market.

The reported sales and costs of each department for the past three months are as follows.

	Department P	Department Q
	£	£
Sales	300,000	400,000
Costs	240,000	325,000
Profit	60,000	75,000

On an initial look at these figures, you might suppose that both companies have achieved exactly the same performance is the three-month period. However, this is not at all the case. In company X, both profit centres sell all their output to external customers. In company R, department P sells half its output internally to department Q.

When one department in a company sells output to another department, there has to be an agreed cost or price of transfer. Since departments P and Q are treated as profit centres, the output from department P to department Q will be sold at an internal price - known as a **transfer price** - that gives department P some profit margin on top of its costs. Here, it is assumed that the transfer price charged for output from P to Q is the external market price for the items.

The internal sales at the transfer price is recorded as revenue for department P, and also as a cost for department Q. These are internal sales between departments, not sales to external customers. The internal sales of department P in fact 'cancel out' the internal costs of department Q. For the purpose of monitoring company R performance, they should be ignored altogether.

A proper comparison of the results of company X and company R for the three-month period would be as follows. (Remember, department P transfers exactly one half of its output to department Q, and sells them at the external market price.)

	Company X	Company R
	£	£
Sales	700,000*	550,000
Costs	565,000**	415,000
Total profit	135,000	135,000

* (50% of £300,000 + £400,000)

** (£240,000 + £325,000 – 50% of £300,000)

The total profit of the two companies is the same, but company R has achieved its profits on a much lower total volume of external sales. Notice how the transfers from department P to department Q are excluded from the company's sales figure, and the cost to department Q of buying the transfers from department P is also excluded from the company's total costs.

Profit centres and transfer pricing systems are just one reason why recording and accounting practices may vary between organisations (and even between different parts of the same organisation). You need to be alert to the characteristics of different accounting systems, and to prepare your reports for management accordingly.

ACTIVITY 1

Brown Ltd manufactures product XYZ which goes through a three-stage manufacturing process. Raw materials are processed in department X to produce units of item X. Some units of X are sold in the external market, and the rest are transferred to department Y.

In department Y, input units of item X are further processed to produce units of item XY. Some units of XY are sold in the external market, and the rest are transferred to department Z.

In department Z, input units of item XY are further processed to produce item XYZ, which is sold in the external market.

Departments X, Y and Z are treated as profit centres for reporting purposes. The results of each department for the year 20X4 and the preceding year 20X3 are summarised below.

	Dept X		Dept Y		Dept Z	
	20X4	20X3	20X4	20X3	20X4	20X3
	£	£	£	£	£	£
Sales	300,000	320,000	560,000	500,000	800,000	780,000
Costs	275,000	280,000	490,000	470,000	750,000	738,000
Profit	25,000	40,000	70,000	30,000	50,000	42,000

All internal transfers are priced at the external market sales price for the item. In 20X3, department X sold one quarter of its output externally and department Y sold 20% of its output externally. In 20X4, department X sold one third of its output externally and department Y sold one quarter of its output externally. All output not transferred externally was transferred/sold internally.

Tasks

1   For each year, 20X4 and the preceding year 20X3, calculate the total profit earned by the company.

2   Calculate the percentage increase in sales revenue and profit for the company as a whole in 20X4 compared with 20X3.

For a suggested answer, see the 'Answers' section at the end of the book.

4   SOURCES OF RELEVANT GOVERNMENT STATISTICS

Much of the information that management needs is extracted from sources within the organisation. However, some information might be obtained externally. The government can be a valuable source of external statistics, normally available free of charge.

You ought to be aware of the types of information that might be available from the government, and how you might obtain it.

Each government department produces statistics relating to its area of responsibility. For example, the Department of Trade and Employment produces business statistics relating to UK trade and the Treasury produces taxation and government spending statistics.

The statistics produced by individual government departments are brought together and published by the Office of National Statistics.

Although government statistics are available in printed form, the quickest and cheapest way of accessing them is by internet. Here are some useful web site addresses.

National Statistics Online (Office of National Statistics): www.statistics.gov.uk

This web site has an enormous range of data. For example, there are sections of the web site for statistics on agriculture, fishing and forestry, commerce, energy and industry, the economy, the labour market, transport travel and tourism, education and training, health and care and so on.

Statistics about the UK's balance of payments (called 'United Kingdom Balance of Payments: The Pink Book') is also available on this web site.

The web site also provides information about the Retail Prices Index, although RPI information is also readily available on non-government web sites, such as www.incomesdata.co.uk.

The Treasury is an important source of information about the UK economy, and taxation and government spending. The web site address is www.hm-treasury.gov.uk.

The section of the web site on 'economic data and tools' includes public spending statistics, public finances statistics and economic indicators.

The Bank of England web site is a source of monetary and financial statistics. (Address: www.bankofengland.co.uk.) The statistics provided on this site include statistics for the exchange rate value of sterling over time, as well as figures for the money supply.

Government statistics for the European Union as a whole are available from **Eurostat**, the Statistical Office of the European Communities, address http://europa.eu.int.

ACTIVITY 2

If you have access to the internet, try visiting some of the web sites listed above, particularly www.statistics.gov.uk, and have a browse through some of the statistics available on the site.

As a second exercise, visit the site of a search engine such as www.google.com or www.yahoo.com and search for either 'retail prices index' or 'UK retail prices index', and see how easily you can find a table giving an index of UK retail prices.

There is no feedback to this activity.

4.1 NON-GOVERNMENT SOURCES OF STATISTICS

The government is not the only source of business statistics, and some organisations provide information free of charge. For example, there are hundreds of trade associations in the UK. A list is available on the web site www.taforum.org. You can use this site to access the web site of any of the listed trade associations, such as the Brick Industry Association, the British Ceramic Confederation, the Association of Electricity Producers, British Biogen, the British Hydropower Association and so on.

CONCLUSION

This chapter sets out the framework for the rest of the text. Briefly summarised, the points to note are that:

- Information is provided by organisations to both external users and internally to management. Information to external users might be required by law, or might be provided voluntarily.

- When information is provided regularly, an organisation should have established procedures for extracting the information and particular individuals or work sections responsible for providing it.

- Since much information in reports and returns is financial in nature, accountants are important information providers within their organisation.

- Much information for inclusion in reports and returns comes from internal data sources. However external sources of information, particularly the government, might be used for certain purposes. For example, retail prices index statistics might be used for reporting to management.

- Systems for recording and accounting can vary between different types of organisation. It is important that the data used to prepare reports and returns should be gathered, analysed and presented correctly.

SELF TEST QUESTIONS

Paragraph

1	What are reports?	1
2	What are returns?	1
3	Give some examples of external organisations that could ask for information from a company.	2
4	Identify four broad aspects of performance measures.	3.1
5	State at least three sources of government statistics.	4
6	State some examples of non-government sources of statistics.	4.1

KEY TERMS

Returns – Standard forms for an organisation to complete that provide information to external organisations.

Reports – Information supplied to internal management. Reports are often in a standard format and produced regularly as a matter of routine.

Performance measures – Include effectiveness, efficiency, economy and quality.

Effectiveness – Measures of effectiveness show what an organisation has achieved. Measures of achievement can be compared with planned targets, to assess how well or badly actual results have turned out.

Efficiency – It is important that results are achieved in the most efficient way possible, avoiding excessive waste of materials or cash, and with an efficient work force.

Economy – Refers to spending wisely and avoiding unnecessary expense that provides no benefit.

Quality – Refers to the quality of the goods or services the organisation has provided.

Transfer price – When one department within a company sells goods or services to another department within the same company the agreed cost or price is referred to as transfer price.

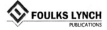

Chapter 2

PRESENTING INFORMATION: TABULATION

The purpose of this chapter is to remind you of some mathematical techniques that are used for analysing data, and to look at techniques for presenting summarised information in tabular form.

CONTENTS

KNOWLEDGE AND UNDERSTANDING

		Reference
1	Use of standard units of inputs and outputs	Item 8
2	Methods of presenting information: ... tabular	Item 14

PERFORMANCE CRITERIA

		Reference
1	Consolidate information derived from different units of the organisation into the appropriate form	Item A, element 7.1
2	Reconcile information derived from different information systems within the organisation	Item B, element 7.1

LEARNING OUTCOMES

At the end of this chapter, you should be able to:

- present data and information in different ways, clearly and concisely

- present numerical data in tables

- consolidate information, derived from different sources into the appropriate form

- reconcile information obtained from different systems.

1 PRESENTING INFORMATION

The aim of Unit 7 is that you should be able to prepare clear reports for management or external agencies. To be able to do this, you have to know how to present data clearly and correctly.

There are various methods of presenting data, including:

- tabulation

- diagrams

- graphs

- percentages and ratios.

To deal with numerical data and to present it in an effective and understandable form, you must be familiar with a number of basic mathematical techniques.

This chapter begins by reminding you of some of the techniques you should know already.

2 AVERAGES

An average is a middle value. There are different types of average, but the most common is the 'arithmetic mean'. The arithmetic mean of a value for a number of different items is calculated as:

$$\frac{\text{Sum of the values of the items}}{\text{Number of items}}$$

Averages might be rounded to the nearest whole number, or nearest decimal place or two.

Example

A business has a fleet of seven delivery vans. The cost of these vans, all bought within a fairly short period of time, was:

Van	Cost
	£
1	15,435
2	14,410
3	14,719
4	15,810
5	16,005
6	14,621
7	15,016

What was the average cost per van, to the nearest £1?

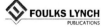

Solution

Here there are seven items (vans) and we are trying to calculate an average cost. To do this, we need the total of the costs of all seven vans.

Van	Cost
	£
1	15,435
2	14,410
3	14,719
4	15,810
5	16,005
6	14,621
7	15,016
Total	106,016

$$\text{Average} = \frac{£106,016}{7} \quad £15,145$$

ACTIVITY 1

A company manufactures two products, widgets and fidgets. Production and cost data for the month just ended are as follows.

	Widgets	Fidgets
	£	£
Direct material costs	24,510	31,402
Direct labour costs	32,791	18,934
Overhead costs	47,567	27,454

During the month the company produced 12,450 widgets and 31,550 fidgets. What was the average cost per widget and the average cost per fidget, to the nearest £0.01?

For a suggested answer, see the 'Answers' section at the end of the book.

2.1 WEIGHTED AVERAGE

The simple average that was calculated in above might not always be appropriate for the type of data given.

Example

Suppose that a group of six employees in an office have the following monthly salaries:

Monthly salary	Number of employees
£2,000	3
£2,200	2
£2,400	1

The simple average of these three monthly salaries is:

$$\frac{£2,000 + £2,200 + £2,400}{3} = £2,200$$

However this is not the true average monthly salary as more employees earn less than £2,200 than above it.

FOULKS LYNCH
PUBLICATIONS

The true average wage must take account of the number of employees earning each salary. This is known as a weighted average as the figures used are weighted according to the number of times they appear.

The reality is that three employees earn £2,000, two earn £2,200 and only one earns £2,400. The true average is therefore:

$$\frac{(2,000 + 2,000 + 2,000) + (2,200 + 2,200) + 2,400}{6}$$

= £2,133.33

The salary levels are weighted according to the number of employees earning at each level. Thus the £2,000 salary appears in the calculation three times whereas £2,400 appears only once. This is because three times as many employees earn £2,000 as earn £2,400. £2,000 is given three times the weight of £2,400.

A weighted average calculation is normally made in a tabular calculation.

Salary £		Number of employees	£
2,000	×	3	6,000
2,200	×	2	4,400
2,400	×	1	2,400
		6	12,800

Weighted average = $\dfrac{£12,800}{6}$

= £2,133.33

ACTIVITY 2

A large company purchases calculators for its staff on a fairly regular basis. In the past year, its purchases have been as follows.

Model	Quantity bought	Price per unit
QS102	34	£9.50
QS105	24	£12.70
QS110	15	£16.90
QS114	11	£21.00

What was the average cost per calculator purchased, to the nearest £0.01?

For a suggested answer, see the 'Answers' section at the end of the book.

2.2 MOVING AVERAGES

A moving average is an average value for a given period of time that is re-calculated at regular intervals, so that a picture emerges of how the average is changing or 'moving' over time.

For example, a business might calculate its average daily sales as a moving average. Suppose that the business week consists of seven days. The first average will be calculated by taking the average of the daily sales for the seven days in the first week that records are kept. Suppose that this is Sunday week 1 to Saturday week 1. The next moving average is calculated the next day from sales for the previous seven days, by

taking the daily sales on Sunday week 2 and dropping the sales for Sunday week 1. The next moving average is then calculated on the following day, by including sales for Monday week 2 and dropping the sales figure for Monday week 1.

Example

Daily sales in Draper's Department Store have been recorded as follows.

Day	Sales
	£
Week 1	
Sunday	5,780
Monday	3,109
Tuesday	3,250
Wednesday	4,109
Thursday	6,241
Friday	8,566
Saturday	10,723
Week 2	
Sunday	5,982
Monday	3,011
Tuesday	3,106
Wednesday	4,435
Thursday	6,499
Friday	8,623
Saturday	10,470

Required:

Calculate a moving average of daily sales, from the data provided.

Solution

We can calculate a moving daily average by first of all calculating moving weekly totals. A moving weekly total is simply the total of sales for the past week. A new weekly total can be calculated each day.

By convention, a moving total and a moving average are associated with the mid-point of the period they cover. For example, the moving weekly total and moving daily average for Sunday week 1 to Saturday week 1 is assumed to be Wednesday week 1.

Here, the moving daily averages are shown to the nearest £1.

Day	Sales		Moving weekly total	Moving daily average (Total/7)
	£		£	£
Week 1				
Sunday	5,780			
Monday	3,109			
Tuesday	3,250			

Wednesday	4,109	(Sun week 1 – Sat week 1)	41,778	5,968
Thursday	6,241	(Mon week 1 – Sun week 2)	41,980	5,997
Friday	8,566	(Tue week 1 – Mon week 2)	41,882	5,983
Saturday	10,723	(Wed week 1 – Tue week2)	41,739	5,963
Week 2				
Sunday	5,982	(Thur week 1 – Wed week 2)	42,064	6,009
Monday	3,011	(Fri week 1 – Thur week 2)	42,322	6,046
Tuesday	3,106	(Sat week 1 – Fri week 2)	42,379	6,054
Wednesday	4,435	(Sun week 2 – Sat week 2)	42,126	6,018
Thursday	6,499			
Friday	8,623			
Saturday	10,470			

This table shows that over the period, average daily sales have risen slightly.

ACTIVITY 3

You are given the following information about sales per quarter for Grapple Ltd.

Quarter	Sales
	£000
Year 1	
Quarter 1	435
Quarter 2	427
Quarter 3	449
Quarter 4	452
Year 2	
Quarter 1	455
Quarter 2	446
Quarter 3	450
Quarter 4	459
Year 3	
Quarter 1	464
Quarter 2	470
Quarter 3	463
Quarter 4	478

Task

Use this data to calculate the moving average sales per quarter for Grapple Ltd. Calculate your averages to the nearest £1,000.

For a suggested answer, see the 'Answers' section at the end of the book.

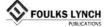

3 STANDARD UNITS OF INPUTS AND OUTPUTS

In recording data or processing data into information, it is sometimes necessary to convert different items into standard units, in order to make sense of the figures.

A widely used example of standardisation of units is found in data relating to work statistics and productivity.

3.1 STANDARDISING LABOUR INPUTS

An employer might have employees who work part-time. In addition to full-time employees, there might be some employees working a three-day week, others a four-day week and others working half-days only, mornings or afternoons.

It might be appropriate to state the size of the work force in terms of full-time equivalent employees.

Example

A small business has been asked to submit statistics to a government department about the number of its employees. The instructions with the return state that part-time employees should be converted to full-time equivalent numbers.

The business operates a five-day week, and its work force is made up of the following numbers.

Time worked each week	Number of employees
Full time	45
2 full days each week	10
3 full days each week	16
5 half days each week	7

Required:

Determine what number should go into the following box on the return?

Number of full time employees and full-time equivalents	

If you think you can answer this question, attempt your own solution before reading on.

Solution

Time worked each week	Full time equivalent per employee	Number of employees	Total full-time equivalents
Full time	1.0	45	45.0
2 full days each week	0.4	10	4.0
3 full days each week	0.6	16	9.6
5 half days each week	0.5	7	3.5
			62.1

This total will probably be rounded to the nearest whole number, for the purpose of filling in the return

Number of full time employees and full-time equivalents	62

3.2 STANDARDISING LABOUR OUTPUTS

When measuring the amount of work that a work force has completed during a given period of time, it is common to measure the work in terms of **standard hours of work done**.

Regular items of output or routine jobs of work are each measured in terms of the number of hours they should be expected to take. For example, if it is expected to take 2 hours to perform a task, and the task is performed five times, then we would say that 10 standard hours of work have been done.

Example

A manufacturer makes three products, A, B and C. One unit of product A is expected to take 3 hours to make, one unit of B is expected to take 2 hours and unit C is expected to take 1.5 hours. During one particular week, the manufacturer makes 200 units of A, 150 units of B and 400 units of C.

This output can be measured in standard hours, as a common measure of work done.

Product	Units made	Standard hours per unit	Standard hours total
A	200	3.0	600
B	150	2.0	300
C	400	1.5	600
			1,500

3.3 OTHER STANDARD MEASURES OF OUTPUT

Different businesses use different standard measures of output. There are no rules about what standard measures of output should be, and not all businesses use them.

For illustrative purposes, here are a few more standard measures of output.

- Road haulage firms transport goods by truck or lorry. Each journey will be a different length, and the amount of goods carried each time will be different. To standardise output, haulage businesses measure the work they do in terms of tone-miles carried. A tonne-mile represents transporting one tonne of goods (in weight) for one mile. So, if a truck carries a load weighing 5 tonnes for 140 miles, it has transported 700 tonne-miles ($5 \times 140 = 700$). Similarly, if another truck has carries 3 tonnes for 50 miles, 150 tonne-miles have been transported. Haulage firms can measure all the transport work they do in tonne-miles (or tonne-kilometres) in this way.

- Hospitals might consider the usage that is made of their beds to be very important. The amount of care provided to patients might therefore be measured in the number of patient-days. One patient-day represents having a patient filling a hospital bed for one day. So if a hospital ward with 12 beds is full for seven days in a week, the ward will have cared for 84 patient-days in the week. If one of the beds had been empty for 3 days, then the ward would have cared for just 81 patient-days in the week.

- Transport companies, notably railway companies, might measure the service they provide customers in terms of passenger-miles. A passenger-mile represents carrying one passenger for one mile. For example, suppose a railway company puts on two trains. Train A takes 150 passengers from London to Bristol which is a journey of 110 miles, and Train B takes 90 passengers from Oxford to Birmingham which is, say, 80 miles. We can say that Train A did 16,500 passenger-miles (150×110), and Train B did 7,200 passenger-miles (90×80).

FOULKS LYNCH
PUBLICATIONS

3.4 WHAT IS THE PURPOSE OF STANDARD MEASURES?

Standard measures of input and output are useful for a number of reasons.

- They can be used as a way of **measuring the cost of output**. Businesses can measure the cost of the work they do in terms of the cost per standard hour. In this way, all work done can be costed on a comparable basis.

- They can be used to **measure productivity**. The actual hours worked by an organisation or a department can be compared with the standard number of hours produced. For example, suppose that a department employs 10 people each working a 37-hour week, and that during one particular week, the department does work that is measured as 390 standard hours of output. Productivity can be measured by comparing the standard hours of output produced with the number of hours actually worked. In this example, if a department produces 390 standard hours of work during 370 hours of actual working time, it would be considered more efficient than expected or average.

- They can be used to measure **resource utilisation**. Resource utilisation means the extent to which available resources are being used. For example, suppose that a hospital has 50 beds and during June it cared for 1,280 patient-days. Maximum capacity, if all the beds are fully occupied for all 30 days of the month, is 1,500 patient-days. In this example, we could measure that actual bed usage was 220 patient-days short of capacity, and capacity utilisation was just $(1,280/1,500) \times 100\% = 85.3\%$.

4 PERCENTAGES, RATIOS AND PROPORTIONS

Figures presented in reports are often given as percentages, ratios or proportions. You might be required to deal with any of these, and so you should check that you understand the arithmetic involved.

4.1 PERCENTAGES

Definition Per cent means 'out of 100' and is written as '%'.

Rules for calculation:

(a) To express number X as a percentage of number Y, divide X by Y and multiply the result by 100.

(b) To calculate a percentage amount (P%) of a total number Z, multiply Z by the percentage P and divide by 100.

Example

(a) Express 20 as a percentage of 50.

(b) What is 15% of 600?

Solution

(a) $\dfrac{20}{50} \times 100 = 40\%$

(b) $600 \times \dfrac{15}{100} = 90$

ACTIVITY 4

(a)   An article cost £206 last year and has increased in price to £225 this year. What is the percentage price increase? (Give your answer to one decimal point of one per cent.)

(b)   Employees are currently paid £240 per week and are claiming a 5% pay increase. How much is the increase that they are claiming in £s?

For a suggested answer, see the 'Answers' section at the end of the book.

4.2   RATIOS

A ratio is really an alternative way of expressing a fraction. Ratios compare the size of one thing with the size of something else. For example:

	£
Sales	500
Cost of sales	300
Gross profit	200

The size of the gross profit can be compared with the value of sales in any of four ways:

(a)   **Fraction** $\dfrac{200}{500} = \dfrac{2}{5}$

In other words, gross profit is two-fifths of sales revenue.

(b)   **Decimal** $\dfrac{200}{500} = 0.4$

In other words, gross profit is 0.4 times the size of sales revenue.

(c)   **Percentage** $\dfrac{200}{500} \times 100 = 40\%$

In other words, gross profit is 40% of sales. Percentages are commonly referred to as 'ratios', so here we might say that the gross profit ratio is 40%.

(d)   **Ratio** $200 : 500 = 2 : 5$

Here the comparative sizes of gross profit and sales are stated as 2:5, meaning that for every £5 of sales, gross profit is £2.

Using a ratio to show how a total amount is divided up

Ratios are often used to show how a total amount is shared between different elements or parts. For example, in a business run as a partnership, with three partners X, Y and Z, we might say that the total profits of the business are shared between the partners in the ratio 3 : 5 : 2 between X, Y and Z respectively.

Similarly, we might say that a work force is made up in the ratio 60:40 men to women.

Example

Ace, Brace and Case is a business partnership. Last year its profits were £385,000. Profits are divided in the ratio 2 : 4 : 5 between Ace, Brace and Case.

What was the share of the total profit for each partner?

Solution

Add the three ratio numbers: 2 + 4 + 5 = 11.

If we divide the total profit by 11, and establish the value of 1/11, we can then go on to establish the total share for each partner.

Ace receives 2/11, Brace receives 4/11 and Case receives 5/11.

One part share = 1/11 of £385,000 = £35,000.

The three parts are therefore:

(a) Ace: 2 × £35,000 = £70,000

(b) Brace: 4 × £35,000 = £140,000

(c) Case: 5 × £35,000 = £175,000

(d) Total profit = £70,000 + £140,000 + £175,000 = £385,000.

ACTIVITY 5

The total sales of an organisation are £400,000. These sales are made by four divisions, (North, South, East and West) in the ratio of 2 : 4 : 9 : 5.

What are the total sales for each of the four divisions?

For a suggested answer, see the 'Answers' section at the end of the book.

4.3 PROPORTIONS

Definition   A **proportion** is the ratio of a part to the whole. It is usually expressed as a fraction or decimal.

Example

A total bonus of £1,000 is to be split between Jo and Jack in the proportions of $\frac{1}{4}$ to Jo and $\frac{3}{4}$ to Jack.

How much will each receive?

Solution

Jo	=	$\frac{1}{4} \times £1,000$
	=	£250
Jack	=	$\frac{3}{4} \times £1,000$
	=	£750

ACTIVITY 6

Banks Ltd sells its goods in the UK and abroad. In the year just ended, its total sales were £574,000 of which £82,000 were export sales and the rest were sales in the UK.

(a) What is the ratio of export sales to domestic (UK) sales?

(b) What percentage of total sales were export sales?

(c) What proportion of total sales were export sales?

For a suggested answer, see the 'Answers' section at the end of the book.

5 STATISTICAL TERMINOLOGY

Much of Unit 7 is concerned with the using and presenting figures or 'statistics'. You are unlikely to come across statistical terms at this stage in your studies, but it might be useful to know about the following one or two.

The word statistics can be used in a variety of different ways but its essential meaning is quite simple.

Definition The word **statistics** refers to collections of numerical facts or estimates. Statistics are data in the form of numbers.

Population and sample

Information might be collected about every item so that the figures are comprehensive. Alternatively, information might be gathered about a selection of all the items, in the expectation that the selection is representative.

Definition The term **population** is used to denote all of the items under consideration in a particular enquiry.

Definition A **sample** is a selected group of items drawn from that population and intended to be a representative selection.

Primary and secondary data

There are two types of statistical data, primary data and secondary data.

Definition **Primary data** is data that has been especially collected for a particular enquiry.

Definition **Secondary data** is data that has not been collected for a particular enquiry, but has been obtained from an existing available source. Government statistics, obtainable from The Office of National Statistics, are an example of secondary data.

6 TABLES IN REPORTS

When numerical information is presented in a report, perhaps the most common method of presenting it is in the form of a table (or several tables). A table can be used to set out figures in an organised and structured way, so that they can be understood by the reader.

Definition **Tabulation** is the systematic arrangement of numerical data that has been obtained, providing a logical account of the results of an analysis. In other words, tabulation means putting figures (or words) into a table.

6.1 RULES OF TABULATION

If you are required to produce a clear table, there are a number of basic rules of tabulation that you should always use. A good table should always have the following:

(a) **Title:** The table must have a clear title, indicating what the figures in the table are intended to show.

(b) **Source:** Where appropriate, the source of the data used to draw up the table should be stated (usually in a footnote underneath the table).

(c) **Units:** Where there are figures in the table, it should always be clear what they represent. The units of measurement that have been used should be stated, for example if the figures in a table are in thousands of pounds, a clear note should state that 'all figures are in £000s'. Alternatively, the units of measurement can be included in the column headings in the table.

(d) **Headings:** All column and row headings should be labelled clearly but concisely.

(e) **Totals:** Totals should be shown where appropriate. Totals can be either or both column totals or row totals. The column or row should be headed clearly 'Total'. Where appropriate, sub-totals should also be included. However, sub-totals need only be shown where they are meaningful for making comparisons.

(f) **Percentages and ratios:** These are sometimes called **derived statistics** and should be shown if meaningful, with an indication of how they were calculated.

7 USING TABLES TO CONSOLIDATE INFORMATION

A common use of tables in business reporting is to bring together information from different units of an organisation. The table can be used to:

• set the information from each unit of the organisation side by side, so that they can be compared, and

• present total figures for the organisation as a whole.

Example

Driver Limited sells its services throughout the UK. It is organised into four sales regions, North, South, East and West. It sells three services, plumbing services, electrical services and pest control services. In September 20X4, sales in North region were plumbing services £56,000, electrical services £60,000 and pest control services £17,000. Sales in South region were plumbing services £42,000, electrical services £36,000 and pest control services £23,000. Sales in East region were plumbing services £76,000, electrical services £53,000 and pest control services £45,000. Sales in West region were plumbing services £36,000, electrical services £14,000 and pest control services £25,000.

Required:

Prepare a table showing:

(a) the sales for each region for each type of service and in total for the month and

(b) total company sales, analysed between the three services.

Solution

The table below consolidates the sales figures of the four sales regions for the three services, to produce total sales figures for the month.

To prepare the table, you need to decide what should go in the columns and what should go in the rows. As a general rule, we try to limit the number of columns, to fit them all easily on to a single sheet of paper or a computer screen. However, this is not a compulsory rule, by any means.

In this example, we need to present information about sales in each region and sales of each service. The columns could be for the sales regions and the rows for the type of service. Alternatively, the columns could be for type of service and the rows could be for the regions. There should be a total column and a total row.

In the example below, the columns are used for the services and the rows for the regions, but you might prefer to have the columns and rows the other way round. The table is constructed simply by entering the appropriate figure into each middle box of the table, and then adding up the row figures to get row totals and adding up the column figures to get column totals. The sum of the row totals and the sum of the column totals equals the grand total figure for sales.

Driver Ltd				
Sales figures for September 20X3				
	Plumbing services	*Electrical services*	*Pest control services*	*Total*
Region	£000	£000	£000	£000
North	56	60	17	133
South	42	36	23	101
East	76	53	45	174
West	36	14	25	75
Total	210	163	110	483

ACTIVITY 7

Carter Professional Services is a firm that provides professional advice to clients. It employs accountants, solicitors, IT specialists and general staff in each of three regional departments, North, Central and south regions.

The chief executive officer has asked for a report on the numbers of staff employed by the business. You have received the following information.

(a)   North Region employs 12 solicitors, 16 accountants, 8 IT specialists and 14 support staff.

(b)   Central Region employs 60 staff, of whom 15 are accountants, 6 solicitors, 20 IT specialists and the rest are support staff.

(c)   South Region employs 15 IT specialists, 18 accountants, 11 solicitors and 17 support staff.

Task

Prepare a table showing the total number of employees in the business analysed by both region and type of employee.

For a suggested answer, see the 'Answers' section at the end of the book.

7.1   CONVERSION OF NARRATIVE DATA INTO TABULAR FORM

A report writer might have some numerical data in narrative form. Numerical data is often difficult to understand and analyse, and it is therefore usual to convert it into a table of figures, or a diagram or a graph.

Example

Alpha Products plc has two departments, A and B. The total salaries bill in 20X7 was £513,000, of which £218,000 was for department A and the rest for department B. The corresponding figures for 20X8 were £537,000 and £224,000. The number employed in department A was 30 in 20X7 and decreased by 5 for the next year. The number employed in department B was 42 in 20X7 and increased by 1 for the year 20X8. Tabulate this data to show the changes over the two-year period for each department and the company as a whole.

Required:

Present this information in tabular form, showing in addition:

(a)   the percentage changes from 20X7 to 20X8, and

(b)   the average salary per employee each year, to the nearest £100, and the percentage increase in average salary between 20X7 and 20X8.

Solution

Alpha Products plc

Changes in Labour Force 20X7 to 20X8

	Dept A			Dept B			Dept C		
	20X7	20X8	% change	20X7	20X8	% change	20X7	20X8	% change
Total salaries (£000)	218	224	+ 2.8	295	313	+ 6.1	513	537	+ 4.7
Numbers employed	30	25	- 16.7	42	43	+ 2.4	72	68	- 5.6
Average salary per employee (£000)	7.3	9.0	+22.3	7.0	7.3	+ 4.3	7.1	7.9	+ 11.3

Note: The average salary is shown in thousands of pounds. Since the average should be shown to the nearest £100, the figure is given to one decimal place.

ACTIVITY 8

The marketing and sales division of Reptar Ltd is divided into four geographical areas, North, South, East and West. The products that Reptar Ltd sells fall into three main categories being security systems, contract maintenance and general electrical work.

In 20X2 the North and West divisions both had turnovers of £200,000 for security systems, whilst South had a security systems turnover of £269,000 and East only £140,000. The contract maintenance turnover was greatest in the South at £165,000, with the North, East and West earning £110,000, £130,000 and £80,000 respectively. The general electrical work turnover was only £12,000 in the West, £48,000 in the North, £32,000 in the East and £21,000 in the South.

Task

Prepare a table showing the actual amounts of turnover, for each division and for the company as a whole, for each of the three categories. In addition, show the percentage of total turnover for each division that each category makes up.

For a suggested answer, see the 'Answers' section at the end of the book.

7.2 CONSOLIDATING FINANCIAL RESULTS

When a table is used to consolidate the financial results of different regions or departments of a company, you might need to take care with any internal sales between one department and another.

Study the following example carefully. Attempt your own solution before reading ours, if you think you can do the task.

Fashion Shops has three sales outlets, in Chelsea, Hampstead and Mile End.

Transactions for the week ended 12 November 20X4 are shown overleaf.

Transactions for the week ended 12 November 20X4

	Chelsea	Hampstead	Mile End
	£	£	£
Sales	34,941	41,099	27,619
Purchases	9,815	8,477	9,456
Salaries	9,790	9,036	7,280
Rent	3,800	4,500	2,700
Telephone	933	812	402
Electricity	876	734	790
Equipment lease costs	2,077	2,319	2,653
Security services	1,560	1,370	1,000
Sundry expenses	2,901	3,886	4,065
Opening stock	2,176	4,022	1,908
Closing stock	2,980	3,400	2,745
Transfers to Mile End	600		
Transfers to Hampstead			800
Transfers from Chelsea			600
Transfers from Mile End		700	

Goods costing £100 were transferred from Mile End to Hampstead on 12 November. The transfer was recorded in the accounts of the Mile End shop. However, although the goods were received in the Hampstead shop on 12 November, they were not recorded in the accounts of the Hampstead shop until 15 November.

Task

Prepare a summary of sales, cost of goods sold, gross profit and net profit for each shop and for the company as a whole, for the week ended 12 November 20X3.

Solution

You need to remember the basic format for presenting a trading, profit and loss account.

	£	£
Sales		X
Opening stock	X	
Plus: Purchases	<u>X</u>	
	X	
Less: Closing stock	<u>(X)</u>	
Equals: Cost of sales		<u>(X)</u>
Gross profit		X
Other expenses		<u>(X)</u>
Net profit		<u>X</u>

A problem with presenting the results in this example is deciding what to do with the transfers of goods between shops. For example, if the Chelsea shop transfers some goods to Mile End:

- Chelsea bought the goods, so the cost is included in its total for purchases.

- Mile End did not buy the goods, but will get the benefit of the revenue from selling the goods.

Transfers should be adjusted for by subtracting the transfers from the cost of purchases for the shop making the transfer, and adding the transfers to the cost of purchases for the shop receiving the transfer.

There is also the problem of the goods that are still 'in transit' between Mile End and Hampstead at the end of the week. This can be dealt with by assuming that Hampstead has received the goods, and so both its purchases and its closing stock should be increased to allow for the goods in transit. In the table below, purchases for the Chelsea shop are therefore reduced by the £800 of transfers to Mile End and purchases by Mile End are reduced by the transfers to Hampstead (£800) less the transfers from Chelsea. Finally, the purchases by Hampstead are increased by the transfers from Mile End, including the £10 of goods in transit.

The goods in transit are added to Hampstead's closing stock.

Transactions for the week ended 12 November 20X4

	Chelsea		Hampstead		Mile End		Total	
	£	£	£	£	£	£	£	£
Sales		34,941		41,099		27,619		103,659
Opening stock	2,176		4,022		1,908		8,106	
Purchases	9,815		8,477		9,456		27,748	
Transfers	(600)		800		(200)		-	
	11,391		13,299		11,164		35,854	
Closing stock	(2,980)		(3,500)		(2,745)		(9,255)	
Cost of sales		8,411		9,799		8,419		26,629
Gross profit		26,530		31,300		19,200		77,030
Salaries	9,790		9,036		7,280		26,106	
Rent	3,800		4,500		2,700		11,000	
Telephone	933		812		402		2,147	
Electricity	876		734		790		2,400	
Equipment lease costs	2,077		2,319		2,653		7,049	
Security services	1,560		1,370		1,000		3,930	
Sundry expenses	2,901		3,886		4,065		10,852	
		21,937		22,657		18,890		63,484
		4,593		8,643		310		13,546

ACTIVITY 9

A company has two divisions, X and Y, whose results for the year ended 31 December 20X3 are shown below, together with the overall results for the company in the previous year to 31 December 20X2.

	Year ended 31 December 20X3		Year ended 31 December 20X2
	Division X	Division Y	Company as a whole
	£	£	£
Sales to external customers	138,050	135,400	268,700
Internal transfers to Y at cost	2,800		
	140,850		
Opening stock	5,700	6,150	22,450
Transfers from X at cost		2,300	
Purchases	76,300	82,100	157,300
	82,000	90,550	179,750
Closing stock	(5,100)	(6,650)	(11,850)
Cost of sales	76,900	83,900	167,900
Gross profit	63,950	51,500	100,800
Other expenses	59,350	43,900	92,100
Net profit	4,600	7,600	8,700

At the end of 20X3, there were £500 of goods in transit from Division X to Division Y. The transfer has been recorded by Division X but has not yet been recorded in the accounts of Division Y.

Tasks

1   Produce a trading, profit and loss account for the company as a whole for the year ended 31 December 20X3.

2   Compare the results for the year ended 31 December 20X3 with the results for the year ended 31 December 20X2, and show the percentage amount by which each item increased (+) or fell (-) in value in 20X3 compared with 20X2.

For a suggested answer, see the 'Answers' section at the end of the book.

7.3   RECONCILING INFORMATION FROM DIFFERENT SOURCES OR SYSTEMS

Sometimes, a report has to be prepared using data from different sources. When data comes from different sources, it might not all be in exactly the same form, and each source might present its data in a slightly different way. If you have to bring the information together, for inclusion in a table or a graph, **your first step should be to convert all the data to the same basis**.

Examples of data from different sources being in different forms are:

- Figures for sales for a company that operates in two or more countries. The sales figures from each country might be given in different currencies, for example with some sales figures in sterling, some in euros and some in US dollars.

- Examination marks might be collected from different university departments. Some marks might be given as percentage scores, some as grades (A, B, C and so on) and some might be given as marks (for example, 15 out of 20, or 38 out of 60, and so on).

Whatever, the nature of the data, however, the guiding rule should be to decide on a common basis for measurement. You need to work out how to convert the data in different forms into the common basis you have selected. Once you have worked out how to do this, the process of converting the data to a common basis and putting it into a table should be reasonably straightforward.

An example is given below. You might like to try your own solution before reading ours.

Example

A small software company is currently working on five IT projects. It employs systems analysts, programmers and support staff on each project, and staff are regularly switched from one project to another. Every month, the chief accountant collects data about the time worked by each category of employee on each project.

For April 20X4, the following data has been submitted on time sheets.

Systems analysts

	Project PJ1	Project PJ2	Project PJ3	Project PJ4	Project PJ5
	days	days	days	days	days
Employee A	6	1	0	2	10
Employee B	3	5.5	4.5	2	6

Systems analysts work an eight-hour day.

Programmers

	Project PJ1	Project PJ2	Project PJ3	Project PJ4	Project PJ5
	hours	hours	hours	hours	hours
Employee C	17	58	0	62	24
Employee D	52	0	48	12	40

Support staff worked a total of 76 days in the month: 5 man-days on project PJ1, 18 man-days on project PJ2, 23 man-days on project PJ3,11 man-days on project PJ4 and 19 man-days on project PJ5. Support staff work a 7½-hour day.

Required:

Tabulate this data to show the total time spent by staff on each of the projects and in total during the month.

Solution

The data is presented differently for each category of staff. Basically, however, some times are given in days and some are given in hours. You could choose to convert all times into days, but as we are not told how many hours a day are worked by programmers, it is probably much simpler to convert all times to hours. To do this, multiply the days worked by the systems analysts by 8 and the number of days worked by the support staff by 7½.

	Project PJ1	Project PJ2	Project PJ3	Project PJ4	Project PJ5	Total
	hours	hours	hours	hours	hours	hours
Systems analysts	72.0	52	36.0	32.0	128.0	320
Programmers	69.0	58	48.0	74.0	64.0	313
Support staff	37.5	135	172.5	82.5	142.5	570
Total	178.5	245	256.5	188.5	334.5	1,203

8 FREQUENCY DISTRIBUTIONS IN TABLES

A **frequency distribution** shows the number of times (frequency) that given values occur, in either a population or a sample. It can be presented in the form of a table, a diagram such as a bar chart or a graph.

Definition A **frequency distribution** is the measure of the number of times that each particular occurrence takes place.

The original data for this will often be in a fairly unmanageable form and as a first step to producing a frequency distribution, it might have to be summarised. One way of doing this is to count the frequencies using tally marks.

For example, suppose that you are given a list of all the scores in the day's professional football matches, and you are asked to work out how many matches ended as home wins, how many were away wins and how many were draws. You could obtain the information by going through the list of scores one by one, and adding each score to a tally of home wins, away wins or draws as appropriate. When you have worked your way through the list, you can then add up the tally count for each type of result, to obtain the totals you require.

It is common practice when making a tally count to build 'five-bar gates'. Each time a value or score occurs, it is recorded with a I. The first four times the value occurs it is recorded each time with a I. So after four of the same value have been counted, we have IIII. The fifth time the value occurs, it is marked as a diagonal line across the other four: HHt

In this way the items are grouped in fives, which makes them easier to add up at the end of the exercise.

Example

A survey was made of the 20 employees in a department, to find out how long, to the nearest year, each of them had worked there. The survey revealed that the length of service of each of the 20 employees was as follows.

5	1	3	2	3
2	2	6	5	5
1	2	0	3	2
2	1	6	0	4

Task: Record this information in a table.

Solution

The range of years of service goes from 0 up to 6, and we want to count the frequency of each of the values 0, 1, 2, 3, 4, 5 and 6. A count can be made by going through the 20 items of data one by one, building up a count with tally marks.

Frequency distribution – years of service

Years	Number of times
0	II
1	III
2	HHt I
3	III
4	I
5	III
6	II

The table to record the frequency distribution can now be prepared as follows:

Frequency distribution – years of service

Years	Number of times
0	2
1	3
2	6
3	3
4	1
5	3
6	2
	20

ACTIVITY 10

The performance of a team of 30 sales representatives has been monitored, to establish a frequency distribution of the number of new clients won by individual representatives during the past 12 months. The following list shows the number of new clients won by each of the sales representatives.

2	7	8	3	5	6
5	6	1	0	5	7
2	4	4	5	1	8
5	4	8	6	3	1
5	4	8	2	8	5

Task: Prepare a frequency distribution table for this data.

For a suggested answer, see the 'Answers' section at the end of the book.

9   GROUPED FREQUENCY DISTRIBUTION

In many cases the number of possible 'scores' or occurrences is so large that recording the frequency of each score would be of little use. For example, suppose that the managers of a supermarket chain wanted some information about weekly sales in each of its stores, presented as a frequency distribution. It would be useless to record the frequencies of different amounts of weekly sales turnover to the nearest £1, or even to the nearest £100 or even £1,000, because no two stores will have such identical weekly sales turnover.

Instead, we can record the number of 'scores' or occurrences within a particular band or range of values. This is known as a grouped frequency distribution.

In our example of supermarket sales, we might count the number of stores with weekly sales from £20,000.00 - £29,999.99, and from £30,000.00 to £39,999.99 and £40,000.00 to £49,999.99, and so on.

9.1   PREPARING A GROUPED FREQUENCY DISTRIBUTION

If you are required to produce a grouped frequency distribution in a table, you might find the following guidelines helpful.

Step 1   Find the highest and lowest values in the data.

Step 2   Calculate the range of values – in other words, calculate the difference between the highest and the lowest data value.

Step 3   Decide how to divide up the range into groups or 'bands'. You should normally try to limit the number of groups or bands in a grouped

frequency distribution to somewhere between 5 and 15. Wherever possible, the range of values in each band should be of equal amounts. The exception will often be for the lowest and highest value bands.

Step 4   Work through the data recording tally marks in the same way as for normal frequency distributions.

Step 5   Add up the tally marks to find the number of occurrences that fall within each band of values.

Open-ended bands

For the lowest and highest value bands, it might be appropriate to have an open-ended range of values.

- At the bottom end, the lowest range of values would be 'less than ...'

- At the top end, the range of values would be 'more than ...'

For example if the heights of a group of adult males is measured in a grouped frequency distribution, the most suitable lowest band or 'class interval' of heights might be 'less than 1.50 metres' and the most appropriate upper class interval might be '2 metres or more'. The class intervals between the bottom and the top might be either 5 or 10 centimetres (0.05 or 0.10 metres).

Class limits

Class limits are the starting and finishing values in the band. They therefore show which values from the data are included the band or class.

For *continuous data* the best method of expressing the class intervals is in the following manner:

1.50 metres and less than 1.55 metres
1.55 metres and less than 1.60 metres
1.60 metres and less than 1.65 metres, and so on.

This is quite clear and there is no ambiguity concerning which class any piece of data would fall into. This method of classification can also be abbreviated to:

1.50 - < 1.55 metres
1.55 - < 1.60 metres
1.60 - < 1.65 metres, and so on.

Note: The symbol < means less than. The symbol > means 'more than'.

If the data has exact whole number values (if the data is 'discrete') then 'less than 5' would in fact mean any number up to and including 4. In this case therefore the classes could therefore be shown as:

0 - 4
5 - 9
10 – 14, and so on

Example

A group of 30 accountancy students have recently sat an examination and their percentage marks are recorded below:

55	61	32	74	80	41
43	58	82	38	45	59
34	36	68	63	55	66
48	41	46	87	63	44
31	49	52	54	75	70

Organise these results into suitable class intervals and show the number of scores within each class interval.

Solution

Step 1   Find the highest and lowest figures from the data.

Highest 87

Lowest 31

Step 2   Determine the range of values between the highest and lowest.

Range = 87 – 31 = 56

Step 3   Decide upon the class intervals to be used. The most appropriate size of class interval will be either 5 or 10. Here, class intervals or bands of 5 are chosen, except with a larger band of 10 at the lowest end (30 – 39) and the top end (80 – 89).

This is because there are only a few results that are below 40 or above 80 and therefore class intervals of 10 have been used for these opening and closing classes rather than the intervals of 5 for the other classes.

30 - 39

40 - 44

45 - 49

50 - 54

55 - 59

60 - 64

65 - 69

70 - 74

75 - 79

80 - 89

Step 4   Work through the raw data inserting a tally mark in each class interval whenever a score falls within the class interval.

Class interval	Tally
30 - 39	H̶H̶
40 - 44	IIII
45 - 49	IIII
50 - 54	II
55 - 59	IIII
60 64	III
65 - 69	II
70 - 74	II
75 - 79	I
80 - 90	III

Step 5   Total the tally marks in order to find the class or group frequencies.

Exam mark	Number of students
30 - 39	5
40 - 44	4
45 - 49	4
50 - 54	2
55 - 59	4
60 - 64	3
65 - 69	2
70 - 74	2
75 - 79	1
80 - 89	3

ACTIVITY 11

An organisation is concerned about the output of one of its production departments and has recorded output in units each day for 25 days. The units of output for each of the 25 days are as follows:

560	613	598	575	587
571	567	612	600	639
624	558	583	603	584
562	574	626	572	551
618	582	592	571	588

Produce a grouped frequency distribution showing these results.

For a suggested answer, see the 'Answers' section at the end of the book.

CONCLUSION

This chapter has introduced some important mathematical techniques for summarising data, and has explained a number of different ways in which data can be presented in tabular form.

For accountants, presenting numerical data in tables is possibly the most common method of data presentation for report writing you will use. It is important to feel comfortable preparing tables from numerical data. To a large extent, an ability to tabulate data depends largely on:

•   an ability to understand what the data is intended to show, and then

•   deciding on the columns and rows for the table.

When you are consolidating information from two or more sources, make sure that the data from each source is consistent with the data from the other sources. If you are consolidating data for two or more divisions in the same business, remember that internal transfers of goods between the divisions should not be included in the consolidated values for total sales.

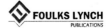

SELF TEST QUESTIONS

KEY TERMS

Average – a middle value of figures.

Weighted average – the figures used are weighted according to the number of times they appear.

Moving average – an average value for a given period of time that is re-calculated at regular intervals, so that a picture emerges of how the average is changing or 'moving' over time.

Standard units of input and output – when recording or processing data into information, it is sometimes necessary to convert different items into standard units, in order to make sense of the figures.

Measuring the cost of output – businesses can measure the cost of the work they do in terms of the cost per standard hour.

Measuring productivity – actual hours worked by an organisation or a department are compared with the standard number of hours produced.

Resource utilisation –the extent to which available resources are being used.

Per cent –'out of 100' and is written as '%'.

Ratio – an alternative way of expressing a fraction. Ratios compare the size of one thing with the size of something else.

Proportion – the ratio of a part to the whole. It is usually expressed as a fraction or decimal.

Statistics – collections of numerical facts or estimates.

Primary data – data that has been especially collected for a particular enquiry.

Secondary data – data that has not been collected for a particular enquiry, but has been obtained from an existing available source.

Frequency distribution – the measure of the number of times that each particular occurrence takes place.

FOULKS LYNCH
PUBLICATIONS

Chapter 3

PRESENTING INFORMATION: DIAGRAMS

This chapter describes the most common methods of presenting information in a report in the form of a diagram.

CONTENTS

KNOWLEDGE AND UNDERSTANDING

		Reference
1	Methods of presenting information: ... diagrammatic	Item 14

PERFORMANCE CRITERIA

		Reference
1	Prepare reports in the appropriate form and present them to management within the required timescales	Item F, element 7.1

LEARNING OUTCOMES

At the end of this chapter, you should be able to:

- construct a pictogram
- construct and interpret a pie chart
- explain the uses of a pie chart
- construct a simple bar chart
- construct a component bar chart
- construct a percentage bar chart

- explain the uses of bar charts

- construct a histogram, and explain what a histogram might be used for.

1 USING DIAGRAMS IN REPORTS

Tables are used in reports to present a quantity of numerical information in an organised and readily-understandable form. Sometimes, however, tables are not necessarily the best way of presenting data. Key information might possibly be presented more clearly in the form of a diagram or a graph.

Types of diagram used in reports include:

- pictograms, although these are not common

- pie charts

- bar charts

- histograms.

You might be familiar with most of these already. However, you also need to appreciate when each type of diagram might be useful in a report, and you also need how to construct each type of diagram yourself, from given data.

1.1 THE NATURE OF THE DATA IN DIAGRAMS

A diagram is most suitable for presenting fairly basic data that can be readily-understood by looking at it quickly. A diagram that is hard to understand is of little or no value.

1.2 RULES FOR PREPARATION OF DIAGRAMS

Diagrams should be as clear as possible. To achieve clarity, a number of rules should be followed:

- Each diagram should be given a name or a title, describing what it is showing

- The source of the data should be given, if it is an external source

- The units of measurement should be stated

- Where appropriate, a scale should be shown so that sizes and values can be seen

- The presentation should be neat. Where suitable, different parts of a diagram should be shaded or coloured differently.

2 PICTOGRAMS

Pictograms are a simple way of showing the numbers of an item, where the item can be easily represented by a picture. For example, a report about a shipping company can show the number of ships that it owns by presenting pictures of a quantity of ships. Similarly, the number of oil wells in a country can be portrayed by drawing pictures of oil wells. One picture or symbol is used to represent a unit or a quantity of the item.

For example, in a report about a shipping company, each picture of one ship might represent 10 ships that the company owns, so if the company owns 30 ships, this could be portrayed in a report by drawing three ships.

Pictograms might be useful in showing how numbers have changed over time, as the following example illustrates.

Example

The following pictogram represents the car sales for British Mayland for the three consecutive years 20X1 to 20X3:

Car sales by British Mayland, 20X1 to 20X3

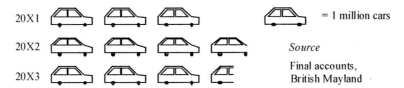

A higher value is shown by a bigger number of pictorial units. In the example above, we can see immediately that sales were 3 million cars in 20X1, went up to nearly 4 million cars in 20X2 but then declined to about 3.5 million in 20X3.

It might also be apparent, however, that a pictogram is not very accurate, and in the example above, it is not possible to understand what numbers exactly are represented by a fraction of a picture of a car. It is probably better to use complete diagrams only (and round the figures to the nearest suitable multiple of pictures).

Another common use of pictograms is for representing numbers of people. For example, a pictogram could be used to represent the population of a country, or the numbers of employees in a business. Where pictograms are used to represent numbers of people, it might also be useful to show numbers of men and numbers of women with different pictures.

ACTIVITY 1

The following information is provided about the numbers of staff in an organisation for 20X1 to 20X3.

Year	Men	Women
20X1	400	100
20X2	550	200
20X3	600	170

Task

Show this data in the form of a pictogram.

This activity covers performance criterion F in element 7.1.

For a suggested answer, see the 'Answers' section at the end of the book.

2.1 CONCLUSION ABOUT PICTOGRAMS

Pictograms are an excellent way of presenting visual data about quantities to create an instant and lasting impression. They are particularly useful for showing how total numbers increase over time. However they are also difficult to both present and interpret exactly.

3 PIE CHARTS

The main purpose of a pie chart is to illustrate the relative sizes of different components elements of a total. It shows how the total ('the pie') is divided up into its different components or parts.

It gets its name because it is the shape of a pie (a round circle) and the component elements are portrayed as slices of the pie. A larger component element is drawn as a bigger slice.

Definition   A **pie chart** is a circle that is divided into different portions in order to represent different components of the total.

3.1 USES OF A PIE CHART

If you are wondering when a pie chart might be used in a report, the key point to remember is that it is used to show **how a total is divided up**. Here are some possible uses:

- A business might sell a number of different products. A pie chart can be used to show what proportion of total sales revenue comes from sales of each of the individual products.

- A company might be organised into four different sales regions. A pie chart could be used to show what proportion of total sales were made in each of the regions.

- An accountant might be writing a report about aged debtors. A pie chart could be used to show what proportion of total debts have been outstanding for, say, less than 30 days, 31 – 60 days, 61 – 90 days and over 90 days.

- A pie chart can be drawn to show how much of a partnership business is owned by each of the individual partners.

3.2 CONSTRUCTING A PIE CHART: CALCULATING THE DEGREES IN EACH SEGMENT OR SLICE

A pie chart should be drawn as accurately as possible and the slices of the pie should be the right size.

One way of drawing an accurate pie chart is by computer. It is possible to input some data into a spreadsheet program, and then instruct the program to present the numbers in pie chart form. The computer-produced pie chart can then be copied into the report you are writing.

However, you also need to understand how to draw a pie chart by hand, using a protractor.

The starting point for drawing a pie chart is that a pie is drawn as a circle, and a circle has 360 degrees (360°). The degrees in a circle are measured from the exact centre spot in the middle of the circle.

The first steps are as follows.

- Decide what the segments of the pie chart will represent.

- Obtain the data for the total value represented by the pie, and the size of each segment. The data might be in actual numbers, such as sales revenue figures or numbers of employees, and so on, or they might be given to you as percentage values.

- For each segment of the pie chart, calculate the number of degrees of the circle (i.e. the number of degrees out of the total of 360) that should be represented

by the segment. Calculating the number of degrees for each segment is found by calculating:

$$\frac{\text{Size of segment}}{\text{Total size}} \times 360$$

If you do this for each segment, you should find that the total number of degrees for all the segments together is 360.

Example

An organisation has three divisions and the proportion of sales in each division are 20%, 35% and 45%.

Task

Convert these percentages into the degrees of a circle that would be necessary in order to construct a pie chart.

Solution

There are three segments for the pie chart, each representing the sales in one of the regions. Here, we are given the data as percentage values, so the total for all three segments is 100%.

In order to convert a percentage to a number of degrees, each percentage must be multiplied by 360/100.

The calculations are therefore as follows:

20% × 360/100	=	72°
35% × 360/100	=	126°
45% × 360/100	=	162°
		360°

ACTIVITY 2

A business achieved the following results for the year just ended.

	£	£
Sales		420,000
Production costs	160,000	
Administration costs	75,000	
Selling and distribution costs	104,000	
Research and development costs	63,000	
		402,000
Profit		18,000

You are asked to construct a pie chart showing what proportion of total revenue is made up by each category of cost, and what proportion represents profit.

As a first step to constructing a pie chart, you need to decide the size of each segment of the pie, in degrees.

Task

Calculate the size of each segment of the pie chart in degrees, giving your figures to the nearest whole number of degrees.

This activity covers performance criterion F in element 7.1.

For a suggested answer, see the 'Answers' section at the end of the book.

FOULKS LYNCH
PUBLICATIONS

3.3 CONSTRUCTING A PIE CHART: DRAWING THE SEGMENTS

The next step in drawing a pie chart is to draw a circle to represent the pie. You might have a template for a circle, which you can use to draw your circle simply by drawing round the shape. Alternatively, you might need to draw a circle with a compass. The size of the circle doesn't matter.

(You might even be given a blank circle in your answer sheets and asked to use it to construct a pie chart.)

To draw a pie chart by hand, you also need a protractor. A protractor is a see-through (plastic or perspex) semi-circle, on which the degrees in the half-circle (from the centre of the circle) are marked around its curved edge.

If you draw a line through the exact middle of the circle, from one edge of the circle to the opposite edge, you will have drawn a line showing the circle's diameter. The diameter you draw will cut circle into two equal halves, and measured from the centre spot, each half of the circle consists of 180° (360°/2).

- You can place the protractor on one half of the circle, with the centre of the flat side of the protractor positioned exactly on the mid-point of your circle.

- Take the size of the first segment you want to draw, and mark off the angle from the centre of the circle using the protractor. You should mark the angle by making a dot with your pencil. Then join up the centre of your circle and the dot you have marked, and take the line you draw to the edge of the circle. When you have done this, you should have drawn the first segment of your pie chart.

- To draw the next segment, move the base of the protractor (the flat side) round until it lies along the segment line you have just drawn. Keep the centre of the base line of the protractor on the centre of your circle.

- You can now draw the next segment, by marking off the number of degrees from the line you have just drawn. Use the same methodology as for drawing the first segment.

- Repeat this process for each segment that you have to draw.

This might seem a bit complicated, but an example might clarify the process for you.

Example

Hubble Farm grows a variety of crops. The amount of its land dedicated to each type of crop is shown below.

Wheat	43%
Barley	20%
Rye	16%
Oats	12%
Other	9%

Task

Construct a pie chart to illustrate this data, showing the proportion of the farmland used for growing each type of crop.

Solution

Step 1   Calculate the size of each segment in degrees.

Grain	%	Angle of sector (degrees)
Wheat	43	$360 \times \dfrac{43}{100}$ = 155
Barley	20	$360 \times \dfrac{20}{100}$ = 72
Rye	16	$360 \times \dfrac{16}{100}$ = 58
Oats	12	$360 \times \dfrac{12}{100}$ = 43
Other	9	$360 \times \dfrac{9}{100}$ = 32
	100	360

Step 2   Draw the pie chart.

The following pie chart represents the proportion of each type of grain produced on the land of Hubble Farm. Notice that:

- The pie chart has been given a title
- Each segment of the pie is labelled to show what it represents
- The size of each segment is also shown. Here, the segment sizes are shown as percentage figures, but in other pie charts, actual numbers might be shown instead.

Hubble Farm

Allocation of farmland to different types of crop

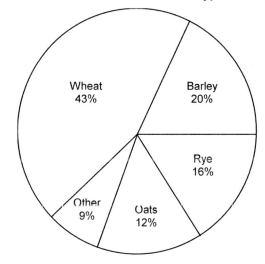

The segments are drawn as follows.

- Draw a circle and then draw a line from one edge of the circle to the opposite edge, which goes through the exact centre of the circle. (One half of this line will not be needed in the pie chart, and will have to be rubbed out later with an eraser.)
- Place your protractor on the centre of the circle, along the line you have drawn. Mark an angle of 155° to represent the segment for wheat. Mark this angle with a dot on the outside edge of the protractor. Draw a line between the centre of

the circle and your dot. The line should go from the centre of the circle to the outer edge (the circumference.)

- Now place the bottom edge of the protractor along the new line you have just drawn, with the centre of its base line on top of the centre of your circle. Now mark an angle of 72° to represent the segment for barley. Again, draw a line between the centre of the circle and your dot, taking the line to the outer edge (the circumference) of the circle, but no further.

- Repeat the process for rye (58°) and oats (43°).

- You should find that when you have drawn your fourth segment for oats, you will also have drawn the fifth and final segment for other crops (32°).

3.4 CONSTRUCT A PIE CHART USING A COMPUTER

Pie charts can be drawn using a spreadsheet program, for example Excel. Open a blank document and type in the values, e.g. 43, 20, 16, 12, 9. Select these values using the mouse and then click on icon 'Chart Wizard' in the tool bar. You will have four steps to complete before your pie chart is finished.

Step 1	You need to select what type of chart you want – in this case it will be pie chart. (You can also select a bar chart or a column chart etc.) At this stage you will be able to select a sub-type of a pie chart. When completed click next.
Step 2	Gives you an option of having the slices of the pie presented in the form of columns or rows. In the case of pie chart you need to choose columns. Click next.
Step 3	Here you are given an option of inputting the title of your pie chart. This step also gives you possibility of choosing how you want the legend on your chart displayed and whether you want the data labelled (here percentages of crops) and in what form. When completed click next.
Step 4	You need to select where you want your pie chart created: on the separate sheet in your Excel document or as an object in sheet one. Click finish.

You can change values in your pie chart by simply changing the values that you had originally inserted, without creating a new pie chart. Try changing your values to 20, 20, 16, 12, 9 instead of 43, 20, 16, 12, 9. This will automatically change the sizes of the slices in the pie chart, as needed. The created chart can be copied and pasted in another document, for example a Word document.

You can also adjust the size of the pie chart and the whole image by clicking and dragging the outside borders of the image.

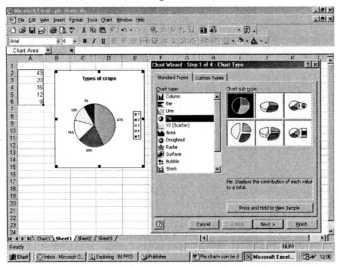

FOULKS LYNCH
PUBLICATIONS

ACTIVITY 3

The following information is available about the profitability for 20X4 of the six different divisions of an organisation.

Division	Profit - 20X4
	£000
A	240
B	380
C	140
D	170
E	290
F	180
	———
	1,400
	———

Illustrate this data using a pie chart.

This activity covers performance criterion F in element 7.1.

For a suggested answer, see the 'Answers' section at the end of the book.

4 BAR CHARTS

Another form of diagram for presenting quantitative information is a bar chart. As its name suggests, a bar chart consists of one or more bars. Each bar demonstrates the size of an item. When there are several bars in the diagram, all the bars have the same width (which has no significance) but different lengths. The lengths of the different bars provide an easily-understandable comparison of relative sizes.

A bar chart is usually drawn up in the form of a graph. The vertical axis is normally used to indicate size, and the bars are drawn vertically. In other words, larger items are drawn with taller bars. The horizontal axis is normally used for the bases of the bars.

Sometimes, each bar represents a period of time, such as a month or a year. In such cases, the horizontal axis represents time, with the bar for each period shown to the right of the bar for the previous period.

There are several types of bar chart:

- simple bar charts

- component bar charts

- percentage component bar charts

- compound bar charts.

4.1 SIMPLE BAR CHARTS

In a simple bar chart, each bar shows the overall size of an item. For example, a simple bar chart might be used to show the total profit earned in each of five sales regions, North, South, East and West. This would be drawn as four bars, one for each sales region. The length of each bar would represent the amount of profit earned in each region.

 **FOULKS LYNCH**
PUBLICATIONS

Similarly, a bar chart might be used to illustrate total sales revenue earned by a business each year over the past five years. This would be drawn as five bars, one for each year. The length of each bar would represent the amount of sales revenue for the year. The bars would be drawn in sequence, with the earliest year on the left and the most recent year on the right.

Normally, an indication of size is given in the bar chart, with a measuring scale shown on the vertical axis of the chart.

A simple bar chart is drawn as follows:

Step 1   Plan the diagram. Decide what bar or bars need to be drawn, and what each bar represents. In a simple bar chart, each bar can represent just one value for one item. Decide the measurement scale that you will be using, so that the chart will be a good size (neither too big nor too small) when it is drawn.

Step 2   Draw the two axes of a graph. The vertical axis will show the measurements of size. The size of the largest item, which will have the longest bar, should be used to decide what the scale of the measurements should be. For example, if the largest item is 768, you might decide that the vertical axis should go up to 800, and that the chart should show the measurement scale in units of 100. You might then decide that each 100 units can be represented by 1 centimetre of height on the chart, so that your chart will be 8 centimetres high. Clearly label the chart with the scale you are using.

For the horizontal axis, decide how many bars will be drawn and space them out in a suitable way. Each bar should have the same width.

Step 3   Draw each of the bars with equal widths and with their heights representing the size of the item. The bars can be either separated by a space or they can be drawn side by side with no space between them.

Step 4   Give the bar chart a title and label each bar clearly to show what it represents. If the bar chart represents results over a period of months or years, each bar should be labelled as the month or year that it represents. Where appropriate, indicate in a footnote the source of any data you have used.

You can create a bar chart using a computer. The procedure is the same as when creating pie charts except that in Step 1 when selecting what type of chart you want, you select 'column' instead of 'pie chart'.

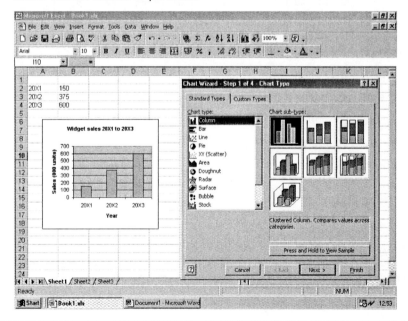

Example

Sales of widgets by GH Daniels in the years 20X1 to 20X3 were as follows:

Year	Sales of widgets
	000s units
20X1	150
20X2	375
20X3	600

Task

Illustrate this data using a simple bar chart.

Solution

Step 1   The simple bar chart will consist of three bars, one for each year, and each bar will indicate the volume of sales in the year.

Step 2   The vertical axis will be used to represent the volume of sales. The largest value is 600,000 units, so the height of the chart does not need to exceed 600,000. However, in the solution below, the scale is extended to 700,000.

The horizontal axis is used to represent time, with the bar for 20X1 on the left, followed by the bars for 20X2 then 20X3.

Step 3   Draw the bars with equal widths, and with their heights representing the volume of sales in the year. Label each bar clearly to show the year it represents.

Step 4   Give the bar chart a title. Here, the data has been gathered internally, and so there is no need to show its source.

GH Daniels

Widget sales 20X1 to 20X3

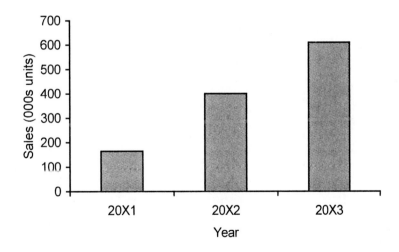

Interpretation of a simple bar chart

A simple bar chart shows not only the size of each bar and so the amount of a particular item. It also shows the relative size of different bars, so that an easy visual comparison can be made. In the example above, for instance, the bar chart shows clearly that annual sales of widgets have grown substantially over the past three years.

If the chart had shown longer bars on the left and shorter bars in the right, this would have indicated declining annual sales.

Simple bar charts are most effective when they are used to make such comparisons.

Another common use of a simple bar chart is to demonstrate cyclical or seasonal patterns.

Example

The monthly sales of Vic's Garage have been as follows during 20X5.

Month	Sales £000
January	15
February	15
March	25
April	35
May	40
June	35
July	10
August	10
September	20
October	40
November	35
December	5

Task

Show this information in a simple bar chart and interpret the data.

Solution

The chart will consist of 12 bars, each representing sales in a month.

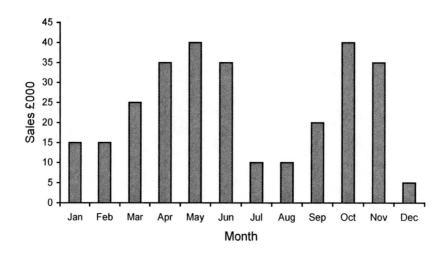

Vic's Garage
Monthly sales

FOULKS LYNCH
PUBLICATIONS

The bar chart shows that the business has two peak periods for sales, I April to June and in October-November. The pattern in this year can be compared with the monthly sales patterns in other years, to establish whether the pattern in regular every year.

ACTIVITY 4

The annual sales for Akia Ltd for the last six years have been as follows:

Year	Sales
	£000
20X4	42
20X5	50
20X6	75
20X7	70
20X8	80
20X9	94

Task

Illustrate this data using a simple bar chart.

This activity covers performance criterion F, element 7.1

For a suggested answer, see the 'Answers' section at the end of the book.

4.2 COMPONENT BAR CHART

A component bar chart is another type of bar chart. In a component bar chart, each bar shows the component elements of the total value of each bar. For example:

- A bar chart might be used to show total annual sales as the bars in a bar chart, but each bar representing total sales for a particular year might then be sub-divided to show the sales from each of the products or services sold by the business.

- A bar chart might be used to shown the changes in the total size of a work force over time, but each bar representing the total number of employees in a particular year is also analysed into the numbers of different types of employee within the total work force.

Example

Continuing with the previous example of annual sales of widgets by GH Daniels, suppose that annual sales can now be split into regional sales as follows.

Year	Total	South region	Central region	North region
		Sales (000 units)		
20X1	150	20	60	70
20X2	375	25	150	200
20X3	600	40	250	310

We can draw a component bar chart to illustrate this data. This is done by drawing a simple bar chart to begin with, and then dividing each bar into its component elements, which are here the sales for each of the three regions.

FOULKS LYNCH
PUBLICATIONS

Solution

GH Daniels

Sales of widgets 20X1 to 20X3

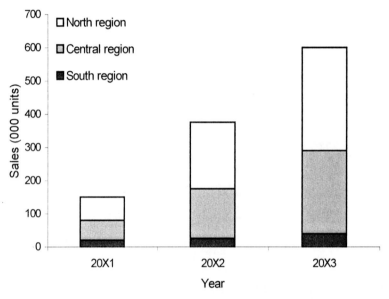

Tutorial note: Note the following points about a component bar chart:

- There must be a key to explain what each element of the bar represents.

- The bar chart should be drawn by drawing the total length of each bar, the same way as for a simple bar chart, and then dividing each bar into its component elements.

- From this type of chart, changes in the constituent elements of the total values can be seen. For example, the chart above shows that the growth in total sales is due mainly to sales growth in the central and northern regions, whereas sales growth in the sales region has been much more modest.

ACTIVITY 5

The annual sales for Akia Ltd for the last six years can be broken down into three different product groups as follows:

Year	Total sales	Product group		
		A	B	C
	£000	£000	£000	£000
20X4	42	12	10	20
20X5	50	18	12	20
20X6	75	30	15	30
20X7	70	30	15	25
20X8	80	35	20	25
20X9	94	37	27	30

Task

Illustrate this data using a component bar chart.

This activity covers performance criterion F in element 7.1.

For a suggested answer, see the 'Answers' section at the end of the book.

4.3 PERCENTAGE COMPONENT BAR CHARTS

A percentage component bar chart is a component bar chart where the one where the actual value of each bar is irrelevant. Instead, each bar in the chart is drawn with the same length.

As its name might suggest, the purpose of a percentage component bar chart is to show what percentage of the total is made up of each component element. The bars in this type of chart are all the same height (representing 100%) and are split according to the proportions of each component element.

A percentage component bar chart is therefore of no use for measuring actual values but can be a useful indicator of changes in the component elements of data.

Example

A business sells three products, X, Y and Z. Annual sales for the years 20X1 to 20X3 can be split into sales of X, Y and Z as follows:

Year	Sales (units)			
	Total	X	Y	Z
20X1	150	20	60	70
20X2	375	25	150	200
20X3	600	40	250	310

Task

From the information given above, draw a percentage component bar chart.

Solution

Step 1 Convert the absolute numbers each year into percentages of the annual total. The actual units of sales each year are of no significance for a percentage component bar chart.

Year	Total units	X units	%	Y units	%	Z units	%
				Sales			
20X1	150	20	13	60	40	70	47
20X2	375	25	7	150	40	200	53
20X3	600	40	7	250	42	310	51

Step 2 Draw up the percentage component bar chart. The height of each bar should be the same, and the scale on the vertical axis should be from 0% to 100%.

Annual sales 20X1 to 20X3

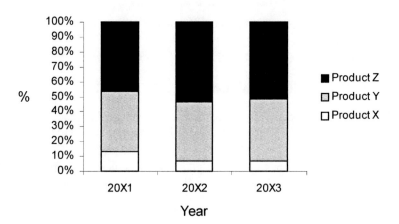

This shows that the proportions of sales product X have declined since 20X1, and the proportion of sales of Y and Z have increased slightly.

ACTIVITY 6

The information from a previous activity is shown again below.

The annual sales for Akia Ltd for the last six years can be broken down into three different product groups as follows:

Year	Total		Product group	
	sales	A	B	C
	£000	£000	£000	£000
20X4	42	12	10	20
20X5	50	18	12	20
20X6	75	30	15	30
20X7	70	30	15	25
20X8	80	35	20	25
20X9	94	37	27	30

Task

Draw a percentage component bar chart to illustrate this data.

This activity covers performance criterion F in element 7.1.

For a suggested answer, see the 'Answers' section at the end of the book.

4.4 COMPOUND BAR CHARTS

Compound bar charts are sometimes called multiple bar charts. In a compound bar chart, there is more than one bar for each sub-division of the chart.

Typically, each sub-division of the chart represents a time period, such as a month or a year. Instead of having one bar representing the time period, there are several. For

example, if the chart shows annual sales of each product, then for each year there could be a separate bar for sales of each product.

With a component bar chart, the component elements are all shown as part of the same bar. With a compound bar chart, the component elements are shown as separate bars.

The measurements for the bars can be either actual figures (for example units of sale or annual sales revenue) or percentages.

Example

An example used before is given again below.

Annual sales by a business for the years 20X1 to 20X3 can be split into sales of three products, X, Y and Z.

Year	Sales (units)			
	Total	X	Y	Z
20X1	150	20	60	70
20X2	375	25	150	200
20X3	600	40	250	310

Task

Illustrate this data in a compound bar chart.

Solution

Here the maximum annual sales of any product is 310, which were the sales of product Z in 20X3. The vertical scale of the chart therefore only needs to go to 310. In the chart below, the vertical axis is drawn up to 350.

For each year, sales of each product are shown in a separate bar. Actual units of sale are illustrated here, not percentages. The products can be shown in any order for each year, but you should keep the same order for each year.

Annual sales 20X1 to 20X3

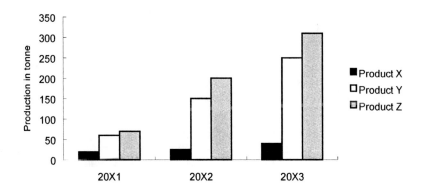

Note: the following points about a compound bar chart:

*   A key is required to explain what each of the bars represents. Here, each bar represents sales of a particular product. Shading is used to distinguish each product from the other.

*   The chart does not show the grand total for each year, so any changes in the total figures are not clearly represented.

*   The changes in comparative size of each component are clearer than with a component bar chart.

ACTIVITY 7

The information from a previous activity is given below.

The annual sales for Akia Ltd for the last six years can be broken down into three different product groups as follows:

Year	Total sales £000	Product group		
		A £000	B £000	C £000
20X4	42	12	10	20
20X5	50	18	12	20
20X6	75	30	15	30
20X7	70	30	15	25
20X8	80	35	20	25
20X9	94	37	27	30

Task

Prepare a compound bar chart to illustrate this data.

What information is readily apparent from the chart?

This activity covers performance criterion F in element 7.1.

For a suggested answer, see the 'Answers' section at the end of the book.

5   HISTOGRAMS

A histogram is a special kind of chart that is used to portray a frequency distribution, and is used to represent the frequencies in a grouped frequency distribution. It is similar to a bar chart, but there are some key differences.

- The horizontal axis is used to represent the values whose frequencies are being measured. There is a bar for each frequency range. For example, a histogram might be used to show the frequencies of the monthly earnings of the employees of a company. The selected ranges of salary might be £700 - £899.99, £900 - £1,099.99, £1,100 - £1,299.99, £1,300 - £1,499.99 and £1,500 - £1,699.99. The numbers of employees earning a monthly salary in each of these selected ranges might be measured. If so, this particular histogram would have five bars.

- Another key point about a histogram is that the frequency of each value range is represented by the **area** of the bar rather than the height of the bar. Therefore if the class intervals are unequal then the heights of the bars will differ.

Example

Data is collected about the results of eight students in an examination. Four of them scored marks in the range 55 – 59 and the other four scored marks in the range 60 – 69.

Notice here that one range of values (55 – 59) covers just five possible scores (55, 56, 57, 58 and 59) whereas the range 60 – 69 covers ten possible scores, and so is twice as big a range. To draw this in a histogram, we would adjust the height of one of the bars to allow for the difference in ranges. In the histogram below, the height of the 60 – 69 bar has been halved, from 4 to 2, to make this adjustment.

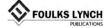

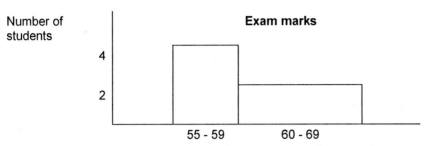

Here, although there are four students in each range of marks, the height of the bar for the range of 10 marks is only half that of the bar for the range of five marks.

This means that there are two types of histogram, those with equal class intervals and those with unequal class intervals.

5.1 HISTOGRAMS WITH EQUAL CLASS INTERVALS

If all the ranges of values ('class intervals') in a frequency distribution are the same size, then there is no need to make any adjustments to the height of any bars to allow for differing ranges. The bars can simply be drawn in the same way as for a bar chart. However, there should be no gaps between bars, and the horizontal axis should represent a continuous range of values.

Example

A company is looking at the age distribution of its work force, and has collected the following data.

Class interval Age (years)	Range of class (years)	Frequency Number of employees
21 and less than 26	5	9
26 and less than 31	5	17
31 and less than 36	5	22
36 and less than 41	5	18
41 and less than 46	5	10

Task

Show this data in a histogram.

Solution

The standard width of a class interval is five years. Notice how the width of each bar coincides with the range of values, here the ages of the employees.

Part of the horizontal axis has been omitted for clarity. The omission is shown by a jagged line.

Note: The bars in the histogram cover a continuous range of values (ages 21 to 46) and there must be no gaps between the vertical bars. In this respect, histograms differ from bar charts, where gaps between bars are permissible.

5.2   HISTOGRAMS WITH UNEQUAL CLASS INTERVALS

If the class intervals of the frequency distribution are not equal, a histogram should be drawn with care, because it differs significantly from a bar chart.

In a histogram, the area of the bar, and not its height, is equal to the frequency. Therefore if the width of the frequency (or class interval) is half of the normal frequency (or class interval) then the height of the bar must be twice the actual frequency of this class.

Example

The examination results of a group of accountancy students has been collected and presented in the following frequency distribution.

Mark	Frequency
30 - 39	5
40 - 44	4
45 - 49	4
50 - 54	2
55 - 59	4
60 - 64	3
65 - 69	2
70 - 74	2
75 - 79	1
80 - 89	3

Task

Represent this data as a histogram.

Solution

The first and the last group frequencies are twice the size of the standard group frequencies. (This is often the case with grouped distributions in order to avoid either very few or no frequencies at extreme levels.)

Step 1   Decide the standard class interval that you will use. For a standard class interval, the height of the bar will be equal to the frequency.

In this case the standard class interval is the most common of 5 marks. This means that if there are four students with a mark in the range, the height of the bar will be 4.

Step 2   Calculate the heights for each bar to be shown on the histogram, bearing in mind the class intervals. If a class interval is twice the standard range, the height of the bar should be the frequency divided by two, as shown in the table below.

Class interval	Range of class	Frequency	Height of bar
30 - 39	10	$5 \times \frac{1}{2}$	2.5
40 - 44	5	4	4
45 - 49	5	4	4
50 - 54	5	2	2
55 - 59	5	4	4
60 - 64	5	3	3
65 - 69	5	2	2
70 - 74	5	2	2
75 - 79	5	1	1
80 - 89	10	$3 \times \frac{1}{2}$	1.5

For the first and last class intervals, in order to give the correct overall area, the height will be only half of the frequency as the width is twice the standard class interval.

Step 3   Draw the histogram.

Accountancy students' examination marks

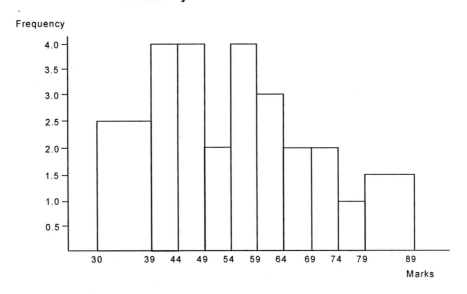

ACTIVITY 8

The information from a previous activity is given again below.

The distribution of output for a production department has been recorded for a period of 25 days and the results are as follows:

Units	Number of days
550 - 559	2
560 - 569	3
570 - 579	5
580 - 589	5

590 - 599	2
600 - 609	2
610 - 619	3
620 - 639	3

Task

Draw a histogram to illustrate this data.

This activity covers performance criterion F in element 7.1.

For a suggested answer, see the 'Answers' section at the end of the book.

CONCLUSION

Data might be presented in the form of a diagram when it might help the reader to see the key information more easily than if the data is presented in another form, such as in a table of figures. The most commonly used types of diagram in business reporting are probably the pie chart and the bar chart.

Computer software, in particular spreadsheet packages, can draw pie charts and bar charts automatically from input data. However, you might have to draw a diagram yourself 'by hand' without the help of a computer program, so you need to understand the basic rules for drawing them.

In addition, you might need to recognise what might be the most appropriate type of diagram for representing any given set of data, a pie chart, a type of bar chart or a histogram.

SELF TEST QUESTIONS

Paragraph

1	Why do we use diagrams in reports?	1
2	State the rules for presentation of diagrams.	1.2
3	What are pictograms used for?	2
4	State an example when it would be useful to present data in the form of a pictogram.	2
5	What are pie charts used for?	3
6	State an example when it would be useful to present data in the form of a pie chart.	3
7	What are bar charts used for?	4
8	State an example when it would be useful to present data in the form of a bar chart.	4
9	What are histograms used for?	5
10	State an example when it would be useful to present data in the form of a histograms.	5

KEY TERMS

Diagram - a suitable way for presenting fairly basic data that can be readily-understood by looking at it quickly.

Pictogram - a simple way of showing the numbers of an item, where the item can be easily represented by a picture.

Pie chart - a circle that is divided into different portions in order to represent different components of the total.

Bar chart - consists of one or more bars, each bar demonstrates the size of an item. All the bars have the same width but different lengths - the lengths of the different bars provide an easily-understandable comparison of relative sizes.

Histogram - a special kind of chart that is used to portray a frequency distribution, and is used to represent the frequencies in a grouped frequency distribution.

Chapter 4

PRESENTING INFORMATION: GRAPHS

This chapter describes methods of presenting information in a report in the form of a graph.

CONTENTS

KNOWLEDGE AND UNDERSTANDING

		Reference
1	Time series analysis	Item 9
2	Methods of presenting information: ... diagrammatic	Item 14

PERFORMANCE CRITERIA

		Reference
1	Prepare reports in the appropriate form and present them to management within the required timescales	Item F, element 7.1

LEARNING OUTCOMES

At the end of this chapter, you should be able to:

* draw a simple graph, including a time series analysis graph

* construct a frequency polygon

* construct and interpret a cumulative frequency curve (an ogive)

- construct and interpret a Z chart

- draw a break even chart with graph lines for total costs and total sales revenue

- construct a simple graph from narrative data.

1 INTRODUCTION TO GRAPHS

A graph is a form of diagram. The purpose of a graph is to demonstrate the relationship between the values of two 'variables'. A variable can be anything at all, provided it can be measured. A graph has two axes, a horizontal axis (the x axis) and a vertical axis (the y axis). Each axis is used to represent one of the two variables.

The variable on the horizontal axis is sometimes called the independent variable, and the variable on the y axis is called the dependent variable. This is because when a graph is drawn, it is often assumed that the value of the variable represented by the y axis is somehow dependent on the corresponding value of the variable on the x axis.

A common type of graph shows how the value of a variable changes over time. For example, a graph might be used to show how total annual sales revenue has changed over a number of years or months, or how profits have changed over a number of years. In these graphs, the x axis represents time and the y axis (the dependent variable) represents sales or profits. Graphs where the x axis represents time are called a **time series**.

1.1 RULES FOR DRAWING A GRAPH

Graphs present information as a type of diagram, so they must be clear and readily-understandable. They must also be drawn accurately. There are a few basic rules for the construction of a graph.

- If graphs are drawn by hand, you should use graph paper. The squares on graph paper are to help you to draw the graph accurately, by plotting the points correctly.

- A graph should be clearly labelled. It should have a title. Each axis must be labelled and the units used must be stated e.g. £000, years, hours, miles etc.

- You need to decide what the two variables in the graph should be, and which should go on the x axis and which on the y axis.

y axis

x axis

The dependent variable must always be plotted on the vertical (y) axis and the independent variable on the horizontal (x) axis.

Definition   **Dependent variables** are those whose value are dependent upon the value of the other variable.

Definition   **Independent variables** are those whose value are not dependent upon another variable.

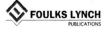

Dependent
variable

Independent
variable

Examples

(a)   When a graph is used to show changes in the value of an item over time, for example sales each month or profits each year over a period of time, the graph will show a time series. **With a time series, time is always the independent variable**, and is plotted on the horizontal axis (x axis). Each square on the graph paper along the horizontal axis represents a day, a month, a quarter or a year, depending on how frequently data is measured.

(b)   Sometimes, a graph is used to show total costs in relation to the volume of production, the volume of sales or the volume of another activity. The assumption is that total costs might rise or fall with the volume of activity. In this sort of graph, the independent variable on the horizontal axis (x axis) should be the volume of activity (production in units, sales in units or money terms, number of hours worked or some other activity measurement). Total costs are the dependent variable and should be plotted on the vertical axis (y axis).

Scales of the axes

Once you know what each axis of the graph will represent, you need to decide on the scale to use for each axis. In other words, what scale should each square on the graph paper represent? To decide this, you need to look at the data you will be drawing on the graph, to see how high the values of the variables go. There are four rules to remember:

-   Try to fill as much of the page of graph paper as possible. A tiny graph on an A4 sheet looks ridiculous and is also difficult to draw and interpret.

    If you are drawing a time series, it is usually sensible to mark each square on the graph paper horizontally as a unit of time (a month or a year etcetera).

-   Use sensible numbers for the scale. Each square of the graph paper, which might be a centimetre, should represent a small number such as 1 or possibly 2 units, or a round number such as 10, 100 or 1,000. This makes the graph easier to draw and to interpret.

    As a guiding rule, take the largest number for data you will be plotting on the graph, and count the number of squares on the graph paper. Then divide the number of squares into this largest value. For example, suppose that on the y axis you will be plotting total annual sales over a period of years and the maximum annual sales in any of the years has been £87,600. You should then count the number of large squares on the graph paper (y axis, in this case). Suppose there are 20 squares. Divide the number of squares into the maximum value for annual sales, and you get £4,380. A suitable scale for each square might therefore be £5,000 (taken to the nearest round figure value up). You might therefore decide that every two squares on the y axis should represent sales of £10,000.

-   There is no need for the same scale to be used on each axis. Even if the units on the x and y axes are the same a different scale for each axis is acceptable.

- The scale must be continuous. For example if the scale on the x axis starts at one square or 1 cm = £100 then it must not change to one square or 1 cm = £1,000 part way along the axis.

Starting point of axis

The scales on both axes should normally start at zero. However in some circumstances this might not be appropriate. For example if the items to be plotted on the y axis are £4,600,000, £4,900,000 and £5,000,000 then it might not be practical to start the scale at zero. In such cases, show that you are not drawing the complete scale from 0 by indicating a break in the scale with a zig-zag line, as follows:

1.2 PLOTTING THE GRAPH

Once the axes and the scale of the graph have been decided and written on to a piece of graph paper, the next step is to record your data on the graph.

The data will consist of several 'pairs of data'. In other words, there will be a value for the variable on the x axis and a corresponding value for the variable on the y axis. Each pair of data should be marked on the graph with a dot or a cross.

This is done by taking a pair of variables, one at a time, and reading along to the value for the x axis variable and then reading up vertically to the corresponding value for the y axis variable. A dot or cross is marked on the graph where the two lines intersect.

For example, to draw a time series analysis showing sales each month for the past 12 months, to plot the sales data for August, read across the x axis of the graph to where August is marked, and then read up from there to the y axis value for the amount of sales. Put a dot or a cross at this point.

When all the pairs of data have been plotted on the graph with dots or crosses, the points can then be joined together. This will usually be done by drawing straight lines between each pair of points. Start with the point on the extreme left hand side and join it with a straight line to the next point to the right that is nearest. Then join this point to the nearest to the right again, and so on until you have joined all the points from left to right on the graph.

In some instances, it might be more appropriate to join the points on a graph with a curved line. However as a general rule join the points with straight lines.

Example

The following data is to be plotted on a graph:

Monthly sales

Month	£
January	6,800
February	7,200
March	5,600

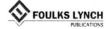

April	6,900
May	7,500
June	8,000

Draw a graph to show this information.

Solution

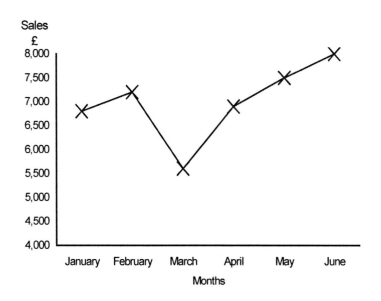

Do not draw a line from the point of intersection of the two axes to the first plotted point. The graph should start at the furthest x point to the left hand side that you have plotted.

ACTIVITY 1

The total cost of production at various levels of production for an organisation are shown below:

Production level	Total cost of production
500 units	£50,000
1,000 units	£90,000
2,000 units	£160,000
3,000 units	£320,000

Draw a graph to show this information.

This activity covers performance criterion F in element 7.1.

For a suggested answer, see the 'Answers' section at the end of the book.

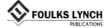

ACTIVITY 2

Sales revenue for each of the past 12 months has been as follows:

Year 20X4	Sales revenue
	£
January	18,400
February	17,200
March	24,900
April	35,200
May	38,800
June	24,700
July	19,600
August	17,100
September	29,500
October	35,500
November	39,400
December	21,000

Task

Plot this data on a graph. You can use the graph paper provided below if you wish. Otherwise use graph paper from another source.

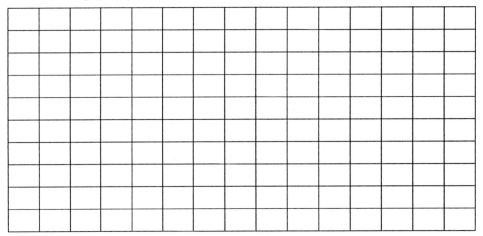

This activity covers performance criterion F in element 7.1.

For a suggested answer, see the 'Answers' section at the end of the book

2 MULTIPLE GRAPHS

You might be required to plot more than one set of data on one graph, with each set of data shown as a separate line. A graph with more than one line is called a multiple graph.

A multiple graph is only possible of the same x axis and the same y axis can be used for all the graph lines you draw.

If more than one line is to appear on a graph, they must be drawn to the same scale. The different lines should be clearly distinguished from each other. If all the lines are drawn in

the same colour, they can be distinguished by drawing one as a continuous line, another as a broken (dashed) line and another as a line of dots, and so on.

_____	continuous line
- - - - - - - - - - - - -	broken line
....	dotted line

If your report uses colour, the lines can be distinguished by giving each a different colour.

A typical example of a multiple graph is a graph showing monthly sales for the year just ended, and also monthly sales for the previous year. The graph then presents in a visual form a comparison month by month between sales in the two years.

Another type of multiple chart is a Z chart, which is explained later.

3 LINE OF BEST FIT

In the graphs illustrated so far, the points next to each other on the graph are joined by a straight line, but the graph line from one end to the other is not a straight line. The line goes up and down between the various points.

Sometimes, a graph might be used to show an estimated straight line across its entire length. An example of this is where data is collected about total costs at different volumes of sales. It might be assumed that there is a direct relationship between total costs and total sales, so that as the volume of sales rises, the amount of total costs rises at a steady rate ('in a straight line'). In such cases, the data collected about actual total costs and total sales volume might be used to estimate a line of best fit, which would be a best estimate from the available data about how costs vary with volume of sales.

There are several ways of drawing a line of best fit, but the method illustrated here uses the 'scatter graph' method.

3.1 SCATTER GRAPH METHOD

A graph that plots a number of points from pairs of data might show that the points lie all over the graph, in an apparently random fashion, and there is no meaning in joining up the points with straight lines. This type of graph is known as a scatter graph.

However, some form of trend might be identified. For example, a scatter graph is used to plot recorded pairs of data for total costs and the corresponding volume of sales over a number of months. The graph would have total sales volume as the x axis and total costs as the y axis.

The points on the graph will be scattered, but it might be possible to detect a trend. As a general rule, we would expect to see higher total costs at higher volumes of sales. The scatter graph should therefore indicate an upward trend. The scatter graph might also indicate an approximate rate of increase in total costs. For example, do total costs appear to rise very sharply as total sales increase, or do total costs rise but at a fairly slow rate as total sales increase?

A line of best fit is a straight line that is drawn on to a scatter graph that is an estimate of how the graph should be drawn as a continuous straight line. To draw such a line, it is necessary to make a visual judgement of where the straight line should go. It is entirely a matter of common sense and judgement. The best advice is to try to keep the number of points above and below the line approximately similar and of similar distances from the line of best fit.

Example

The following data are to be plotted on a graph and a line of best fit then drawn to approximate the trend of the data.

Year	Annual sales total £000
20X0	100
20X1	150
20X2	130
20X3	170
20X4	140
20X5	130
20X6	160
20X7	190
20X8	150
20X9	180

Solution

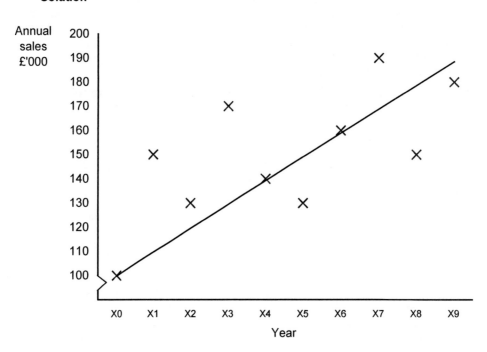

ACTIVITY 3

A scatter graph might be used with a time series, in order to estimate into the future. Here is an example.

The following data are available concerning the output from a factory for a period of 12 weeks.

FOULKS LYNCH
PUBLICATIONS

Week	Output in £000
1	120
2	100
3	150
4	200
5	140
6	190
7	150
8	210
9	200
10	160
11	170
12	200

Task

Plot this data on a scatter graph and draw a line of best fit to approximate the trend of the data.

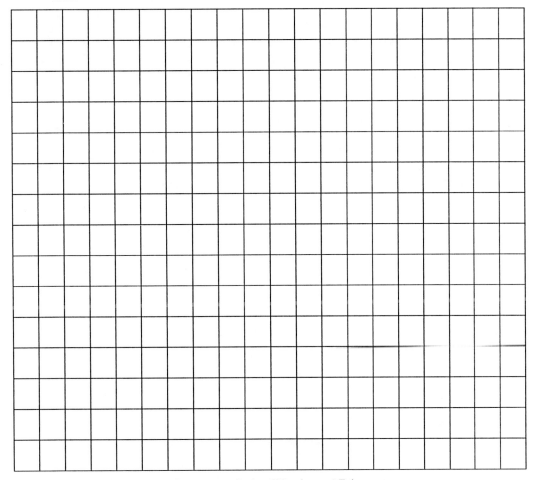

This activity covers performance criterion F in element 7.1.

For a suggested answer, see the 'Answers' section at the end of the book.

4 FREQUENCY POLYGON

Histograms were explained in the previous chapter. A frequency polygon is a graph drawn from a histogram for a grouped frequency distribution. You are unlikely to be required to draw this type of graph, but a brief explanation is given here. (They are quite commonly found in statistics.)

If the mid-points of the tops of the rectangles in a histogram are joined by straight lines, the figure is known as a **frequency polygon.**

The lines at each end of the diagram must be taken to the base line at the centres of the adjoining corresponding class intervals. This is because these two class intervals have, in effect, a zero frequency since they contain no items.

4.1 CONSTRUCTING A FREQUENCY POLYGON

The rules for drawing a frequency polygon are as follows:

Step 1   Draw a histogram from the frequency distribution data. Leave enough space at the start and end of the x axis for one more class interval.

Step 2   Mark the middle point of the top of each bar of the histogram with a cross. Join these mid-points with straight lines.

Step 3   At the left hand side and the right hand side of the histogram, join the cross at the mid-point of the top of the bar to the base line (the x axis). On the left hand side, the graph should be joined to the x axis at the mid point of the class interval to the left of the histogram. On the right hand side, the graph should be joined to the x axis at the mid point of the class interval to the right of the histogram.

Example

The following grouped frequency data were used in the previous chapter to construct a histogram.

A group of 30 accountancy students sat an examination and their percentage marks were grouped as follows:

Percentage mark	Frequency
30 - 39	5
40 - 44	4
45 - 49	4
50 - 54	2
55 - 59	4
60 - 64	3
65 - 69	2
70 - 74	2
75 - 79	1
80 - 89	3

Task

Draw a frequency polygon for this data.

Solution

Make sure you remember how to construct a histogram. To draw a frequency polygon, leave a class interval to the left and a class interval to the right. Since the class intervals on the extreme left-hand side and extreme right-hand side of the histogram are 10 marks (30 – 39 and 80 – 89) leave a class interval of 10 marks to the left of the histogram (20 – 29 marks) and a class interval of 10 marks to the right hand side (90 – 99 marks).

Mark the middle point of the top of each bar of the histogram with a cross. Then join the crosses.

On the left-hand side of the histogram, join the cross at the mid-point for the histogram bar for 30 – 39 marks to the x axis at the mid-point of the class interval for 20 – 29 marks. Similarly, on the right hand side of the histogram, join the cross at the mid-point for the histogram bar for 80 – 89 marks to the x axis at the mid-point of the class interval for 90 – 99 marks.

The lines you have joined form the frequency polygon.

Accountancy examination marks

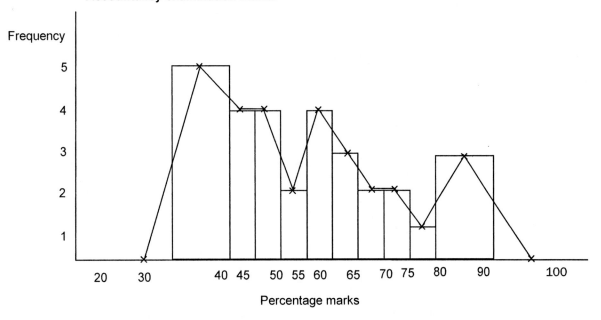

Conclusion: frequency polygons

You might wonder what the purpose of frequency polygons is. Simple frequency polygons are not often used in reports. However, in statistics frequency curves, which are essentially frequency polygons with curved lines instead of straight lines, are commonly used.

5 CUMULATIVE FREQUENCY CURVE: OGIVE

Another way of showing a frequency distribution on a graph is by drawing a cumulative frequency curve. Cumulative frequency curves are also called ogives.

There are two types of cumulative frequency curve or ogive:

• the 'less than' ogive

• the 'more than' ogive.

With an ogive, the x axis represents a range of values. It might represent the marks of students in an examination, or a range of weekly production output volumes at a factory, and so on. The x axis should have the class intervals drawn to scale, in the same way as for any other graph.

The y axis represents the frequencies, for example the numbers of students with marks of a certain amount, or the number of weeks in which certain production volumes were achieved, and so on.

With an ogive, however, the graph shows cumulative frequencies. For each value on the x axis, the ogive shows the total frequencies either above or below the given value.

The 'less than' ogive is more common and therefore is explained here.

5.1 'LESS THAN' OGIVE

A 'less than' ogive shows the frequency (number) of items that are less than or equal to any given amount. This is done by plotting the cumulative frequency of occurrences against the upper class limits of the classes or groups.

A 'less than' ogive is constructed as follows:

Step 1   Calculate the cumulative frequency for each class or range of values.

Step 2   Plot the cumulative frequencies on a graph using the highest value for each class interval on the x axis to plot the cumulative frequency. for example, for a range 40 to 50 (over 40 and not exceeding 50) the cumulative frequency should be plotted on the ogive at the point where x = 50, the highest value for the range.

Some care should be taken with this, because the class limits can be expressed in different ways.

- If the class limits are expressed as 'from 10 to 20' then the upper class limit to be used is 20.

- Alternatively if the class limits are expressed as '10 or more but less than 20' , and vales are whole numbers only, then the upper class limit to be used for the ogive would be 19.

Step 3   Join the points you have plotted. This gives you your cumulative frequency distribution.

Example

The following frequency distribution has been used already, but will now be used to construct a 'less than' ogive.

A group of 30 accountancy students sat an examination and their percentage marks were grouped as follows:

Percentage mark	Frequency
30 - 39	5
40 - 44	4
45 - 49	4
50 - 54	2
55 - 59	4
60 - 64	3
65 - 69	2
70 - 74	2
75 - 79	1
80 - 89	3

Task

Prepare a 'less than' ogive or cumulative frequency curve for this data.

Solution

Step 1   Calculate the cumulative frequency for each class.

Class marks	Frequency student numbers		Cumulative frequency student numbers
30 – 39	5		5
40 – 44	4	(5 + 4)	9
45 – 49	4	(9 + 4)	13
50 – 54	2	(13 + 2)	15
55 – 59	4	(15 + 4)	19
60 – 64	3	(19 + 3)	22
65 – 69	2	(22 + 2)	24
70 – 74	2	(24 + 2)	26
75 – 79	1	(26 + 1)	27
80 – 89	3	(27 + 3)	30

Step 2   Plot the cumulative frequencies on a graph using the upper class limit to plot each frequency.

In this example the upper class limits will be 39, 44, 49 and so on.

Step 3   Join the points you have plotted to draw the ogive.

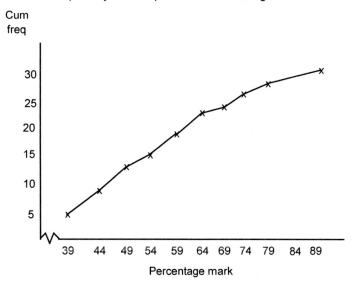

Interpreting what an ogive shows

A 'less than' ogive shows the total number of frequencies up to and including any value. In the example above, the ogive shows the total number of students with marks up to a certain level. For example, it shows that 5 students scored a mark up to and including 39, 9 students scored up to and including 44, 13 students scored up to and including 49 marks, and so on. Thus it can be seen that 19 students scored less than 60 marks (up to and including 59) and 26 students scored less than 75 marks (up to and including 74).

The ogive can be used to read off certain frequencies of occurrences. For example suppose that the pass mark for this examination was 45%. It would be possible to read off from the ogive the approximate number of students who failed.

Alternatively the ogive could also be used to estimate the mark that say the 5th highest student scored, or the mark below which (say) 50% of the group scored.

FOULKS LYNCH
PUBLICATIONS

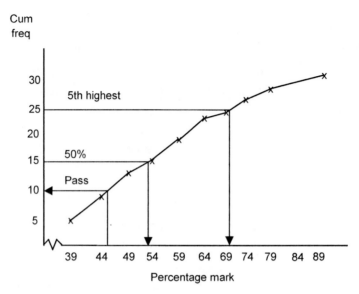

From the graph:

If the pass mark was 45% then approximately 10 students failed.

The score of the 5th highest student was 71%.

50% of the students scored below 54% (this is known as the 'median' value).

ACTIVITY 4

The grouped frequency distribution for units of output each day from a production department, used previously, is reproduced below.

Daily units of output	Frequency
	Number of days
550 - 559	2
560 - 569	3
570 - 579	5
580 - 589	5
590 - 599	2
600 – 609	2
610 – 619	3
620 - 639	3

Task

Construct a cumulative frequency curve (a 'less than' ogive) to illustrate this data. From the graph you draw, estimate:

(a)   the number of days where output is less than 605 units, and

(b)   the level of output that is achieved 50% of the time.

This activity covers performance criterion F in element 7.1.

For a suggested answer, see the 'Answers' section at the end of the book.

6   Z CHARTS

Definition   A Z chart consists of three lines drawn on the same graph. One of the lines is higher on the graph than a second line. The third line joins the left hand end of the lower line with the right hand end of the upper line, so that the three lines together resemble a letter Z.

A Z chart is often drawn to show sales performance, typically over a one-year period. In such a graph:

(a)   the lower line shows the monthly sales figures for each month of the year

(b)   the higher line shows, at each month of the year, the cumulative annual sales for the previous 12 months

(c)   the middle line shows the cumulative sales for the year to date.

The three lines will look something like this:

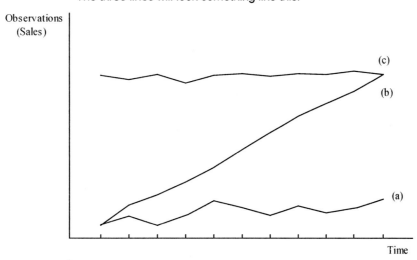

6.1   CONSTRUCTING A Z CHART

The following steps should be followed to draw a Z chart. To draw a Z chart for sales for a given year, you need monthly sales data for a two-year period – the year to be shown on the Z chart and the preceding year. Monthly sales for the preceding year are needed in order to calculate (for each month) the cumulative annual sales for the previous 12 months.

Step 1   Produce a table showing the following three totals:

- Monthly sales for the year under consideration

- The cumulative sales for the year to date

- A moving annual total of sales. This is the total of the sales for the previous twelve months ending with the month under consideration.

Step 2   Decide the scale to use in the Z chart. The x axis needs 12 points (so 12 squares), one for each month. For the y axis scale, look at the largest figure for cumulative annual sales. This shows you the maximum value to be plotted vertically on the graph. Having done this, you can decide on a suitable scale in the usual way as for other types of graph.

Step 3   Plot the three sets of figures from the table on to the graph. All points are plotted at the end of their time interval as they are totals up to the end of each month rather than averages for a month.

Step 4   Join each of the points for each of the three graph lines with straight lines. This gives you the Z chart.

Tutorial note: Z-charts are normally drawn up to show monthly sales figures. However this need not always be the case. A Z-chart could be drawn for quarterly figures or for the seven days in the week. The method applied to draw the Z chart would be the same.

Example

The following table shows the monthly sales (in £000) of Zabra Ltd for 20X4 and 20X5.

A Z chart will be drawn from this information for 20X5.

Month	Jan	Feb	Mar	Apr	May	Jun
20X4	20	20	25	18	16	25
20X5	18	21	26	16	20	26

Month	Jul	Aug	Sep	Oct	Nov	Dec
20X4	18	17	19	18	19	26
20X5	24	28	28	32	33	41

Solution

Step 1   Produce a table showing the required figures

Month (20X5)	Sales in month	Cumulative sales for the year		Sales for the previous 12 months	
				(Moving annual total)	
	£000		£000		£000
January	18		18	(note 1)	239
February	21	(21 + 18)	39	(239 + 21 – 20)	240
March	26	(26 + 39)	65	(240 + 26 – 25)	241
April	16	(16 + 65)	81	(241 + 16 – 18)	239
May	20	(20 + 81)	101	(239 + 20 – 16)	243
June	26	(26 + 101)	127	(243 + 26 – 25)	244
July	24	(24 + 127)	151	(244 + 24 – 18)	250
August	28	(28 + 151)	179	(250 + 28 – 17)	261
September	28	(28 + 179)	207	(261 + 28 – 19)	270
October	32	(32 + 207)	239	(270 + 32 – 18)	284
November	33	(33 + 239)	272	(284 + 33 – 19)	298
December	41	(41 + 272)	313	(298 + 41 – 26)	313

Note

The figure for January is the sum of the monthly sales for February 20X4 to January 20X5, inclusive. Subsequent monthly moving annual totals can be calculated by adding the sales for the new month and subtracting the sales for the corresponding month in the previous year. These workings are shown in the table.

January:

239 is the total of the 12 months from Feb 20X4 to Jan 20X5 inclusive, (20 + 25 + 18 + 16 + 25 + 18 + 17 + 19 + 18 + 19 + 26 + 18 = 239)

February:

240 is the total of the 12 months from March 20X4 to February 20X5 inclusive. It is found by subtracting the February 20X4 value (20) and adding the February 20X5 value (21) instead, giving an increase of 1 to 240.

The moving total for the subsequent months are calculated in a similar way, as shown in the workings in the table.

Step 2   Decide the scales to be used for the graph. Here the y axis needs to go up to at least £313,000.

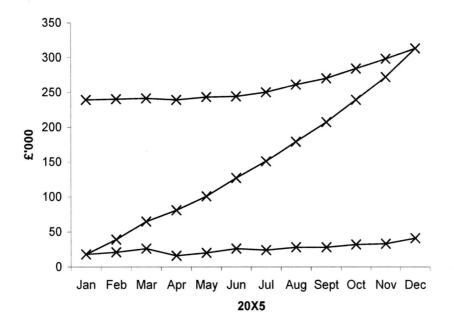

Step 3   Plot the three sets of figures from the table.

The monthly sales figures line starts at 18,000 for January 20X5.

The cumulative annual sales figures also starts at January and 18,000.

The moving annual total sales starts at 239 for January.

Since the moving annual total is the total of the preceding 12 months' sales, the moving annual total for December 20X5 must be the same as the cumulative monthly total up to December 20X5 and the two lines will therefore meet at this point, £313,000.

Step 4   Join each of the points of each of the graph lines and you should have a Z chart.

6.2   INTERPRETING A Z-CHART

The Z-chart shows three specific pieces of information.

* The monthly sales line shows the fluctuations in sales from month to month. Many businesses have seasonal sales patterns, so the monthly figures will usually go up and down.

* The line showing the cumulative monthly sales for the year to date can be compared to the budgeted sales to date by also drawing a line for cumulative budgeted sales on to the same graph. (Alternatively, you can draw a Z chart for the previous year as well as the current year, and the cumulative sales for the year just ended and for the previous year can be seen.) If you draw two Z

charts, remember to distinguish one chart from the other, by using a broken line or dotted line for the previous year's results.

- The moving annual total of sales shows the trend in annual sales, eliminating any seasonal effects. If this line is rising then this shows that sales performance is better than in the previous 12 months. However, when the moving total line is falling, sales performance is not so good and might be a cause for some concern.

ACTIVITY 5

Below are the monthly sales figures for George Ltd for 20X8 and 20X9. From this information prepare a Z-chart for the 20X9 sales figures and briefly interpret the results.

	20X8	20X9
	£'000	£'000
January	100	90
February	80	80
March	70	80
April	100	90
May	110	120
June	120	120
July	120	130
August	140	150
September	150	140
October	130	120
November	120	120
December	100	90

Tasks

1   From this information prepare a Z-chart for the 20X9 sales figures.

2   Briefly interpret the results.

This activity covers performance criterion F in element 7.1.

For a suggested answer, see the 'Answers' section at the end of the book.

7   GRAPHS OF COSTS AND SALES

It is fairly common business reporting practice to present a graph that shows both the sales revenue from a product and the total costs of that product on the same graph. This type of graph is sometimes called a **break even chart**.

7.1   COSTS

The cost of producing a product or line of products during a period of time is often assumed to consist of a combination of:

- a fixed cost for the period, plus
- an amount of cost that is variable depending upon the number of products that are made.

The total cost of the product is equal to the fixed cost plus the variable cost for the particular level of production. These total costs can be drawn on a graph as a straight line. The formula for this straight line is:

$$y \quad = \quad a + bx$$

FOULKS LYNCH
PUBLICATIONS

This can be applied to the total costs of a product as follows:

x	=	the number of units produced in the period
y	=	the total cost of producing those units
a	=	the fixed costs in the period
b	=	the variable costs of the units produced

Example

Suppose that the total monthly cost of producing widgets was a variable cost of £6 per widget produced and £3,000 of fixed costs.

Task

Express total production costs in terms of a straight-line equation.

Use this equation to calculate the total cost of producing 200 widgets and 1,000 widgets in a month.

Solution

The total cost of producing widgets can be expressed as:

$$y \text{ (in £)} = 3,000 + 6x$$

The total cost of producing 200 widgets in a month therefore equals, in £:

$$3,000 + (6 \times 200) = £4,200$$

The total cost of producing 1,000 widgets in a month equals, in £:

$$3,000 + (£ \times 1,000) = £9,000$$

Drawing a graph of total costs

A straight line graph for total costs, given the equation for total costs, can be drawn very easily. To draw a straight line, you need to plot just two points on the graph and join them up. Volume of production/sales is the independent variable on the x axis, and costs are the dependent variable on the y axis.

Make sure that your line starts on the left where x = 0. The line should end on the right hand side at a sensible level of production/sales volume.

Example

Suppose that the total monthly cost of producing widgets was a variable cost of £6 per widget produced and £3,000 of fixed costs. If the possible production levels range from 1 widget to 1,000 widgets then show this total cost on a graph.

Solution

It is only necessary to plot two points on a straight line graph and then to join those two points.

- When x = 0, y = (fixed costs only) £3,000.

- When x = 1,000, y = £3,000 + (£6 x 1,000) = £9,000.

These can now be plotted on the graph.

Total costs of production of widgets

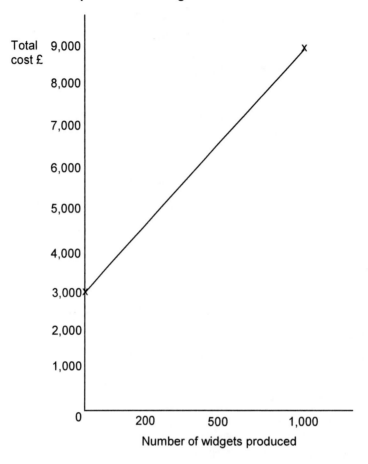

Tutorial note: The line of the graph cuts the y axis at £3,000 (variable a). This is the value of the fixed costs.

7.2 DRAWING A GRAPH OF SALES REVENUE

A straight-line graph can be drawn of the expected revenue from selling a particular number of products. It is assumed that the sales price per unit is the same, regardless of the volume of units sold.

Drawing a graph of sales revenue is even more straightforward than drawing a graph for costs. You need to plot just two points on your graph and join them up to make a straight line.

- If no units are sold then revenue is zero. The graph line for sales revenue therefore always starts at x = 0, y = 0.

- Total sales revenue is simply the number of units sold multiplied by the selling price. Take any volume of sales and calculate the total revenue. Plot this on the graph. You now have your two points to join up.

Example

Continuing with the example above of widgets, suppose that the selling price is £14 for each unit sold.

Task

Express the sales revenue function as an equation.

Draw a graph to show the total sales revenue at different levels of sales, up to a level of 1,000 units of sale.

Solution

Total sales revenue can be expressed as:

$$y \quad = \quad £14x$$

Therefore:

When x   =   0,   y   = £0
When x   =   1,000,   y   = £14,000

This can be shown on a graph as follows:

Sales revenue from widgets

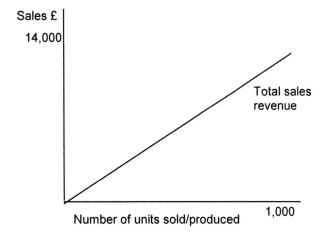

7.3   BREAK EVEN CHART

If a graph line for total costs and a graph line for total sales revenue are shown on the same graph, the graph is usually called a break even chart. The reason for this name is that the graph will show the level of sales and the costs at which no profit and no loss is made by producing and selling the product. In other words, the graph will show, amongst other things, what volume of production and sales is necessary to 'break even' during the period.

Definition   The **break-even point** for a product is the number of units of production and sales where the total sales revenue is equal to the total costs. This is the point where the product makes no profit or loss.

This break even point can be shown graphically as the point where the total sales and total costs lines for a product intersect.

Example

Using an example of widgets the information given to date is as follows.

The total cost of producing widgets is a variable cost of £6 per widget produced and £3,000 of fixed costs.

The selling price is to be £14 per widget no matter how many are sold. Production is limited to 1,000 units and the number that are produced are the number sold so that there are no closing stocks.

Prepare a break even chart and show the number of widgets that must be produced for the product to break even.

Solution

Step 1	Draw up a graph so that the scale of the y axis is big enough to include total revenue as well as total costs. Remember that the sales line starts at the origin of the graph (x = 0, y = 0).
Step 2	Plot the total cost line on the graph.
Step 3	Plot the total sales revenue line on the graph.
Step 4	You can indicate the break even point on the graph, as the point where the costs and sales lines intersect.

Break even chart for widget production

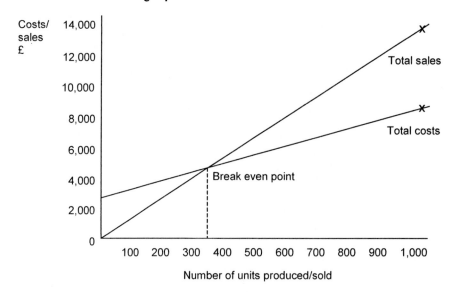

The break even point is 375 units.

This can be proved as follows:

	£
Sales (£14 × 375 units)	5,250
Costs (£3,000 + (£6 × 375 units))	(5,250)
Profit	-

This means that if sales and production are less than 375 units then the product makes a loss but if they rise above this figure then the product makes a profit.

From the graph it can be seen that if the total cost line is above the total sales line then a loss is being made, whereas if the total sales line is above the total cost line then a profit is being made.

ACTIVITY 6

An organisation produces splodgets and the demand for splodgets could range from 1,000 per annum to 10,000. The selling price of the splodget will remain the same no matter how many are produced or sold and this price has been set at £25.

The fixed costs of running the splodget factory are £50,000 and the variable costs are £12.50 per splodget.

The following tasks should now be performed:

(a)   Produce a break even chart to illustrate this cost and sales information.

(b)   Estimate the break even point from the graph.

For a suggested answer, see the 'Answers' section at the end of the book.

8   GRAPHS FROM NARRATIVE DATA

Occasionally, you might be asked to include a graph in a report where the data is given to you in narrative form. The task is similar in many ways to preparing a table of figures from narrative data. You have to understand the narrative and convert it into a suitable graphical form.

See if you can do the activity below.

ACTIVITY 7

Below is an extract from a report concerning the levels of profits of a company for the eight years from 20X1 to 20X8.

'... The 20X1 profit level of £100,000 was maintained for the next twelve months. The following three years then saw an increase of 10%, 15% and 20% respectively over the previous year's profits. This sort of growth however could not be maintained and in 20X6 profits slumped to just 75% of their 20X5 level. This fall in profits continued for the following two years with further drops of £4,600 and £3,800 in 20X7 and 20X8'.

Task

Illustrate this information in the form of a graph.

For a suggested answer, see the 'Answers' section at the end of the book.

9   MEASURES OF AVERAGES OF GROUPED DATA

In this section we summarise the different ways of calculating the central measure of grouped data.

CONCLUSION

In this chapter you have learned how to:

*   draw a simple graph, including a time series graph

*   draw a frequency polygon

- construct and interpret an ogive

- construct and interpret a Z chart

- draw a breakeven chart.

These are the most common forms of graph used in periodic performance reports.

A slightly more complex form of graphical reporting is time series analysis. This is described in the next chapter.

SELF TEST QUESTIONS

		Paragraph
1	What is the purpose of a graph?	1
2	State the rules for presenting a graph.	1.1
3	What is the dependent variable and what is the independent variable?	1.1
4	Which variable is plotted on the y axis of a graph: the dependent or the independent variable?	1.1 – 1.2
5	What are multiple graphs and when do we use them?	2
6	What is line of best fit?	3
7	When do we use scatter graph method?	3.1
8	What is a frequency polygon?	4
9	What is an ogive?	5
10	Which three lines are drawn on a Z chart?	6
11	Define break-even point.	7.3

KEY TERMS

Dependent variable – variable whose value is dependent upon the value of the other variable.

Independent variable – variable whose value is not dependent upon another variable.

Multiple graph – you can plot more than one set of data on one graph, with each set of data shown as a separate line. A graph with more than one line is called a multiple graph.

Line of best fit – an estimated straight line across entire length of the graph. The data collected about actual total costs and total sales volume can be used to estimate a line of best fit, a best estimate from the available data about how future costs might vary with volume of sales.

Scatter graph – a graph that plots a number of points from pairs of data. The points lie all over the graph, in an apparently random fashion, and there is no meaning in joining up the points with straight lines.

Frequency polygon – a graph drawn from a histogram for a grouped frequency distribution.

Cumulative frequency curve (ogive) – an alternative way of showing a frequency distribution on a graph, by drawing a cumulative frequency curve.

Z chart – consists of three lines drawn on the same graph. One of the lines is higher on the graph than a second line. The third line joins the left hand end of the lower line with the right hand end of the upper line, so that the three lines together resemble a letter Z.

Break-even chart – a graph that shows both the sales revenue from a product and the total costs of that product on the same graph.

Break-even point – the number of units of production and sales where the total sales revenue is equal to the total costs. This is the point where the product makes no profit or loss.

FOULKS LYNCH
PUBLICATIONS

Chapter 5

TIME SERIES ANALYSIS

This chapter describes methods of presenting information in a report relating to time series analysis, both in tabular and graphical form. The chapter will also explain how an underlying trend can be measured, and how historical data collected over time can be used to make forecasts for the future.

CONTENTS

KNOWLEDGE AND UNDERSTANDING

		Reference
1	Time series analysis	Item 9
2	Methods of presenting information: ... diagrammatic; tabular	Item 14

PERFORMANCE CRITERIA

		Reference
1	Prepare reports in the appropriate form and present them to management within the required timescales	Item F, element 7.1

LEARNING OUTCOMES

At the end of this chapter, you should be able to:

- Construct a graph that illustrates a time series and be able to use it for forecasting

- Identify the trend of a time series using the line of best fit or moving average calculation

- Estimate the trend using time series analysis and seasonal variations.

1 INTRODUCTION TO TIME SERIES ANALYSIS

Definition   A **time series** is a set of observations or measures taken at equal time intervals.

The measurements might be taken hourly, daily, weekly, monthly, quarterly or annually.

Examples of time series might include the following:

- quarterly sales revenue totals over a number of years
- annual profit figures over a number of years
- weekly payroll totals over a year
- hourly temperature readings over a day or a week
- daily production output over a month
- monthly employee numbers over a period of one year or longer

A time series can be drawn as a simple graph, as illustrated in the previous chapter.

Definition   **Time series analysis** describes techniques for analysing a time series, to identify whether there is any underlying trend and if there is, measuring it. A trend over time, established from historical data, can then be used to make predictions for the future.

2 GRAPH OF A TIME SERIES

A time series is often shown on a graph. Examples were shown in the previous chapter. Time is always plotted on the horizontal axis (x axis) and the measurements on the vertical axis.

Example

The following data are the quarterly sales figures for Barb Ltd, a retailer of barbecue equipment and accessories, for three years.

	Quarter 1 £000	Quarter 2 £000	Quarter 3 £000	Quarter 4 £000
20X1	121	188	290	88
20X2	125	201	301	102
20X3	146	227	318	103

Plot this data on a graph.

Solution

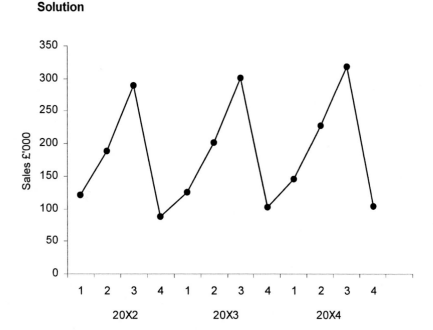

Tutorial note: To be strictly accurate, each point is plotted at the end of the relevant quarter.

ACTIVITY 1

Ski Fun Ltd owns a number of chalets in Switzerland that it lets out for holidays. Given below is data showing the number of people who stayed in the chalets each quarter for a period of 3½ years.

	Quarter 1	Quarter 2	Quarter 3	Quarter 4
20X5	Not available		92	195
20X6	433	324	95	202
20X7	486	347	98	218
20X8	499	360	104	236

Task

Plot this time series on a graph.

This activity covers performance criterion F in element 7.1

For a suggested answer, see the 'Answers' section at the end of the book.

3 TRENDS AND VARIATIONS

A time series might be analysed in order to make forecasts or predictions for the future. In analysing a time series, certain assumptions are made as a starting point for the analysis. These assumptions are that:

- A time series will show a **long-term trend**. The trend might be a rising trend, a declining trend or a stable trend, going neither up nor down. It is often assumed that this long-term trend can be represented graphically as a straight line.

- Actual data measurements will rarely be exactly on the long-term trend line. This is because there are **variations** in actual results, above or below the trend.

There are three types of variation, and all three could exist.

- A **seasonal variation**. This is a variation in results arising because of normal rises or falls in certain seasons or months of the year, or in some days of the week. For example, a manufacturer of swimwear might expect higher sales in the spring and summer seasons than in autumn and winter. Most businesses find that they have higher sales in some months of the year than others, due to the nature of customer demand. Similarly, a shop or department store might have higher sales on certain days of the week than on others. All such variations caused by the time of day, week or year are called seasonal variations. Seasonal variations will help to explain why actual results are higher or lower than we would expect from the underlying long-term trend.

- A **cyclical variation**. A cyclical variation is similar in concept to a seasonal variation, but is longer-term in nature. A cycle can cover a period of several years. A significant cyclical variation could be a variation caused by the economic cycle. If an economy is in recession, or even just slowing down, actual results might fall below the long-term trend. If the economy is booking, actual results might be higher than the long-term trend. Cyclical variations are difficult to measure accurately.

- A **residual variation** or **random variation**. If we could make estimates for the expected seasonal variation and the expected cyclical variation for any given period of time, we might expect these variations to explain the difference between what actually happened and the underlying long-term trend. The seasonal and cyclical variations might explain most of the difference, but will not explain all the difference exactly. Any remaining difference between actual results and the underlying long-term trend is called a residual variation.

Given that the residual variation is a balancing figure, we can therefore explain the difference between actual results in any time period and the results that would have been expected from the underlying long-term trend. This difference is the sum of the seasonal, cyclical and residual variations.

Time series analysis involves trying to measure the long-term trend and the seasonal and cyclical variations.

Example

A company has used time series to estimate its future sales in each quarter of next year. It has estimated that the company is growing and that on the basis of the long-term trend, its sales should be £4 million in the first quarter of next year, rising by £100,000 a quarter in each of the next three quarters.

The company has also estimated that there are seasonal variations, and that sales in each quarter will be above or below the long-term trend by the following amounts.

Quarter	Seasonal variation Above (+) or below (-) trend £
1	+ 50,000
2	+ 250,000
3	- 120,000
4	- 180,000
Total	0

There are no estimated cyclical variations.

Note that the total of all the seasonal variations is 0. This should always be the case, because variations around an underlying trend should average out to nothing.

The estimated sales in each quarter of the year will therefore be:

Quarter	Trend line sales	Seasonal variation Above (+) or below (-) the trend	Forecast sales
	£000	£000	£000
1	4,000	+ 50,000	4,050
2	4,100	+ 250,000	4,350
3	4,200	- 120,000	4,080
4	4,300	- 180,000	4,120

ACTIVITY 2

DR Limited uses time series to estimate its future monthly sales, and is now preparing a forecast of monthly sales next year to go in the annual budget. It has estimated that there is a rising trend in sales, and has made an estimate of what the long-term trend will be. Sales are expected to be £300,000 in January, rising by £10,000 each month throughout the year.

The company has also estimated that the following monthly variations in sales, above or below the long-term trend.

Month	Seasonal variation Above (+) or below (-) trend
	£
January	- 30,000
February	- 10,000
March	+ 5,000
April	+ 15,000
May	+ 35,000
June	0
July	- 8,000
August	- 12,000
September	- 5,000
October	+ 14,000
November	- 6,000
December	+ 2,000
Total	0

There are no estimated cyclical variations.

Task

Estimate the monthly sales in the year, using the trend line and estimates of monthly variations.

This activity covers performance criterion F in element 7.1.

For a suggested answer, see the 'Answers' section at the end of the book.

4 CALCULATING THE TREND IN A TIME SERIES

The trend of a time series is the way that the time series tends to move overall. The trend is an estimate of how the time series increases or decreases over time, and it is often assumed to rise or fall at a constant rate over time.

- If the figures in a time series are on the whole tending to increase as time progresses then such a time series will have an upwards trend.

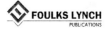

- If the figures are generally falling over a period of time then the trend will be downwards.

- Finally it is not necessarily the case that the figures will be either increasing or decreasing as they may appear to be reasonably similar for each of the periods under review. In this case the trend is said to be static.

If the underlying trend is assumed to be linear, it can be represented on the graph of a time series by drawing a straight line that appears to represent the general or overall 'shape' of the graph. This is known as a line of best fit.

Definition   A **line of best fit** is a straight line that would appear to be the best approximation or general description of the entire time series.

One way of establishing a line of best fit is to record historical data in a time series, and then use this as a scatter graph and estimate the line of best fit by judgement.

Example

Suppose that the following information is available about the number of employees in a manufacturing concern for each of six months:

	Number of employees
Month 1	50
Month 2	54
Month 3	65
Month 4	58
Month 5	70
Month 6	68

There appears to be an upward trend in employee numbers.

Plot this information on a graph and draw a line of best fit in order to show an estimate the trend.

Solution

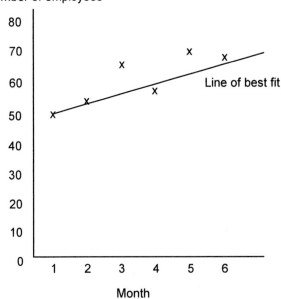

Tutorial note: The line of best fit is drawn by judgement and is therefore only an approximation of the trend of a time series.

4.1 MOVING AVERAGES

When a linear trend cannot be assumed, another method for estimating future trends is based on moving averages.

Definition   A **moving average** is an average taken from a time series representing the average of several time periods in the series.

- A moving average can be taken as the average of any number of time periods. For example, we can calculate a moving average of two, three, four, five or six (etc) time periods.

- A moving average is calculated by adding up the values for each of the time periods, and then finding the average by dividing this total by the number of time periods. In other words, it is a simple average calculation. For example, suppose that a moving average of monthly sales is calculated from three time periods and the monthly sales for a three-month period are £40,000, £55,000 and £49,000. The moving average from these three monthly figures will be £(40,000 + 55,000 + 49,000)/3 = £144,000/3 = £48,000.

- When a moving average is calculated for several time periods, the average value is normally associated with the mid-point of the time periods. For example, suppose that a moving average is taken for three months, and sales for months 1, 2 and 3 are £40,000, £55,000 and £49,000 respectively. The moving average is £48,000, and this would be the moving average value for month 2, which is the middle point of the period months 1 – 3.

- A moving average figure is calculated for each time period. For example, if we take a moving average of monthly sales, and the moving averages are based on three months of sales, we would use the sales for months 1, 2 and 3 to calculate the moving average value for month 2. Then we would use the sales for months 2, 3 and 4 to calculate the moving average value for month 3. Then we would use the sales for months 3, 4 and 5 to calculate the moving average value for month 4. To calculate each successive moving average value, we drop the value for the earliest time from the previous moving average and replace it with the most recent time's value.

The best way to illustrate the calculation of a moving average is perhaps with an example.

Example

Suppose that the following information is available about the number of employees in a manufacturing business for each month over a period of six months. Management suspect that there is an upward trend in employee numbers, and as a starting point for estimating this trend, they would like to see a moving average of employee numbers, based on moving averages for three months.

Number of employees

Month 1	50
Month 2	54
Month 3	65
Month 4	58
Month 5	70
Month 6	68

Tasks

(a)   Calculate the trend of these figures using a three-figure (three-month) moving average and then

(b)   Plot the trend on the time series graph.

Solution

Step 1   Moving averages are to be based on a three-month moving average. We must therefore calculate a three-month total for each successive three-month period. Then calculate the moving average by dividing the total by three (the number of months in the moving average.) Each moving average should be related to the middle of the three months in the average.

Month	Three-month total		Moving average
1			
2	(50 + 54 + 65)	169	56
3	(54 + 65 + 58)	177	59
4	(65 + 58 + 70)	193	64
5	(58 + 70 + 68)	196	65
6			

Note that the three-month moving total and the three-month moving average are shown in the middle of the time period, i.e. on the line of, or against, the middle figure for the three months. Therefore the month 1 to month 3 moving figures are shown in the month 2 line and the month 2 to month 4 figures in the month 3 line. There are no moving totals or moving averages for month 1or month 6.

The moving averages have been rounded to the nearest whole number.

We can draw a time series showing the monthly employment numbers for the six-month period, and we can use the same graph to show the trend based on moving averages, for the period month 2 to month 5.

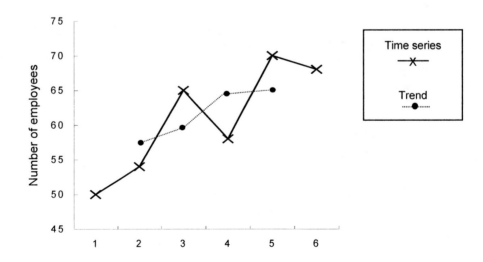

FOULKS LYNCH
PUBLICATIONS

ACTIVITY 3

The data given is the daily temperature reading for one week in July.

	Temperature (F)
Monday	68
Tuesday	74
Wednesday	70
Thursday	71
Friday	78
Saturday	73
Sunday	80

Tasks

(a) Calculate the trend of these temperatures using a three-figure (three-day) moving average.

(b) Plot the trend on the time series graph.

This activity covers performance criterion F in element 7.1.

For a suggested answer, see the 'Answers' section at the end of the book.

ACTIVITY 4

Billy's Bakery has recently opened and the shop is having enormous success. The shop opens seven days a week and daily sales for the past two weeks are shown below. Billy thinks that the upward trend in daily sales will continue into the foreseeable future. He would like to see a moving average trend line of daily sales, calculated on a seven day moving average.

	Sales
Week 1	£
Sunday	250
Monday	266
Tuesday	248
Wednesday	270
Thursday	290
Friday	364
Saturday	489
Week 2	
Sunday	262
Monday	293
Tuesday	280
Wednesday	340
Thursday	370
Friday	378
Saturday	502

Task

Calculate seven-day moving averages of daily sales from this data.

This activity covers performance criterion F in element 7.1.

For a suggested answer, see the 'Answers' section at the end of the book.

4.2 EXAMPLES OF MOVING AVERAGE PERIODS

When moving averages are used to calculate a trend, an important issue is the choice of the number of time periods to use to calculate the moving average. How many time periods should a moving average be based on?

There isn't a definite or correct answer to this question, however, where there is a regular cycle of time periods, it would make sense to calculate the moving averages over a full cycle.

- When you are calculating a moving average of daily figures, it is probably appropriate to calculate a seven-day moving average.

- When you are calculating a moving average of quarterly figures, it is probably appropriate to calculate a four-quarter moving average.

- When you are calculating a moving average of monthly figures, it might be appropriate to calculate a 12-month moving average, although a shorter-period moving average might be preferred.

4.3 MOVING AVERAGES AND EVEN-NUMBER PERIODS

When we calculate a moving total and moving average, each moving total and moving average value relates to the mid-point of the time period chosen. If the moving average period is an odd number of periods then the mid-point will be a specific time period. For example, the mid-point of a seven-day moving average is day 4 of the period and the mid-point of a three-month moving average is month 2.

However if an even number of time periods is chosen for a moving average, then the mid-point for the moving total and moving average will not correspond with an actual time period.

For example, suppose we calculate the four-quarter moving average of sales in each quarter. The moving total and the moving average for quarters 1, 2, 3 and 4 of year 1 will be half-way between quarter 2 and quarter 3.

Example of the problem

The following six years of sales figures are given:

	£000
20X1	100
20X2	120
20X3	160
20X4	180
20X5	192
20X6	204

We want to calculate four-year moving averages.

- The moving total for the first four years 20X1 to 20X4 is 560, and the four-year moving average is therefore 140 (560/4).

   This average of 140 relates to the middle of the four-year period and this is half-way between 20X2 and 20X3.

FOULKS LYNCH
PUBLICATIONS

- Similarly, the moving total for the four years 20X2 to 20X5 is 652, and the four-year moving average is therefore 163 (652/4).

   This average of 163 relates to the middle of the four-year period and this is half-way between 20X3 and 20X4.

- Similarly, the moving total for the four years 20X3 to 20X6 is 736, and the four-year moving average is therefore 184 (736/4).

   This average of 184 relates to the middle of the four-year period and this is half-way between 20X4 and 20X5.

These moving total and moving averages should be shown in the averaging table between the lines for the years, to show their mid-way position. In this example, the table should be as follows:

Year	Sales	Moving total	Moving average
20X1	100		
20X2	120		
		560	140
20X3	160		
		652	163
20X4	180		
		736	184
20X5	192		
20X6	204		

There is a problem with this. The trend line must relate to specific time periods in order to be used in further calculations with seasonal variations.

The problem is solved by taking a two-figure moving average of the moving averages. This is known as **centring the moving average**.

In the example above, we would take the first two-figure moving average, which is (140 + 163)/2. This is 151.5, say 152. This average of moving averages should relate to the mid-point in time between the two moving averages. In this case, it is the year 20X3. A sales figure of 152 would therefore be the moving average trend value for 20X3.

Similarly the next two-figure moving average is (163 + 184)/2 = 173.5, say 174. This is the centred moving average to associate with the year 20X4.

This now gives us the following two-value moving average trend line.

Year	Sales	Moving total	Moving average	Centred moving average
20X1	100			
20X2	120			
		560	140	
20X3	160			**152**
		652	163	
20X4	180			**174**
		736	184	
20X5	192			
20X6	204			

Example

The sales figures for Barb Ltd have been as follows:

	Quarter 1 £'000	Quarter 2 £'000	Quarter 3 £'000	Quarter 4 £'000
20X1	121	188	290	88
20X2	125	201	301	102
20X3	146	227	318	103

Tasks

(a)   Using a four-period moving average to calculate the trend in quarterly sales.

(b)   Plot the trend on the graph for this time series. Work to the nearest £1,000.

Solution

Step 1   Calculate each four-period moving total and position this figure in the middle of the four-quarter time period.

Step 2   Calculate each four-period moving average by dividing the total by four, and also position this figure in the middle of the four-quarter time period.

Step 3   Calculate a two-period moving average of each of the moving averages. This will give the trend at specific time periods.

Year		Moving total	Moving average	Centred moving average
			(divide by 4)	
20X1, quarter 1				
20X1, quarter 2				
	121 + 188 + 290 + 88	687	172	
20X1, quarter 3				
	188 + 290 + 88 + 125	691	173	
20X1, quarter 4				175
	290 + 88 + 125 + 201	704	176	
20X2, quarter 1				178
	88 + 125 + 201 + 301	715	179	
20X2, quarter 2				181
	125 + 201 + 301 + 102	729	182	
20X2, quarter 3				185
	201 + 301 + 102 +146	750	188	
20X2, quarter 4				191
	301 + 102 +146 + 227	776	194	
20X3, quarter 1				196
	102 +146 + 227 + 318	793	198	
20X1, quarter 2				199
	146 + 227 + 318 + 103	794	199	
20X1, quarter 3				
20X1, quarter 4				

FOULKS LYNCH
PUBLICATIONS

Tutorial note: When calculating the trend all of the numbers have been rounded to the nearest £000.

The trend can now be plotted on the time series graph (showing an **approximate** linear trend).

Barb Ltd – Quarterly Sales

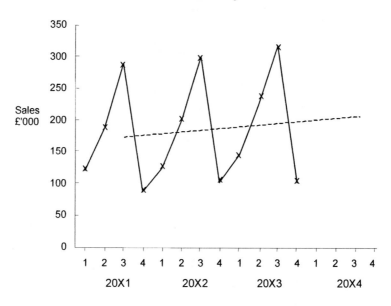

ACTIVITY 5

The information from the earlier activity, Ski Fun Ltd, is reproduced below.

Ski Fun Ltd owns a number of chalets in Switzerland that it lets out for holidays. Given below is data showing the number of people who stayed in the chalets each quarter for a period of 5 years.

	Quarter 1	Quarter 2	Quarter 3	Quarter 4
20X5			92	195
20X6	433	324	95	202
20X7	486	347	98	218
20X8	499	360	104	236

Task

Calculate the trend of the number of visitors and plot it on the graph of the time series. Use a four-period moving average and round to the nearest whole number where necessary.

This activity covers performance criterion F in element 7.1.

For a suggested answer, see the 'Answers' section at the end of the book.

5   USING MOVING AVERAGES TO ESTIMATE A TREND

So far, we have seen that moving averages can be used to establish a trend. However, the moving average trend is not a straight line.

An important use of time series analysis is to make estimates for the future. For example, if we establish a trend line for monthly sales or annual sales, we can use this to estimate what sales might be next month or next year.

So how do we use a trend line calculated from moving averages to make a forecast or estimate for the future?

The explanation that follows assumes that there are no seasonal or cyclical variations to worry about and make adjustments for.

5.1 COMPARING THE ACTUAL FIGURES WITH THE MOVING AVERAGE TREND

When we calculate a moving average trend line, the moving average values for any time period will not usually be the same as the actual results for the time period. This is illustrated in the table below, which shows sales figures month by month for nine months, and a moving average trend line based on a three-month moving average.

Month	Sales	Three-month moving total	Three-month moving average	Difference between trend line and actual sales
	£	£	£	£
1	3,000			
2	3,100	9,300	3,100	0
3	3,200	9,700	3,233	+ 33
4	3,400	10,200	3,400	0
5	3,600	10,900	3,633	+ 33
6	3,900	11,700	3,900	0
7	4,200	12,700	4,233	+ 33
8	4,600	13,900	4,633	+ 33
9	5,100			

Here, there are three months where the moving average value and actual sales for the corresponding month are exactly the same. This is because in each of these three cases, the actual increase in sales each month over the three-month period is the same. For example the increase in sales between month 1 and month 2 and between month 2 and month 3 is exactly £100 in each case, so the moving average for the three-month period equals the actual sales in month 2.

Normally, increases or decreases from one time period to the next are not so constant, so the moving average trend line value and the corresponding actual value for the same time period will not be the same. In the table above, the differences are 33 in four of the months. The differences are given a + value to show that the trend line value is higher than the actual sales for the month.

The + values occur here because the trend in monthly sales is upwards. The increase in monthly sales is getting gradually bigger. It is £100 between month 1 and month 2, and has grown to £500 between month 8 and month 9. When the trend is rising, the moving average will be higher than the corresponding actual value.

If there is a declining trend, we should expect the opposite to happen, and the moving average value will be lower than the corresponding actual value.

When the trend is either up or down, but also quite erratic, we should expect the moving average trend line value to be sometimes higher and sometimes lower than the corresponding actual value.

5.2 MAKING A FORECAST OR ESTIMATE WITH A MOVING AVERAGE TREND LINE

To make a forecast or estimate with a moving average trend line, we should try to allow for an upward or downward trend. We can do this by:

- Adding up the total of the differences between the moving average values and the actual values. Where there are both + and – values, remember to add the plus values and subtract the negative values.

- Calculating an average monthly difference. This is simply the total of the differences divided by the number of values in the moving average trend line.

In the example above, the total of the differences is 0 + 33 + 0 + 33 + 0 + 33 + 33 = + 132.

There are seven values in the moving average trend line, so the monthly average difference is + 132/7 = + 19.

This shows that on average, the moving average trend line value is 19 higher than the corresponding actual sales. This shows that the trend over this period is upward, and we should therefore allow for this in our estimates.

Making an estimate or forecast calls for judgement, but a suitable approach to forecasting is as follows.

- Look at the moving average trend line, and take a view of what this suggests about the general trend into the future. In the example above, the moving average trend line value has risen from 3,100 for month 2 to 4,633 for month 8. This shows that on average, the monthly moving average has been increasing by about 255 [(4,633 – 3,100)/6]. We might therefore assume that the monthly moving average will continue to increase by 255 each month.

- In addition, we should allow for a rising or falling rate of change in the trend line, and make an adjustment for an estimate of what effect this might have. In the example above, the trend is rising, and the moving average is on average 19 higher than the recorded actual figures. To allow for this increasing rate of rise in the trend line, we could add a further amount to our forecast for month 10. From the month 8 trend line figure, we would add (2 × 19) = 38.

- A forecast can be based on an estimate of the trend line value plus or minus an allowance to allow for the rate of change in the trend.

Again, going back to the example above, we could use the month 8 trend line figure to make sales estimates for months 10 and 11. Allowing for a basic monthly increase of 255 and a further 19 to allow for arising trend, the forecasts would be:

Month 10: 4,633 + (2 × 255) + (2 × 19) = 5,181

Month 11: 4,633 + (3 × 255) + (3 × 19) = 5,455.

It is important to remember that estimates and forecasts are based on assumptions. You might not agree with all the assumptions used in the illustrative example above, but hopefully you are able to follow the argument.

If you are required to carry out time series analysis for a report, it is important to make your assumptions clear and logical. Study the following example closely.

Example

You are given the following weekly sales data for a small business.

Week	Sales
	£
1	7,500
2	5,200
3	8,100
4	4,900

5	9,100
6	7,700
7	7,200
8	9,800
9	11,000
10	9,900

Tasks

1   Calculate a trend line for weekly sales based on a three-week moving average.

2   Calculate the average difference each week between the trend line and actual sales.

3   Make a forecast of sales for weeks 11 and 12, assuming no cyclical or seasonal variations in sales each week, and using the trend line as a basis for your estimate.

Solution

The moving averages and the differences between the moving average and actual sales each week are shown below.

Week	Sales	3-week moving total	3-week moving average	Difference
	£	£	£	£
1	7,500			
2	5,200	20,800	6,933	+ 1,733
3	8,100	18,200	6,067	- 2,033
4	4,900	22,100	7,367	+ 2,467
5	9,100	21,700	7,233	- 1,867
6	7,700	24,000	8,000	+ 300
7	7,200	24,700	8,233	+ 1,033
8	9,800	28,000	9,333	- 467
9	11,000	30,700	10,233	- 677
10	9,900			
				+489

The average weekly difference between the moving averages and the actual sales is + 489/8 = + 61.

This suggests that the weekly sales are on an upward trend, and the rate of change in the trend is rising.

Estimating future sales

We might take the view from these figures that weekly sales are simply on a rising trend of £61 each week. If so, we can simply take the trend line value for week 9, and make the following estimates:

Week 11: 10,233 + (2 × 61) = 10,355

Week 12: 10,233 + (3 × 61) = 10,416.

On the other hand, you might want to make higher estimates, on the basis that in spite of fluctuations in sales from week to week, the trend line is clearly upwards and future sales should therefore continue their strong growth.

Whatever estimates you make, state your assumptions clearly.

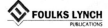

ACTIVITY 6

You are given the following weekly sales data.

Week	Sales
	£
1	10,200
2	11,300
3	7,800
4	6,200
5	9,900
6	12,300
7	11,100
8	11,700
9	10,800
10	12,000
11	13,500
12	12,900

Tasks

1   Calculate a trend line for weekly sales based on a five-week moving average.

2   Calculate the average difference each week between the trend line and actual sales.

3   Make a forecast of sales for weeks 13 and 14, assuming no cyclical or seasonal variations in sales each week, and using the trend line as a basis for your estimate.

This activity covers performance criterion F in element 7.1.

For a suggested answer, see the 'Answers' section at the end of the book.

6   SEASONAL VARIATIONS

In time series analysis, an allowance might have to be made for seasonal variations. These were introduced earlier, but it might now be useful to look in a little more detail at forecasting to allow for seasonal variations.

Sales of many product sales will vary with the season:

- Ice cream sales are highest in the summer months.

- Sales of greetings cards sales in the UK have peaks at Christmas and Easter.

Other types of time series might also have seasonal variations:

- The number of diners in a restaurant is likely to be higher at weekends than during the week.

- Production in a factory might be lower on Fridays than on other days in the week.

Definition   **Seasonal variations** are the amounts by which periodic data normally fluctuate above and below the trend line.

6.1   ADJUSTING FOR SEASONAL VARIATIONS

A common way of presenting a time series analysis is to give the **seasonally adjusted** or **de-seasonalised figures**. By this method, the seasonal variation is taken away from the actual data in order to see how closely the de-seasonalised figures adhere to the trend.

FOULKS LYNCH
PUBLICATIONS

The adjustment to the actual data to find de-seasonalised data is straightforward.

Seasonally adjusted data = Original data − Seasonal variation

Example

The sales figures and trend for 20X2 for Barb Ltd and the seasonal variations are given below.

	Quarter 1 £000	Quarter 2 £000	Quarter 3 £000	Quarter 4 £000
20X2 - sales	125	201	301	102
20X3 - trend	178	181	185	191

The seasonal variations have been estimated as:

Quarter 1	-52
Quarter 2	24
Quarter 3	116
Quarter 4	-88

A minus figure indicates that the actual sales will be lower than the average, because of seasonal factors.

Task

Show the seasonally-adjusted figures for 20X2 and briefly comment on any pattern that they show.

Solution

Seasonally-adjusted figures are figures that are expectations of what actual sales would be if the seasonal factors did not exist. So if the seasonal variation is positive, we should subtract it from actual sales to find the de-seasonalised sales figure. If the seasonal variation is negative, we should add it to actual sales to get the de-seasonalised sales figure.

		De-seasonalised figures	Trend
Quarter 1	125 − (-52)	177	178
Quarter 2	201 − 24	177	181
Quarter 3	301 − 116	185	185
Quarter 4	102 − (-88)	190	191

The de-seasonalised figures show that if the seasonal variations are taken out or ignored then for quarters 1, 3 and 4 the actual figures are pretty much in line with the trend. However the trend figure for quarter 2 is 181 whereas the de-seasonalised figure is only 177.

Something has happened to cause this difference and it can be put down to residual or random variations.

ACTIVITY 7

The number of visitors and trend for Ski Fun Ltd for 20X7 are given below together with the seasonal variations.

	Quarter 1	Quarter 2	Quarter 3	Quarter 4
20X7 - actual	486	347	98	218
20X7 - trend	283	285	289	293

The seasonal variations are as follows:

Quarter 1	196
Quarter 2	62
Quarter 3	-181
Quarter 4	-77

Task

From this data calculate the seasonally adjusted figures for 20X7 and briefly comment upon anything that these show.

This activity covers performance criterion F in element 7.1

For a suggested answer, see the 'Answers' section at the end of the book.

6.2 FORECASTING WITH TIME SERIES ANALYSIS AND SEASONAL VARIATIONS

Where there are seasonal adjustments, forecasting with time series analysis can be done as follows.

Step 1   Estimate the trend for the future period.

One way of doing this is to extend the trend line on the time series graph and read off the figure at the future point in time for which the forecast is to be made. This process of extending the trend line forward into the future is known as **extrapolation**.

Step 2   Apply the appropriate seasonal adjustment to the forecast trend line value in order to reach your forecast figure.

Residual or random variations cannot be forecast, because they are unforeseeable by their very nature.

Example

Given below is the time series graph for Barb Ltd showing the original time series and the trend.

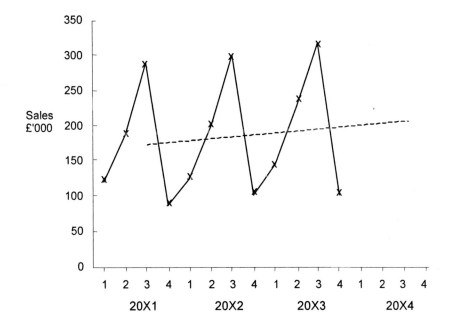

The seasonal variations for Barb Ltd are:

Quarter 1	-52
Quarter 2	24
Quarter 3	116
Quarter 4	-88

Task

From this information estimate the values of sales for each quarter of 20X4.

Solution

Step 1   Estimate the trend figure for each of the quarters of 20X4.

This can be done by extending the trend line on the graph and reading off the relevant figures. This is also known as extrapolation.

Barb Ltd – Quarterly sales

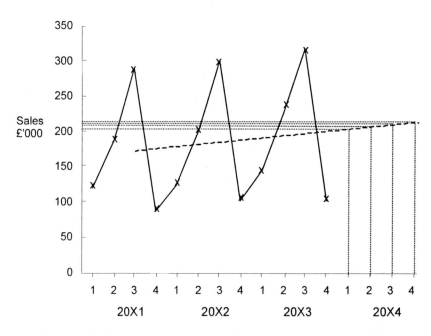

Reading off the results from the graph the trend figures for each quarter of 20X5 are approximately:

	£000
Quarter 1	215
Quarter 2	218
Quarter 3	222
Quarter 4	227

Step 2   Adjust the appropriate trend figures for the seasonal variation.

Quarter 1: The trend figure for this quarter is 215 but the seasonal adjustment for quarter 1 is -52. This means that the actual results for quarter 1 are on average 52 below the trend. The anticipated or forecast sales for quarter 1 are the trend plus the seasonal variation.

Forecast   £215,000 + (- £52,000)   =   £163,000

Quarter 2: Trend 218, seasonal variation +24

Forecast   £218,000 + £24,000   =   £242,000

Quarter 3: Trend 222, seasonal variation +116

Forecast   £222,000 + £116,000   =   £338,000

Quarter 4: Trend 227, seasonal variation -88

Forecast   £227,000 + (-£88,000)   =   £139,000

ACTIVITY 8

Given below is the time series graph for Ski Fun Ltd showing the time series and the trend. The seasonal variations for Ski Fun Ltd are also given.

The seasonal variations are as follows:

Quarter 1	196
Quarter 2	62
Quarter 3	-181
Quarter 4	-77

Ski Fun Ltd – Quarterly chalet occupancy

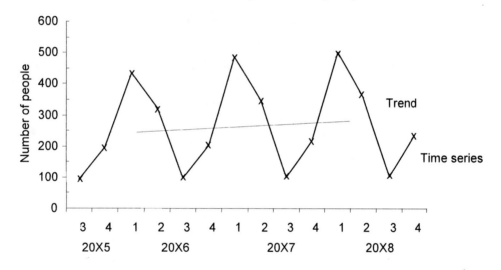

Task

From this information estimate the approximate number of chalet visitors for each of the four quarters of 20X9.

This activity covers performance criterion F in element 7.1.

For a suggested answer, see the 'Answers' section at the end of the book.

6.3   PROBLEMS WITH FORECASTING

There are a number of problems with using time series analysis to estimate or forecast future results.

- The main problem is the inherent weakness of extrapolation. In order to estimate the trend for the future the trend line is extended on the graph and the figures read off. However, although the trend has moved in a particular way in the past, it does not necessarily mean that it will continue to do so in the future.

- The seasonal adjustments used to find the forecast for the future are based on historical figures that might now be out of date. There is no guarantee that the seasonal variations will remain the same in the future.

- If the time series has a large residual or random variation element, then this will make any forecasts even less reliable.

CONCLUSION

In this chapter you have learnt how to:

- draw a graph to illustrate a time series and understand how to use it for forecasting

- identify the trend of a time series, by either line of best fit or moving average calculation

- adjust for a seasonal variation when forecasting.

SELF TEST QUESTIONS

Paragraph

1	What is a time series?	1
2	What is the main use of time series analysis?	1
3	What is meant by long term trend?	3
4	What is meant by variations in actual results and which are the three types of variations?	3
5	What is meant by centering the moving average?	4.3
6	How do we use a trend line calculated from moving averages to make a forecast or estimate for the future?	5
7	How is data de-seasonalised?	6

KEY TERMS

Time series – a set of observations or measures taken at equal time intervals.

Time series analysis – describes techniques for analysing a time series, to identify whether there is any underlying trend and if there is, measuring it. A trend over time, established from historical data, can then be used to make predictions for the future.

Long-term trend – can be shown by time series. The trend might be a rising trend, a declining trend or a stable trend, going neither up nor down. It is often assumed that this long-term trend can be represented graphically as a straight line.

Variations – actual data measurements will rarely be exactly on the long-term trend line, This is because there are variations in actual results, above or below the trend.

Seasonal variation – a variation in results arising because of normal rises or falls in certain seasons or months of the year, or in some days of the week.

Cyclical variation – similar in concept to a seasonal variation, but is longer-term in nature. A cycle can cover a period of several years.

Residual variation or **random variation** – any remaining difference after considering seasonal and cyclical variations between actual results and the underlying long-term trend.

Line of best fit – a straight line that would appear to be the best approximation or general description of the entire time series.

Moving average – an average taken from a time series representing the average of several time periods in the series

Seasonal variations – the amounts by which periodic data normally fluctuate above and below the trend line.

Seasonally adjusted or **de-seasonalised figures** – the seasonal variation is taken away from the actual data in order to see how closely the de-seasonalised figures adhere to the trend.

Chapter 6

INFLATION AND INDICES

The purpose of this chapter is to show you how a price index is constructed and how it can be used to adjust money values for various purposes and restate costs or revenues in different time periods. This will enable us to make comparisons of costs and revenues over time.

CONTENTS

KNOWLEDGE AND UNDERSTANDING

		Reference
1	Use of index numbers	Item 10

PERFORMANCE CRITERIA

		Reference
1	Compare results over time using an appropriate method that allows for changing price levels	Item C, element 7.1

LEARNING OUTCOMES

At the end of this chapter, you should be able to:

- Estimate future costs or revenues to allow for expected inflation

- Use a price index to adjust money values at different time periods to a common price level in order to compare results over time

1   INFLATION AND CHANGING PRICE LEVELS

Prices of goods and services and wages and salaries change over time. Some prices go down, but in general prices tend to go up and some inflation has become an accepted feature of life.

 FOULKS LYNCH
PUBLICATIONS

Over time, inflation can make a big difference to prices. For example, annual inflation of 2% might not seem very much, but over a five-year period this will make a difference of over 10% to price levels.

An aspect of inflation is that it makes money values difficult to compare between one time period and another.

- If you are comparing money values at different times in the past, the comparison might be meaningless. For example, suppose that you are told that X bought a house in London in 1980 for £70,000 and that Y bought a house in the same part of London in 2000 for £350,000. Would you have any idea whose house is worth more today?

- If you are trying to forecast money values in the future, such as sales revenue figures or cost figures, your estimates will not be reliable if you ignore inflation, if the rate of inflation is expected to be high.

Two factors determine the extent to which prices in one time period cannot be easily compared with prices in another time period:

- The *length of time between the two periods*. The longer the time difference, the greater will be the effect of inflation.

- The *annual rate of inflation*. When the annual rate of inflation is 15%, prices between one year and the next will be more difficult to compare than if annual inflation is only say, 1%.

This chapter looks at two methods of dealing with inflation for the purpose of financial reporting:

- Using expected annual rates of inflation to estimate future revenues or costs.

- Using index numbers to adjust revenues or costs in different time periods to a common price level.

2 ESTIMATING FUTURE COSTS OR REVENUES TO ALLOW FOR INFLATION

When you are preparing a forecast, it might be appropriate to allow for inflation. To do this, you simply need to establish what you think the annual rate of inflation will be up to the year for which the forecast is being made.

Prices will rise each year by a factor of $(1 + i)$, between the beginning and the end of the year, where i is the rate of inflation expressed as a proportion. For example, if the expected annual rate of inflation is 5%, i is 0.05 and if the annual rate of inflation is 3%, i is 0.03, and so on.

Example

A business has calculated that its advertising costs in the year just ended were £132,000. It expects advertising costs to rise by 4% next year and by 6% the year after that, due to inflation in advertising rates.

What are the forecast advertising costs for next year and the year after?

Solution

Costs next year = £132,000 (1.04) = £137,280

Costs in the following year = £132,000 (1.04)(1.06) = £145,517.

For forecasting purposes, we might round these figures to the nearest £1,000, giving estimates of £137,000 and £146,000 for the two years.

ACTIVITY 1

The labour costs of a company's work force were £460,000 last year. The company is trying to forecast its labour costs in the next three years, and has made the following estimates.

(a)   Labour pay rates will rise 3% next year, 4% the year after and 4% the year after that, because of inflation.

(b)   Next year and in the year after that, the size of the work force will remain stable. In the third year, the work force will increase in size by 7%.

Task

Produce estimates of labour costs for each of the next three years.

This activity covers performance criterion C in element 7.1.

For a suggested answer, see the 'Answers' section at the end of the book.

3   INDICES AND INDEX NUMBERS

In business reporting, it is very common to compare results in one year with results in another year. Sometimes, comparisons are made between money amounts in one year and money amounts in another year.

For example, a report comparing the costs of providing a service might find that a service costing £185 to provide in 1993 cost £272 in 2003. Similarly, a report into the sales revenue of a business might find that whilst the business earned £870,000 in revenue in 1995, its total revenue had risen to £960,000 in 2000.

Comparisons of this kind, between a money value in one year and a money value in another year, are difficult to interpret. Revenues and costs will be expected to increase over time, due to inflation. From a business point of view, it is important to know how much of the increase is due to inflation, and so probably unavoidable. The most appropriate way of comparing two money values from different years is to try to put them on to a common price level, after adjusting for the effects of inflation.

A **price index** can be used to adjust price levels in different years to a common price level.

Definition   An index is a series of numbers showing the variation in either a price level or a quantity level compared with a common base period. A price index is a series of numbers showing the variation in a price level compared with a common base period.

A **base period** is normally given an index value of either 100 or 1,000.

For example, the base period for a prices index might be January 1991, and the index for January 1991 set at 100. Prices might then be measured every month, and an index number calculated for the month. The index number would show by how much prices have changed, up or down, compared with the base period. For example, if the price index for May 2004 is 152, this would show that prices have risen by a factor of 1.52 (152/100), which is a rise of 52%, over the intervening time.

3.1   SOURCES OF INDEX NUMBERS

Businesses can construct their own price indices if they want to, but this is not usual. A reason why the use of index numbers is widespread is that a number of price indices are readily available, for no cost, from the government.

In the UK, the government produces:

- an index of prices for consumers, the Retail Prices Index or RPI

FOULKS LYNCH
PUBLICATIONS

- an index of prices for consumers, excluding the cost of mortgage interest payments (which is known as the RPI – X index)

- a range of industry-specific price indices

- indices for average earnings (wages and salaries).

A business can select and use a price index that is best-suited to its specific requirements.

3.2 HOW A PRICE INDEX IS CONSTRUCTED?

You will not be expected to construct a price index, but it might help your understanding of indices if you are aware of the basic rules for doing so.

To construct a price index, you need to identify a 'basket' of goods and services whose prices will be monitored by the index. The goods and services selected for measurement should be representative. For example, to construct the Retail Prices Index, the government selects a basket of goods and services that are suitably representative of what consumers spend their money on.

Let's assume, for the purpose of a simple illustration, that a basket of goods and services consists of just three items, two loaves of bread, a litre of unleaded petrol and a small jar of coffee.

The base period might be January Year 1, when a loaf of bread costs £1.00, a litre of petrol 70p and a jar of coffee £1.25.

In December Year 3, a loaf of bread might cost £1.15, a litre of petrol 80p and a jar of coffee £1.20.

We can work out the cost of the basket of goods in January Year 1 and December Year 3, as follows.

	January Year1	December Year 3
	£	£
2 loaves of bread	2.00	2.30
Litre of petrol	0.70	0.80
Jar of coffee	<u>1.25</u>	<u>1.20</u>
	<u>3.95</u>	<u>4.30</u>

If the base period January Year 1 is given an index value of 100, we can calculate the index value for December Year 3 as:

$$\frac{4.30}{3.95} \times 100 = 108.9 \text{ (to one decimal place)}$$

An index value can be calculated in the same way for any other month.

Changes in the price index therefore represent changes in the prices, on average, for a selected group of items.

ACTIVITY 2

A company is constructing its own price index for the selling price of its only product, product XZ. Price index values are calculated annually, and the base year (index = 100) is 20X1. The actual selling price of product XZ in each year from 20X1 to 20X5 was as follows:

Year	Selling price £
20X1	200
20X2	232
20X3	256
20X4	250
20X5	280

The index for each subsequent year must then be calculated by comparing that year's price to the price in 20X1.

Task

Construct a price index for the price of product XZ for each of the five years.

For a suggested answer, see the 'Answers' section at the end of the book.

ACTIVITY 3

A product which cost £12.50 in 20X0, cost £13.65 in 20X1. Calculate the price index for 20X1 taking 20X0 as the base period, index = 100.

For a suggested answer, see the 'Answers' section at the end of the book.

3.3 INDEX POINTS AND PERCENTAGE CHANGES

It is important to make a distinction between index points and percentage values. Confusion can arise because an index often has a base = 100, and percentages are also based on 100.

When there is an increase in a price index, the increase can be stated as either:

- an increase in the number of index points, or

- a percentage increase.

The two figures will be different.

Example

A retail prices index for the past few years has the following index numbers.

Period	Index
January 20X1	560
January 20X2	581
January 20X3	607
January 20X4	622

Task

What is the increase in prices between January 20X2 and January 20X4?

Solution

The increase in the index is (622 − 581) 41 index points.

This does not mean 41%! The increase in the index is 41 points from its January 20X2 level of 581. The percentage increase in price levels can be calculated as:

$$\frac{41}{581} \times 100\% = 7.1\% \text{ (to one decimal place)}$$

ACTIVITY 4

An average earnings index for the past few years has the following index numbers.

Period	Index
20X5	267
20X6	280
20X7	293
20X8	306

Task

What was the increase in average earnings between 20X5 and 20X8?

For a suggested answer, see the 'Answers' section at the end of the book.

4 PRICE INDICES AND INFLATION

In the UK the generally-accepted measurement of general price inflation is the Retail Prices Index or RPI. The RPI and other price indices for specific industries are published by the Office of National Statistics.

An organisation can choose to compare its revenues and costs to a general inflation index such as the RPI or a specific price index for its inputs or outputs. This is done by stripping out the effects of inflation leaving only the 'real' increase or decrease in sales or costs.

The **reason for adjusting actual values to allow for price changes** is to give more meaning to **comparisons** of different money figures between different years.

If the general or specific increases in prices are taken out of an organisation's results then this will leave only the **real** or genuine increase (or decrease) due to changes in selling prices, sales volume and costs.

4.1 ADJUSTING MONEY VALUES TO A COMMON PRICE LEVEL

Measurements of costs or revenues over a period of time are usually adjusted for inflation in one of two ways.

- All the figures can be reduced to base year figures by stripping out the effects of inflation.

- All the figures can be inflated to current year prices.

To adjust the value of an item at period X prices to the prices of the base period, we multiply by a factor:

$$\frac{\text{Index value, base period}}{\text{Index value, period X}}$$

To adjust the value of an item at period X prices to the prices of the current period, we multiply by a factor:

$$\frac{\text{Index value, current period}}{\text{Index value, period X}}$$

Example

Suppose that an organisation has the following sales over a number of years. The specific price index that relates to those sales is also given:

	Sales	Specific price
	£000	index
20X0	122	100
20X1	140	112
20X2	150	118
20X3	154	128
20X4	160	135
20X5	170	140

Tasks

1   Remove from these sales figures the effect of inflation (the specific price changes) by converting the sales figures for this product to base year (20X0) levels.

2   Remove from these sales figures the effect of inflation (the specific price changes) by converting the sales figures for this product to current year (20X5) levels.

3   Use the results you have produced to measure the percentage real growth or decline in sales between 20X1 and 20X5.

Solution

In order to remove the effects of inflation two different methods can be used:

(a)   All the figures can be reduced to base year figures by stripping out the effects of inflation.

(b)   All the figures can be inflated to current year prices.

Task 1:   Reduction or deflation of sales figures

The sales figures for each year are deflated or reduced by dividing by the price index for the year being considered and multiplying by the index for the earliest year.

Year	Sales	Adjustment factor	Sales at base period prices
20X0	£122,000	$\times \dfrac{100}{100}$	£122,000
20X1	£140,000	$\times \dfrac{100}{112}$	£125,000
20X2	£150,000	$\times \dfrac{100}{118}$	£127,119
20X3	£154,000	$\times \dfrac{100}{128}$	£120,313
20X4	£160,000	$\times \dfrac{100}{135}$	£118,519
20X5	£170,000	$\times \dfrac{100}{140}$	£121,429

Task 2:   Adjust all amounts to current year prices

Year	Sales	Adjustment factor	Sales at current (20X5) prices
20X0	£122,000	$\times \dfrac{140}{100}$	£170,800

20X1	£140,000	$\times \dfrac{140}{112}$	£175,000
20X2	£150,000	$\times \dfrac{140}{118}$	£177,966
20X3	£154,000	$\times \dfrac{140}{128}$	£168,438
20X4	£160,000	$\times \dfrac{140}{135}$	£165,926
20X5	£170,000	$\times \dfrac{140}{140}$	£170,000

Task 3:   Comparisons

Taking the figures at 20X0 price levels, there has been a slight decrease in sales, from £122,000 to £121,429. This is a reduction of £571. The percentage reduction in sales between 20X0 and 20X5 is therefore (100% × 571/122,000) 0.47%.

Taking the figures at current price levels (20X5), we get exactly the same analysis. There has been a slight decrease in sales, from £170,800 to £170,000. This is a reduction of £800. The percentage reduction in sales between 20X0 and 20X5 is therefore (100% × 800/170,800) 0.47%.

ACTIVITY 5

Given below are the sales figures of an organisation and the Retail Prices Index for a number of years.

	Sales £000	Retail price index
20X4	500	131
20X5	510	139
20X6	540	149
20X7	580	154
20X8	650	164

Task

Restate the sales figures for each year on the following bases:

(a)   deflating each year's sales to 20X4 levels in order to take out the effect of inflation

(b)   restating each year's figures in terms of current (20X8) prices.

Briefly comment on what your figures show.

This activity covers performance criterion C in element 7.1.

For a suggested answer, see the 'Answers' section at the end of the book.

5   MORE APPLICATIONS OF ADJUSTMENTS FOR CHANGING PRICE LEVELS

Index numbers can be used to compare changes in values over time, and by putting all figures on to a common price level, we can identify and measure any 'real' change over time.

There are many different ways in which comparisons might be made with adjusted money values.

For example, a business might be concerned about cost control. One way of monitoring costs over time is to identify whether increases in costs are attributable to causes that management might have little control over, such as:

- changes in price levels or

- changes in the volume of production or sales.

We can use a price index to put all costs on to the same basis, and then try to identify the extent to which any remaining cost differences are attributable to differences in volume.

Example

A business is looking at its costs by comparing its costs in the current year (year 4, just ended) with costs three years ago. The following data has been collected.

Year	Units of production	Fixed costs	Variable costs	Total costs	Relevant price index (cost index)
		£	£	£	
1	147,000	200,000	294,000	494,000	376
4	194,000	229,500	413,000	624,500	425

Tasks

Re-state the year 1 costs at year 4 price levels.

Give your view as to whether costs are being kept under control or not.

Solution

Year1		Adjustment factor	Sales at current (20X5) prices
Fixed costs	£200,000	$\times \dfrac{425}{376}$	£226,064
Variable costs	£294,000	$\times \dfrac{425}{376}$	£332,313

Fixed costs should be the same regardless of the volume of activity, and the figures suggest that total fixed costs have risen by slightly more than the general level of cost rises. The increase is (£229,500 - £226,064) £3,436 at year 4 prices, which represents a 'real' increase of 1.5% (100% $\times$ 3,436/226,064).

Variable costs go up or down with the volume of activity, and in year 4, production was 194,000 units compared with just 147,000 units in year 1.

Taking year 1 costs as a base point, we would expect total variable costs in year 4 to be:

$$£332,313 \times \frac{194,000}{147,000} = £438,563$$

Actual variable costs were just £413,000 in year 4, suggesting that control over variable costs has improved since year 1.

Another way of making the analysis of variable costs is to say that at year 4 price levels, the variable cost per unit was £2.26 in year 1 (£332,313/147,000 units) but just £2.13 (£413,000/194,000 units) in year 4.

Example

A price index or earnings index is sometimes used in negotiations between employers and trade unions about pay rises for employees.

Suppose that a company pays a grade of employee an annual salary of £37,700, but salaries for comparable workers in a competitor business is thought to be £39,000.

Five years ago, the company paid the same grade of employee an annual salary of £28,000 when salaries of comparable workers in the competitor' business was £30,500.

An earnings index for this type of employee shows that the current index value is 1097 and five years ago it was 825.

Task

(a) Calculate whether salaries for the company's employees have kept pace with the general increase in salary levels for this type of worker over the past five years.

(b) Compare salary increases for the company's workers with those of competitors.

Solution

(a) We can re-state salaries of five years ago at today's levels.

		Adjustment factor	Salaries of five years ago at current prices	Current salaries
Company	£28,000	$\times \dfrac{1097}{825}$	£37,232	£37,000
Competitor	£30,500	$\times \dfrac{1097}{825}$	£40,556	£39,000

(b) The figures for the company show that salaries for employees have just about kept up with the rate of salary increases for this type of worker. The figures for the competitor show that salaries for its employees not kept up with the rate of salary increases for this type of worker.

We can conclude that salaries for the company's employees have been 'catching up' on the salaries of competitor's employees. At current year price levels, the real decrease in salaries for the company's employees has been £232 or 0.6% (100% × 232/37,232). In contrast the real decrease in the salaries of the competitor's employees has been £1,556 or 3.8% (100% × 1,556/40,556).

ACTIVITY 6

You have been asked to comparing the costs of your business in the current year (20X3, just ended) with costs in the previous year. The following data has been collected.

Year	Sales units	Fixed costs	Variable costs	Total costs	Relevant price index (cost index)
		£	£	£	
20X2	214,000	176,000	118,000	294,000	635
20X3	206,000	184,900	121,700	306,600	687

Tasks

1 Re-state the 20X2 costs at 20X3 price levels.

2 Give your view as to whether costs are being kept under control or not.

For a suggested answer, see the 'Answers' section at the end of the book.

FOULKS LYNCH
PUBLICATIONS

CONCLUSION

In this chapter you have learnt:

- how a price index is constructed and what index numbers represent

- how to use indices to adjust money values for inflation, and re-state costs or revenues in different time periods on a common price basis

- that the purpose of adjusting costs or revenues with price index numbers is to make comparisons over time more meaningful.

SELF TEST QUESTIONS

		Paragraph
1	Why is it that prices in one time period often cannot be easily compared with prices in another time period?	1
2	What is a price index?	3
3	State some sources of index numbers.	3.1
4	How is a price index constructed?	3.2
5	What is the difference between index points and percentage changes?	3.3
6	What sort of index is the Retail Price Index (RPI)?	4
7	Explain how the RPI is determined each month.	4

KEY TERMS

Inflation – a general increase in the price level over time.

Index – a series of numbers showing the variation in either a price level or a quantity level compared with a common base period.

Price index – a series of numbers showing the variation in a price level compared with a common base period. Price index can be used to adjust price levels in different years to a common price level.

Retail Prices Index (RPI) – the generally-accepted measurement of general price inflation in the UK.

Office of National Statistics – publishes the RPI and other price indices for specific industries.

FOULKS LYNCH
PUBLICATIONS

Chapter 7

RATIOS AND PERFORMANCE INDICATORS

This chapter describes various ratios and other performance indicators that might be used to report performance in a business.

CONTENTS

KNOWLEDGE AND UNDERSTANDING

		Reference
1	Main types of performance indicators: productivity; cost per unit; resource utilisation; profitability	Item 11
2	Ratios: gross profit margin; net profit margin; return on capital employed	Item 12

PERFORMANCE CRITERIA

		Reference
1	Calculate ratios and performance indicators in accordance with the organisation's procedures	Item E, element 7.1
2	Ensure calculations of ratios and performance indicators are accurate	Item B, element 7.2

LEARNING OUTCOMES

At the end of this chapter, you should be able to:

- Explain and calculate performance indicators relating to productivity

- Explain and calculate performance indicators relating to resource utilisation

- Calculate costs per unit

- Explain and calculate performance indicators relating to profitability, including gross profit margin and net profit margin

- Explain and calculate return on capital employed

- Explain a number of other balance sheet ratios relating to business performance

1 PERFORMANCE REPORTS

Performance reports are produced by businesses to give the managers information about how well or badly the business, or a part of it, is performing.

One way of providing information about financial performance is to present managers with a detailed set of financial statements, full of detailed accounting figures. A problem with providing too much information, however, is that the manager might suffer from 'information overload', and might not be able to take in all the details. A more suitable way of reporting on performance might be to present a few key performance indicators or ratios, which show whether performance has been good, satisfactory or poor.

Many performance indicators are presented as ratios. A ratio is simply a comparison of two values, such as the size of profit as a proportion of total sales revenue. Performance indicators might also be presented in other ways, such as a cost per unit, or as a percentage.

There is a huge range of performance indicators, which can be made up from financial information, non-financial information or a mixture of the two. In this chapter, some of the more common ratios and other performance indicators will be examined.

1.1 THE IMPORTANCE OF COMPARISONS FOR JUDGING PERFORMANCE

A performance report is intended to allow its reader to make a judgement about how good or bad the performance has been, and so indicate whether corrective action needs to be taken.

In order to judge whether performance has been good or bad, there has to be some guideline or yardstick against which actual performance can be compared. Actual measures of performance can be compared with any of the following:

- performance in previous time periods

- a budgeted or planned level of performance

- a target for achievement

- an ideal level of performance

- the performance of similar businesses.

To make comparisons with the performance of similar businesses, there has to be a system for gathering information about other businesses and making a comparison. In many industries, there is a federation or association of employers who provide an 'interfirm comparison' report service. All businesses that join the scheme submit information about their own performance to the central organisers. The information is then assembled and analysed, and then presented to each of the scheme members, showing how the individual scheme member's performance has compared with the average for the other participants in the scheme.

2 WHAT ASPECTS OF PERFORMANCE ARE MEASURED?

Although many aspects of performance can be measured, it is possible to group performance measures for a business into just a few broad categories.

- Efficiency or productivity measures. These are measures of how well or badly the business has made use of the resources it has employed, such as its labour force, equipment and money.

- Capacity utilisation measures. These are measures of how effectively the business has made use of all its available capacity.

- Cost measures. A simple but effective method of measuring performance is to calculate costs per unit of output or per unit of activity.

- Financial measures of profitability and return on capital.

3 MEASURES OF PRODUCTIVITY OR EFFICIENCY

Definition   A **productivity measure** is a measure of the efficiency of an operation or the efficiency with which a resource has been used. They relate outputs obtained to input resources consumed.

Productivity measures relate the amount or value of goods or services produced to the resources that have been used to produce them. The most productive or efficient operation is one that either:

- produces the maximum output for any given set of resource inputs, or alternatively

- uses the minimum inputs for any given quantity or quality of output.

Example

Suppose that three rival bus companies operate a number of buses on the same route, and that during a particular month:

- Green Bus Company uses three buses, which made a total of 350 return journeys on the route.

- Red Bus Company also uses three buses, which made a total of 240 return journeys on the route.

- Blue Bus company uses two buses, which together made a total of 350 return journeys on the route.

- Here, Green Bus Company has been more efficient than Red Bus Company, because it has made more journeys in the period with the same number of buses, so it has used its resources (buses) more productively. Blue Bus Company is even more efficient than Green Bus Company, because it has made exactly the same number of journeys, but with fewer buses.

3.1 PRODUCTION AND PRODUCTIVITY

It is important to distinguish between production and productivity.

- Production is the quantity of goods or services that are produced in a period.

- Productivity is a measure of how efficiently those goods or services have been produced.

Management can control production levels by asking the work force to work more hours or by taking on more employees. Production levels can be reduced by cutting overtime or laying off employees. Increases or decreases in production might therefore be unrelated to changes in productivity.

However, changes in productivity will affect total production or output in a period. For example, suppose that an employee works 160 hours each month and was producing two units an hour. This means that the employee was producing 320 units each month. Now if productivity is improved and the employee is able to make 3 units an hour, monthly production will increase to 480 units.

3.2 PRODUCTIVITY AND INPUT RESOURCES

Productivity is a measure of the relationship between the quantity of outputs produced and the quantity of resources used to produce the output. Outputs are perhaps most easily associated with outputs of products from a manufacturing process, but outputs can also be a volume of activity or a quantity of service provision.

Input resources can be:

- labour, measured either as a quantity of hours worked or a number of employees employed

- equipment, measured perhaps as a quantity of machine time or equipment time operated, or a number of machines used

- money. Productivity can be measured in terms of the amount of output produced per £1 spent.

4 LABOUR PRODUCTIVITY

Businesses often monitor the productivity of their work force. There are several measures of labour productivity, which include:

- output per labour hour

- output per employee per period (day, week, month etc)

- productivity ratio

4.1 OUTPUT PER LABOUR HOUR

Output per labour hour (e.g. production per labour hour) is calculated as the quantity or volume of goods produced in the labour hours worked.

Output per labour hour can be compared with a target rate of output, or a planned output rate, or with productivity in previous time periods.

To measure output per labour hour, there has to be a way of measuring all output in common units. If an organisation produces one standard unit of product, or provides one single service, the calculation is quite simple. However, if an organisation produces widely differing products or non-standard items, or if it provides a range of different services, measuring productivity in this way is difficult, and maybe impossible.

Measurements of output per labour hour are therefore normally restricted in practice to measuring efficiency in the performance of standard, routine and repetitive work.

Production per labour hour is calculated as:

$$\frac{\text{Number of units produced}}{\text{Number of labour hours worked}}$$

Example

An organisation has the following production details for two weeks:

	Week 1	Week 2
Quantity of goods produced (units)	1,500	1,700
Labour hours worked	500	600

Task

Calculate the production per labour hour for each of the two weeks. Comment on what this indicates about productivity.

Solution

Production per labour hour - Week 1

$$\frac{1,500 \, units}{500 \, hours} = 3 \, units \, per \, hour$$

Production per labour hour - Week 2

$$\frac{1,700 \, units}{600 \, hours} = 2.8 \, units \, per \, hour$$

This shows that even though production levels increased in Week 2, productivity decreased from 3 units per hour to only 2.8 units per hour.

ACTIVITY 1

Monthly production details for January to March for an organisation are given below:

	Number of units produced	Labour hours worked
January	24,000	12,000
February	20,000	9,100
March	28,000	15,000

Task

Calculate the production per labour hour. Briefly discuss what these figures indicate about productivity over the three months.

This activity covers performance criterion E in element 7.1.

For a suggested answer, see the 'Answers' section at the end of the book.

4.2 PRODUCTION PER EMPLOYEE

Another method of measuring the efficiency or productivity of the labour force is to calculate the amount of production per employee during a given period of time, such as a week or a month. Output per employee is often measured in relation to an entire work force.

Production per employee is calculated as:

$$\frac{Number \, of \, units \, produced \, in \, the \, period}{Number \, of \, employees \, in \, the \, period}$$

 **FOULKS LYNCH**
PUBLICATIONS

Example

The following production details are available for two weeks of production at a car manufacturing plant:

	Week 1	Week 2
Number of cars produced	2,400	3,000
Number of employees	2,000	2,400

Task

Calculate the production per employee in each week and comment briefly on what this indicates about productivity.

Solution

Week 1 $\dfrac{2,400 \text{ cars}}{2,000 \text{ employees}} = 1.2 \text{ cars per employee per week}$

Week 2 $\dfrac{3,000 \text{ cars}}{2,400 \text{ employees}} = 1.25 \text{ units per employee per week}$

Production levels increased in week 2 by 600 cars or 25% of the week 1 output level. The increase in total production is partly due to an increase (of 400 or 20%) in the numbers employed, but also partly by an improvement in productivity from 1.2 cars to 1.25 cars per employee.

ACTIVITY 2

In June 20X3 a manufacturing organisation produced 168,000 units of its product and employed 50 factory workers. In July 20X3 production levels increased to 180,000 units and 4 additional factory workers were employed for the month.

Calculate the production per employee per month in each of June and July. Comment on what this shows about productivity.

This activity covers performance criterion E in element 7.1.

For a suggested answer, see the 'Answers' section at the end of the book.

4.3   PRODUCTIVITY IN SERVICE INDUSTRIES

Productivity measures in service industries cannot be based on production output per labour hour or per employee, because service industries do not produce goods. However in many service industries some sort of output per employee might be calculated in order to give some indication of productivity.

For example, in a telephone call answering centre, productivity might be measured as number of calls handled per operator per hour. Suppose that a call centre handles 1,085 telephone calls in a day, and employs 25 staff each of whom works a 7 hour day. Productivity could be measured as 6.2 calls per operator per hour (1,085 calls/175 hours worked).

Some forms, such as firms of solicitors or accountants, might measure productivity in terms of the number of 'chargeable hours' per employee each week or month. chargeable hours are the number of hours sent on work for a client, for which the client will be invoiced.

Example

Suppose that the qualified staff in an accountancy firm worked for 2,100 chargeable hours in April and 2,000 chargeable hours in May. Fifteen qualified staff were employed throughout April and sixteen qualified staff were employed throughout May.

Task

Calculate the chargeable hours per qualified staff member for April and May. What do these figures indicate?

Solution

Chargeable hours per qualified staff member:

April $\dfrac{2,100 \text{ hours}}{15 \text{ staff}} = 140$ chargeable hours per staff member

May $\dfrac{2,000 \text{ hours}}{16 \text{ staff}} = 125$ chargeable hours per staff member

Both the total number of chargeable hours for the month in total and also the chargeable hours per employee fell in May compared with April.

ACTIVITY 3

A firm of architects has 3 qualified architects. However in June one was on holiday for the entire month. The chargeable hours for the architects totalled 495 in May and 340 in June.

Calculate the chargeable hours per architect for each month and comment on the figures produced.

This activity covers performance criterion E in element 7.1.

For a suggested answer, see the 'Answers' section at the end of the book.

4.4 PRODUCTIVITY RATIO

Many businesses do not produce just a single product, and do not provide just one service. Instead they make a range of different products or provide a range of different services. This means that measuring productivity is not so easy.

One method of measuring productivity in multi-product or multi-service operations is to:

- Establish expected times for the completion of each product or service. Expected times might be measured in 'standard hours'. For example, if the production of one widget is expected to take three hours in a particular department, one widget will be valued at three standard hours. If the department makes 100 widgets in a week, its output would be measured as 300 standard hours.

- Measure the actual amount of work done or units produced, and convert this into standard hours of work.

- Monitor the actual time it has taken to do the work.

A comparison of the work done (in standard hours) with the number of hours actually worked provides a measure of efficiency or productivity.

$$\text{Efficiency ratio (productivity ratio)} = \frac{\text{Standard hours produced}}{\text{Actual hours worked}} \times 100\%$$

 FOULKS LYNCH
PUBLICATIONS

Example

A business makes three products: X, Y and Z. The expected time to produce them has been estimated as 2.5 standard hours for one unit of X, 1.5 standard hours for one unit of Y and 0.75 standard hours for one unit of Z. During a particular week, the business made:

240 units of X

360 units of Y, and

824 units of Z.

The total number of hours worked in the week by the production team was 1,640 hours.

Tasks

1   How many standard hours of output were produced in the week?

2   What was the efficiency ratio?

Solution

	Standard hours per unit	Standard hours produced
240 units of X	2.50	600
360 units of Y	1.50	540
824 units of Z	0.75	618
		1,758

$$\text{Efficiency ratio (productivity ratio)} = \frac{1,758}{1,640} \times 100\% = 107.2\%$$

An efficiency ratio above 100% means that the work has been done in a shorter time than would normally be expected. An efficiency ratio below 100% indicates some inefficiency.

ACTIVITY 4

A business makes two products, widgets and grommits. Each product goes through two processes, Process 1 and Process 2. The expected time to make them has been estimated as:

Process 1: 45 minutes for one widget and 30 minutes for one grommit

Process 2: 15 minutes for one widget and 75 minutes for one grommit.

During May, the business made 6,200 widgets and 5,500 grommits. 7,500 hours were worked in Process 1 and 8,100 hours were worked in Process 2.

Tasks

1   How many standard hours of output were produced in the month, in Process 1, Process 2 and in total? Present your figures in tabular form.

2   What were the efficiency ratios in Process 1, Process 2 and overall?

This activity covers performance criterion E in element 7.1.

For a suggested answer, see the 'Answers' section at the end of the book.

5 EFFICIENCY OF MACHINE UTILISATION

In many manufacturing and service organisations, processes are highly mechanised or automated, and reliant upon machinery. The efficiency or speed of production is outside of the control of the work force, and so measuring labour productivity might not be a useful way of monitoring performance.

In highly mechanised or automated departments and factories, productivity might be better measured in terms of how efficiently the equipment has been used.

5.1 PRODUCTION PER MACHINE HOUR

A simple measure of the efficiency of using machinery is production per machine hour. This is calculated as:

$$\frac{\text{Number of units produced}}{\text{Number of machine hours operated}}$$

Example

The following production information is available for an organisation for two days.

	Monday	Tuesday
Number of units produced	20,000	21,000
Number of machine hours worked	80	90

Calculate and briefly comment upon the productivity for these two days in terms of machine hours.

Solution

Production per machine hour:

Monday $\dfrac{20,000 \text{ units}}{80 \text{ hours}}$ = 250 units per machine hour

Tuesday $\dfrac{21,000 \text{ units}}{90 \text{ hours}}$ = 233 units per machine hour

The number of units produced in total is larger on Tuesday but the productivity per machine hour is lower.

ACTIVITY 5

A factory produces 3,000 units of its product in week 27 using 480 machine hours. In week 28 the number of machine hours used fell to 440 and production fell to 2,800. What does this indicate about the productivity of the machines? (Work to two decimal places).

This activity covers performance criterion E in element 7.1.

For a suggested answer, see the 'Answers' section at the end of the book.

5.2 PRODUCTION PER MACHINE

In a similar way to producing a production per employee figure, a production per machine indicator can also be produced, in order to reflect the productivity of the machines. This might be particularly relevant in a situation where it is the number of machines or pieces of equipment that is important rather than the number of hours that those machines or equipment work.

 **FOULKS LYNCH**
PUBLICATIONS

Example

A minicab firm has the following information about the number of passengers transported in each of two days.

	Friday	Saturday
Number of passengers	260	350
Number of minicabs in service	10	12

Task

Calculate the number of passengers per minicab for each of the two days.

Solution

Passengers per minicab:

Friday $\dfrac{260 \text{ passengers}}{10 \text{ minicabs}}$ = 26 passengers per minicab

Saturday $\dfrac{350 \text{ passengers}}{12 \text{ minicabs}}$ = 29 passengers per minicab

ACTIVITY 6

A refuse collection organisation had 45 dustcarts in operation in week 31 and only 40 in operation, due to mechanical failures, in week 32. The number of dustbins emptied in week 31 were 22,500 and in week 32 totalled 21,000.

Calculate the number of dustbins emptied per dustcart for each of the two weeks.

This activity covers performance criterion E in element 7.1.

For a suggested answer, see the 'Answers' section at the end of the book.

5.3 CAPACITY UTILISATION

Managers should want to make the best use of the resources at their disposal. Resources include labour and machinery and equipment.

Resource utilisation is partly a matter of efficiency or productivity. It is also partly a matter of capacity utilisation.

Example

A warehouse stores goods for shipping overseas. It is 20,000 square metres in size, employs 14 warehouse staff and has 6 fork-lift trucks.

During the past month, the warehouse used only 15,000 square metres of its available space and two fork-lift trucks have been idle. The work force spent much of its time doing nothing.

This situation should be a matter of concern to the management, because expensive resources – building space, equipment and employees – are being paid for but not fully utilised. The solution should be either to find ways of making more use of the available capacity, or to get rid of the surplus capacity.

5.4 CAPACITY RATIO

Resource utilisation might be measured by means of a capacity ratio:

$$\text{Capacity ratio (utilisation ratio)} = \frac{\text{Hours used}}{\text{Total hours available}} \times 100\%$$

Alternatively, for measuring the utilisation of building space or items of equipment:

$$\text{Capacity ratio (utilisation ratio)} = \frac{\text{Amount used}}{\text{Total quantity available}} \times 100\%$$

Example

A telephone exchange has the capacity to handle 16 million call-minutes of capacity each week. A call-minute is a minute's time of telephone call. During a particular week, the exchange handled 9.65 million call-minutes.

Capacity utilisation was therefore:

$$\frac{9.65\,\text{million}}{16\,\text{million}} \times 100\% = 60.3\%$$

ACTIVITY 7

A taxi firm has 8 taxi cabs, each of which operates for nine hours a day and five days a week. During a particular week, the cabs carried passengers for a total of 211 hours.

What was the capacity utilisation of the cabs during the week?

This activity covers performance criterion E in element 7.1.

For a suggested answer, see the 'Answers' section at the end of the book.

5.5 OTHER MEASURES OF RESOURCE UTILISATION

Measures of resource utilisation vary from business to business. For example, a bus company should want to know whether or not it is making good use of its buses, a road haulage firm should want to know whether it is making good use of its trucks, and a private hospital should want to know about its use of its bed space and operation theatre time.

Resource utilisation can be measured in terms of output per unit of input resource. For example:

- for a bus company, passenger-miles carried per bus

- for a refuse collection company, number of refuse bins emptied per refuse truck

- for a road haulage company, tonne-miles carried per truck

- for a private hospital, operating hours per operating theatre and patient-days per bed per month.

The choice of resource utilisation measure will vary according to the nature of the business but a common feature is that they relate units of output to units of resources input.

Alternatively, resource utilisation might be measured in terms of:

- a cost per unit of output (see later)

- a cost per unit of input (such as a cost per hour worked or a cost per machine hour operated)

- revenue per unit of input resource

- profit per unit (see later)

Example

Suppose that an organisation rents 10,000 square metres of factory and warehouse space and employs 120 employees. If the revenue for the period is £400,000 then what is the amount of:

(a)   revenue per square metre

(b)   revenue per employee?

Solution

(a)   Revenue per square foot $= \dfrac{\text{Revenue}}{\text{Square metres of space}}$

$\qquad\qquad = \dfrac{\text{£400,000}}{\text{10,000 sq m}}$

$\qquad\qquad =$ £40 per square metre

(b)   Revenue per employee $= \dfrac{\text{Revenue}}{\text{Number of employees}}$

$\qquad\qquad = \dfrac{\text{£400,000}}{\text{120 employees}}$

$\qquad\qquad =$ £3,333 per employee

6   COST PER UNIT

Management monitor efficiency (productivity) and resource utilisation so that they can identify what aspects of operations are doing well, and what are not doing well.

Other important aspects of performance are costs and, for commercial businesses, profits.

Information about costs and profits is probably the most important performance information for business managers, and they will often expect to receive regular cost and profit reports.

It is useful to compare actual costs incurred with planned costs, target costs or the costs incurred in previous periods. To make comparisons simpler, it is common practice to report costs incurred as a cost per unit.

There are different ways of measuring costs and costs per unit. Some of these are explained below.

6.1   DIRECT AND INDIRECT COSTS

The costs incurred by an organisation might be separated into direct costs and indirect costs. Indirect costs are also called overheads.

Definition   **Direct costs** are costs that can be directly attributed to units of production or sale. The direct costs of an activity are costs that can be directly attributed to the activity.

Definition   **Indirect costs** are costs that cannot be directly attributed to units of production or sale.

Direct costs

The direct cost of a product will be made up of three elements:

●   Direct materials – these are the materials used to make the product.

●   Direct labour – this is the cost of the hours of labour spent working on the product.

- Direct expenses – these are any costs, other than direct materials and direct labour, that can be directly attributed to a unit of the product.

Indirect costs

Indirect costs or overheads are all the other costs that are not direct costs. These consist of the costs of indirect materials, indirect labour and indirect expenses.

Overheads are often classified by function, according to which part of the business has incurred the expenditure. Three generally-accepted functional classifications of overheads are:

- production overhead

- selling and distribution overhead (or marketing overhead)

- administration overhead.

A business might therefore report its costs as follows.

Cost report for (period)

Number of units produced: 8,000 units

	Total costs	Costs per unit
	£	£
Direct materials	44,000	5.50
Direct labour	28,800	3.60
Total direct costs	72,800	9.10
Production overhead	49,600	6.20
Administration overhead	17,200	2.15
Selling and distribution overhead	27,200	3.40
	166,800	20.85

6.2 FIXED AND VARIABLE COSTS

Costs might also be classified according to whether they are fixed or variable.

Definition   A **fixed cost** is one that should remain the same no matter what the level of production and sales volume. As the volume of output increases, the cost per unit will therefore fall, because the same total fixed costs are spread over a larger number of units.

Definition   **Variable costs** vary directly with the level of production and sales. Total variable costs rise in proportion to increases in volume, but the variable cost per unit is the same.

Example

A factory makes widgets. Fixed costs are £16,000 each week and the variable cost per unit of production is £1.50.

What will be the total costs and the cost per unit if production in the week is:

- 6,000 units

- 8,000 units

- 10,000 units?

Solution

Weekly output (units)	6,000	8,000	10,000
	£	£	£
Variable costs (£1.50/unit)	9,000	12,000	15,000
Fixed costs	16,000	16,000	16,000
Total costs	25,000	28,000	31,000
Cost per unit			
Variable	1.50	1.50	1.50
Fixed	2.67	2.00	1.60
Total	4.17	3.50	3.10

ACTIVITY 8

VZ Limited manufactures and sells Product T. During October, it made 21,800 units of Product T.

Cost data relating to the week are as follows:

Manufacturing costs:

Direct materials	£57,100
Direct labour	£43,700
Production overhead	£68,900

Other costs

Administration overhead	£31,500
Selling and distribution overhead	£68,200

Stocks of goods are valued at manufacturing cost. At the beginning of October, there were units of opening stocks and these were valued at £14,000. At the end of October, there were units of closing stocks, valued at £19,000.

Task

Present this data in tabular form to show the cost per unit of T **sold** during the week. The unit costs of sale should show the production cost per unit sold, administration cost per unit and selling and distribution cost per unit, as well as the total cost per unit.

This activity covers performance criterion E in element 7.1.

For a suggested answer, see the 'Answers' section at the end of the book.

ACTIVITY 9

During month 6, 12,000 units of an organisation's only product were produced. The costs incurred in the production of that product were as follows.

	£
Direct materials	68,000
Direct labour	72,000
Direct expenses	15,000
Production overheads	54,000

Task

Calculate the direct production cost and the total production cost for one unit of the organisation's product in month 6.

This activity covers performance criterion E in element 7.1.

For a suggested answer, see the 'Answers' section at the end of the book.

6.3 STANDARD COSTS AND ACTUAL COSTS

Definition	**Standard costs** of a product are the expected or anticipated costs. Standard costs for each type of product manufactured are recorded on a standard cost card. Standard costs are used to compare actual costs incurred with the standard costs that should have been expected.
Definition	**Actual costs** are the costs actually incurred in producing the product. If the actual costs differ from the standard costs, the differences are quantified as variances.

ACTIVITY 10

Given below are the standard direct costs and actual direct cost information for product Y.

Standard costs:

10 kg of material G56 at £4.50 per kg

3 hours of labour at £5 per hour

Direct expenses of £2.00 per unit

Actual costs

During March 30,000 units of product Y were produced. The costs actually incurred were as follows:

	£000
Direct materials	1,200
Direct labour	480
Direct expenses	80

Task

Show the standard direct cost per unit and the actual direct cost per unit for March.

This activity covers performance criterion E in element 7.1.

For a suggested answer, see the 'Answers' section at the end of the book.

6.4 COSTS OF INPUT RESOURCES

Sometimes, managers might want to monitor the costs of key resources, so that they can assess whether costs are being kept properly under control. Measures of cost per input resource vary between businesses, and depend on what the resources of the business are.

For example:

- A television studio will be interested in monitoring the cost per hour of filming.

- A refuse collection firm will be interested in the cost per refuse bin emptied.

- A warehouse might be interested in the average cost per tonne of materials handled or stored.

- A telephone call answering centre might be interested in the cost per operator hour.

Costs of input resources are calculated quite simply as:

$$\frac{\text{Total costs}}{\text{Quantity of input resources}}$$

7 PROFITABILITY

As well as needing to know about costs, managers also need to know about profits. Just as it is useful to calculate a cost per unit in order to compare actual performance against a target, or standard or previous years' costs, it is also useful to report profits as a profit per unit.

A report on profitability might show both total profit and the profit per unit.

7.1 COST OF SALES, GROSS PROFIT AND NET PROFIT

A report about profitability will show both **gross profit** and **net profit**.

Definition   **Gross profit** is defined as sales revenue minus the cost of goods sold.

Definition   **Net profit** is defined as gross profit minus all other costs.

Businesses measure the cost of goods sold in different ways, but the following guidelines might be useful.

- For a retail business, the cost of goods sold is the purchase cost of the goods sold. In other words, it is the cost of buying the sold items from the suppliers to the business.

- For a manufacturing business, it is the cost of manufacturing the units sold.

'Cost of goods sold' or 'cost of sales' is generally associated with a business that sells goods, as a retailer, trader or manufacturer, and all of these businesses are likely to hold stocks of their items. In order to calculate the cost of goods sold, it is therefore necessary to make an adjustment for opening and closing stocks in the period.

For a retailing business, the cost of goods sold would be measured as follows. (Illustrative numbers are shown):

	£
Opening stock	15,800
Purchases	69,200
	85,000
Less closing stock	(11,400)
Cost of goods sold	73,600

Gross profit is sales revenue less the cost of goods sold, and net profit is gross profit minus all other expenses. These are all the costs that are not included in the cost of goods sold, and will include items such as salaries of employees, rental costs, telephone expenses and so on.

Example

A business has three shops, in Manchester, Glasgow and Cardiff. Transactions for November are as follows:

	Manchester	Glasgow	Cardiff
	£	£	£
Sales	30,400	27,200	27,600
Purchases	10,600	12,700	9,900
Salaries	5,400	5,000	4,100
Shop rental	2,800	2,200	2,000
Telephone	800	900	500
Electricity and gas	700	1,000	400
Equipment lease costs	3,100	2,900	1,800
Sundry expenses	4,400	6,100	4,800
Opening stock	2,900	4,800	1,900
Closing stock	3,600	2,600	1,700
Transfers to Manchester and Cardiff		3,300	
Receipts from Glasgow	1,500		1,800

The transfers of goods from Glasgow to the other two shops were made at their purchase cost.

Task

For each shop and for the three shops combined, show the following for November:

* sales
* cost of goods sold
* gross profit
* net profit

Solution

The cost of goods sold is the purchase cost of the goods. During November, some goods were transferred from Glasgow to the other two shops. These transfers are goods that have been purchased by Glasgow, but sold by the other shops. The cost of the items should therefore be in the cost of goods sold for Manchester and Cardiff, not the cost of goods sold for Glasgow.

An adjustment to the cost of goods sold should therefore be made:

* the cost of the items transferred should be deducted from the cost of goods sold for Glasgow, and
* the cost of the transferred items received should be added to the cost of goods sold for Manchester (£1,500) and Cardiff (£1,800).

	Manchester	Glasgow	Cardiff	Total
	£	£	£	£
Sales	30,400	27,200	27,600	85,200
Opening stock	2,900	4,800	1,900	9,600
Purchases	10,600	12,700	9,900	33,200
Transfers	1,500	(3,300)	1,800	
Closing stock	(3,600)	(2,600)	(1,700)	(7,900)

Cost of goods sold	11,400	11,600	11,900	34,900
Gross profit	19,000	15,600	15,700	50,300
Salaries	5,400	5,000	4,100	14,500
Shop rental	2,800	2,200	2,000	7,000
Telephone	800	900	500	2,200
Electricity and gas	700	1,000	400	2,100
Equipment lease costs	3,100	2,900	1,800	7,800
Sundry expenses	4,400	6,100	4,800	15,300
Net profit/(loss)	1,800	(2,500)	2,100	1,400

ACTIVITY 11

A printing company has two print shops, in Basildon and in Walton. Transactions for February were as follows.

	Basildon	Walton
	£	£
Sales	68,100	95,000
Purchases of paper	21,000	17,500
Purchases of ink	2,600	3,900
Salaries	25,400	31,800
Building rental	1,700	1,900
Printing machine rental	3,300	3,700
Sundry expenses	18,500	26,600
Opening stock of paper and ink	3,800	4,100
Closing stock of paper and ink	5,100	3,400
Transfers of paper to Walton	6,300	
Receipts from Basildon		3,800

The transfers of paper from Basildon to Glasgow were made at their purchase cost. However, as at the end of February, a transfer of £2,500 of paper had not yet been recorded in the accounts of the Walton plant.

Task

For each print shop and for the two shops combined, show the following for February:

- sales

- cost of goods sold

- gross profit

- net profit

This activity covers performance criteria A, B and E in element 7.1.

For a suggested answer, see the 'Answers' section at the end of the book.

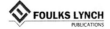

7.2 PROFITABILITY PER UNIT OF INPUT RESOURCE

Profitability is normally measured in terms of the profitability of products or services sold by a businesses.

Sometimes, it might also be useful to have information about the profitability of key input resources. For example:

- A firm of solicitors is likely to measure the profitability of its professional employees, and calculate a profitability per solicitor employed.

- A taxi firm might want to measure the average profitability of its taxis.

The reason for measuring the profitability of input resources is to help managers to assess whether the resources are earning as much as they should.

8 PROFITABILITY RATIOS

When assessing the profitability of a business, key measures are gross profit and net profit. However, these are money values, and on their own, they do not necessarily provide management with the information they need to assess performance properly.

For example, suppose you are told that a business made a gross profit of £600,000 last year and a net profit of £200,000. Without more information, these figures don't really tell you anything. For a small business, these could be excellent results. For a huge multinational company, they would be appalling results.

A better indication of performance would be possible if there were figures for comparison. For example, we might know that in the previous year, the same business had a gross profit of £575,000 and a net profit of £190,000. This comparison would enable us to see that gross profit and net profit have both increased since the previous year (by 4.3% and 5.3% respectively).

However, this could be a misleading comparison, because there is still no information about the size of the business operations. Suppose that last year, the business had sales of £12 million, whereas in the previous year, sales had been just £8 million. Sales therefore increased by £4 million or 50%, but profits grew by a much smaller amount.

To measure profitability in a meaningful way, it is therefore useful to:

- have figures for comparison. These could be budgeted profit figures, or figures for the previous year, or figures for competitor firms.

- relate the profits earned to the volume of sales, and compare these results with a budget, the previous year or the profitability of competitors.

The ratio of profit to sales is sometimes referred to as profit margin ratio. In many businesses, two profit margin ratios are monitored:

- gross profit margin

- net profit margin.

8.1 GROSS PROFIT MARGIN

The gross profit percentage or gross profit margin is the gross profit figure expressed as a percentage of the sales for the period.

This is calculated as follows:

$$\frac{\text{Gross profit}}{\text{Sales}} \times 100\%$$

Example

A profit and loss account is given for an organisation for the year ended 31 December 20X4.

	£	£
Sales		340,000
Cost of sales		226,000
		————
		114,000
Less: Expenses		
Rent and rates	11,000	
Power, heat and light	6,000	
Wages	44,000	
Depreciation	10,000	
	————	71,000
		————
Net profit		43,000
		————

Task

Calculate the gross profit margin, as a percentage.

Solution

$$\text{Gross profit margin} = \frac{\text{Gross profit}}{\text{Sales}} \times 100\%$$

$$= \frac{114,000}{340,000} \times 100\%$$

$$= 33.5\%$$

This should be compared with the gross profit margin the previous year, the gross profit margin being earned by other businesses or the budgeted gross profit margin.

A gross profit percentage might change due to either a change in selling price or a change in the cost of these sales.

If you read business reports about retailing organisations, such as supermarket chains, you might see a reference to gross profit margins. Even small changes in the gross margin for these companies can have an enormous effect on profitability. For example, suppose that a supermarket chain, Asbury's, has monthly sales turnover of £100 million. A decline in gross profit margin by just 1% would reduce gross profits by £1 million each month.

8.2 NET PROFIT MARGIN

The net profit percentage or net profit margin is the net profit figure expressed as a percentage of sales. The calculation is as follows:

$$\frac{\text{Net profit}}{\text{Sales}} \times 100\%$$

Example

Using the profit and loss account from the previous example (reproduced below), what is the net profit percentage?

	£	£
Sales		340,000
Cost of sales		226,000
		114,000
Less: Expenses		
Rent and rates	11,000	
Power, heat and light	6,000	
Wages	44,000	
Depreciation	10,000	
		71,000
Net profit		43,000

Solution

$$\text{Net profit percentage} = \frac{\text{Net profit}}{\text{Sales}} \times 100\%$$

$$= \frac{43,000}{340,000} \times 100\%$$

$$= 12.6\%$$

This should be compared with the net profit margin the previous year, the net profit margin being earned by other businesses or the budgeted net profit margin.

The net profit percentage might change over a period due to either a change in the gross profit percentage or an increase or decrease in expenses.

ACTIVITY 12

Given below is a profit and loss account for Monty & Co for the year ended 31 March 20X9.

	£000	£000
Sales		2,000
Cost of sales		1,575
		425
Less: Expenses		
Selling and distribution expenses	110	
Administrative	126	
Finance	14	
		250
Net profit		175

Task

Calculate, as a percentage, the gross profit margin and the net profit margin.

This activity covers performance criterion E in element 7.1.

For a suggested answer, see the 'Answers' section at the end of the book.

9 COSTS AS A PERCENTAGE OF SALES REVENUE

Gross profit margin and net profit margin ratios measure profits in relation to sales turnover, as a means of providing information for monitoring performance through comparison.

In the same way, we can measure the various items of cost incurred by a business in relation to its sales revenue. This will give an indication of the relative importance of each expense category to the organisation.

For example, it might be useful to know that in Business A, salary costs are 45% of sales revenue, whereas n a rival Business B, salary costs are only 30% of sales. This would suggest that Business A might be spending too much on its salary costs for the volume of business it enjoys.

Example

The profit and loss account of Wert Limited is shown below, for the current year just ended and the previous year.

	Current year £	Previous year £
Sales	130,500	110,000
Cost of sales	63,300	55,500
Gross profit	67,200	54,500
Salaries	43,000	30,700
Rental costs	12,800	10,100
Other expenses	8,700	7,400
Net profit	2,700	6,300

Task

Calculate for each year the gross profit margin percentage, the net profit margin percentage and the cost to sales ratios.

Comment on what these ratios tell you.

Solution

	Current year £	%	Previous year £	%
Sales	130,500	100.0	110,000	100.0
Cost of sales	63,300	48.5	55,500	50.5
Gross profit	67,200	51.5	54,500	49.5
Salaries	43,100	33.0	30,700	27.9
Rental costs	12,800	9.8	10,100	9.2
Other expenses	8,700	6.7	7,400	6.7
Net profit	2,600	2.0	6,300	5.7

- There has been a decline in profit, in spite of an increase in sales by £20,500 or 18.6%.

- Gross profit margin improved from 49.5% to 51.5%.

- The problem appears to be that in spite of the increase in gross profit margin, net profit fell because of higher costs. In particular, salary costs rose from 27.9% of sales revenue to 33% of sales revenue, and there was also some increase in rental costs as a percentage of sales.

ACTIVITY 13

The profit and loss account for Monty & Co for the year ended 31 March 20X9 is again given below.

	£000	£000
Sales		2,000
Cost of sales		1,575
		———
		425
Less: Expenses		
Selling and distribution expenses	110	
Administrative	126	
Finance	14	
	——	
		250
		———
Net profit		175
		———

Task

Calculate the percentage of sales for each of the expense categories, including cost of sales, and show each item in the profit and loss account in terms of percentages of sales.

This activity covers performance criterion E in element 7.1.

For a suggested answer, see the 'Answers' section at the end of the book.

10   RETURN ON CAPITAL EMPLOYED (ROCE)

So far when considering profitability indicators, the profit of the business has been compared to the total sales or turnover in order to give a profitability percentage. The return on capital employed compares the profit to the capital that has been used ('employed') to earn that profit. In other words, it is a measure of profitability that relates the amount of profit earned to the amount of capital that has been invested to earn it.

There are several ways of calculating return on capital employed.

You are strongly advised, before you calculate a ROCE ratio, to check what definition of ROCE should be used.

The return on capital employed (ROCE) is commonly measured as the net profit as a percentage of the capital of the business. ROCE is therefore calculated as:

$$\frac{\text{Net profit}}{\text{Capital employed}} \times 100$$

Capital employed can be measured in different ways, but it is often assumed to be the net assets of the business.

Example

The net profit of a business for a year is £10,000 and the total capital, or net assets, of the business are £80,000 at the end of the year. What is the return on capital employed?

Solution

$$\text{ROCE} = \frac{\text{Profit}}{\text{Capital employed}} \times 100\%$$

$$= \frac{£10,000}{£80,000} \times 100\%$$

$$= 12.5\%$$

10.1 COMPLICATIONS

As stated earlier, ROCE can be calculated in different ways. These include:

(a)   Return on shareholders' capital

This is measured as the net profit (after tax), measured as a percentage of shareholders' capital, which is the share capital plus balance sheet reserves.

(b)   Return on total long term capital

This will be the profit before interest and tax (PBIT), measured as a percentage of both shareholders' capital and also long-term debt capital.

Tutorial note: You will usually be told which measure to use in a devolved assessment. If there is no indication in any task as to which way to calculate return on capital employed then you should simply use whichever method you prefer or seems appropriate. However, make sure to show in words as well as in numbers which figures are being used. So give your definition of ROCE in words before you show the calculation.

10.2 INTERPRETATION OF ROCE

On its own, the ROCE achieved in a given year doesn't tell us much about performance. To get meaning from the figure, we need to compare it with the ROCE in previous years or the ROCE that is being achieved by rival businesses.

11   BALANCE SHEET RATIOS FOR MEASURING PERFORMANCE

A number of ratios for measuring performance are calculated from figures reported in the balance sheet of a business. These are described briefly here. The reasons they are relevant to performance reporting are that:

*   they might be presented to management in regular performance reports

*   they might be used for interfirm comparisons.

11.1 CURRENT RATIO

If an organisation is to succeed in the medium to long term then it must be not only profitable but also liquid. This means that it has enough cash at any point in time to pay off its creditors as they fall due. Without liquidity an organisation cannot survive. Therefore indicators of the liquidity of a business are important: they can also provide useful comparisons between different firms.

The current ratio looks at whether a business has enough current assets to cover its current liabilities.

The current ratio is calculated as:

$$\frac{\text{Current assets}}{\text{Current liabilities}}$$

The current ratio is therefore determining how many times larger the current assets are than the current liabilities.

Example

An organisation has current assets and current liabilities made up as follows at the end of June and July 20X8.

	June £000	July £000
Current assets:		
Stock	230	260
Debtors	338	252
Cash	6	12
	574	524
Current liabilities:		
Bank overdraft	12	16
Trade creditors	200	210
	212	226

Calculate the current ratio at the end of each of these months.

Solution

		June	July
$\dfrac{\text{Current assets}}{\text{Current liabilities}}$	=	$\dfrac{574}{212}$	$\dfrac{524}{226}$
	=	2.7	2.3

Tutorial note: an overdraft is technically a liability that is due on demand.

Interpretation of current ratio

The current ratio measures in general terms how safe an organisation is in terms of liquidity. If it were able to turn all of its current assets into cash would it be able to pay off all of its current liabilities?

A generally quoted figure for a 'safe' current ratio is 2 but this is a guide only and will differ markedly from one type of business to another.

If asked to comment on the current ratios calculated in the example above it would be possible only to say that the current ratio had decreased over the month but still appeared to be fairly safe.

11.2 ACID TEST RATIO (OR QUICK RATIO)

An indication of the liquidity of an organisation can be obtained by calculating the current ratio. This shows the ratio of the total value of current assets to the value of current liabilities. However whereas most of the current liabilities are likely to be trade creditors to whom payment will be due reasonably soon, one of items of current asset is stock. In some businesses, it could take a long time to turn stock into cash, and stock might not be very 'liquid' at all.

If the stock of a business is to be turned into cash then firstly a buyer has to be found and the stock sold and then the money has to be collected from the buyer. All of this may take a considerable amount of time.

If stock is not a particularly liquid asset, an alternative measure of liquidity for a business is the acid test ratio, or quick ratio. This is similar to the current ratio, except that it excludes stocks.

The acid test ratio is calculated as:

$$\frac{\text{Current assets - stock}}{\text{Current liabilities}}$$

Example

An organisation has current assets and current liabilities made up as follows at the end of June and July 20X8.

	June	July
	£000	£000
Current assets:		
Stock	230	260
Debtors	338	252
Cash	6	12
	574	524
Current liabilities:		
Bank overdraft	12	16
Trade creditors	200	210
	212	226

Task

Calculate the acid test ratio at the end of each of these months.

Solution

	£000
June 20X8	
Current assets	574
Less: Stock	230
	344
Current liabilities	212
Acid test ratio	$\dfrac{344}{212}$
=	1.6
July 20X8	
Current assets	524
Less: Stock	260
	264
Current liabilities	226
Acid test ratio	$\dfrac{264}{226}$
=	1.2

Interpretation of the acid test ratio

The acid test ratio is perhaps a better measure than the current ratio of how liquid a business is. In the example above, if the bank were to call in the overdraft and the trade creditors required immediate payment, the acid test ratio provides a guide as to whether the business has enough cash and debtors (who should soon pay what they owe) to satisfy these demands.

It is generally thought that an acid test ratio of 1 is reasonably 'safe' but again this should be treated with caution.

11.3 STOCK TURNOVER

Stock is necessary for most organisations in order to be in a position to satisfy customer demand. However a balance has to be found between holding enough stock to satisfy demand and the cost of having too much capital tied up in stock. The stock turnover ratio can help management in its control of stock levels.

The stock turnover ratio can be calculated in one of two ways:

(1) $$\frac{\text{Cost of sales}}{\text{Average stock level during the period}}$$

This gives a measure of the number of times that stock turns over during the period.

(2) $$\frac{\text{Average stock level during the period}}{\text{Cost of sales}} \times 365 \text{ days}$$

This gives the number of days that stock is on average held in the organisation.

Example

The stock level of an organisation on 1 January 20X5 was £10,200 and on 31 December 20X5 had risen to £11,200. The cost of sales figure for the period was £107,000.

Calculate stock turnover using both methods shown above.

Solution

The average stock level for the period is determined by adding together the opening and closing stock and dividing by two.

Average stock $\quad = \quad \dfrac{10,200 + 11,200}{2}$

$\qquad\qquad\quad = \quad$ £10,700

Stock turnover:

(1) $$\frac{\text{Cost of sales}}{\text{Average stock level during the period}}$$

$$\frac{\text{£107,000}}{\text{£10,700}} = 10 \text{ times}$$

This indicates that stock turns over on average 10 times during the year.

(2) $$\frac{\text{Average stock level during the period}}{\text{Cost of sales}} \times 365$$

$$\frac{\text{£10,700}}{\text{£107,000}} \times 365 = 36.5 \text{ days}$$

This indicates that stock turns over every 36.5 days.

Interpretation of stock turnover

The stock turnover measure gives an indication of the speed at which an organisation uses up and replaces its stock. Different types of business will have different stock turnover periods. For example, a jeweller is likely to have a low stock turnover whereas a seller of fresh fish would hopefully have a very high stock turnover. Management should monitor stock turnover, to make sure that it remains at an acceptable and efficient level.

ACTIVITY 14

Below is an extract from the profit and loss account for an organisation for 20X1.

	£	£
Sales		64,000
Opening stock	3,600	
Purchases	44,000	
	———	
	47,600	

Closing stock	4,100	
Cost of sales		43,500
Gross profit		20,500

Task

Calculate the stock turnover for this period.

This activity covers performance criterion E in element 7.1.

For a suggested answer, see the 'Answers' section at the end of the book.

11.4 DEBTORS TURNOVER (DEBTOR DAYS)

If a business makes sales on credit then it will specify its credit terms on the invoice. However not all debtors will pay up within the specified time scale.

The debtors turnover ratio is also known as the average debt collection period or 'debtor days'. It measures the average collection period for the organisation's debts.

Debtors turnover (debtor days) is calculated as:

$$\frac{\text{Average trade debtors}}{\text{Credit sales for the year}} \times 365 \text{ days}$$

Alternatively closing debtors can be used rather than average debtors giving the calculation as:

$$\frac{\text{Closing trade debtors}}{\text{Credit sales for the year}} \times 365 \text{ days}$$

Example

The debtors at 1 January 20X5 for an organisation were £12,000 and at 31 December 20X5 were £10,000. Credit sales for the year totalled £80,000.

Task

Calculate the debtors turnover figure.

Solution

As both the opening and closing debtors figure is given, the average trade debtors can be calculated:

$$\text{Average trade debtors} = \frac{£12,000 + £10,000}{2}$$

$$= £11,000$$

$$\text{Debtors turnover} = \frac{£11,000}{£80,000} \times 365$$

$$= 50 \text{ days}$$

ACTIVITY 15

Closing debtors at the end of an organisation's accounting year were £460,000. Credit sales for the year were £3 million.

What is the average debt collection period?

This activity covers performance criterion E in element 7.1.

For a suggested answer, see the 'Answers' section at the end of the book.

 **FOULKS LYNCH**
PUBLICATIONS

Interpretation of debtor days

The average debt collection period can be compared with the credit terms of the organisation, in order to assess the effectiveness of its credit control procedures. Any material changes in debtor days should probably be investigated. For example, if a business normally allows 30 days credit but its average debtor days are 50 days, something must be wrong with its debt collection procedures. Similarly, if the average debt collection period slips from 20 days in one month to 35 days the next month, the cause should be investigated.

11.5 NET ASSET TURNOVER

Asset turnover ratios are a measure of the efficiency with which a business has used all its resources. Quite simply, it is a ratio of total sales revenue to the quantity of assets that have been employed to generate the sales.

Net asset turnover is calculated as:

$$\frac{\text{Turnover or sales}}{\text{Net assets}}$$

The resultant figure shows the amount of turnover or sales revenue for every pound of net assets.

Example

The summarised balance sheet of an organisation at 31 December 20X4 is given below. If the turnover for 20X4 is £250,000 then what is the net asset turnover?

Balance sheet summary extract as at 31 December 20X4

	£	£
Fixed assets		340,000
Current assets	58,000	
Current liabilities	38,000	
	——————	20,000
		360,000
Long term liabilities		120,000
		240,000

Solution

$$\text{Net asset turnover} = \frac{\text{Turnover or sales}}{\text{Net assets}}$$

$$= \frac{£250,000}{£240,000}$$

$$= 1.04 \text{ times}$$

Tutorial note: Remember that net assets are fixed assets plus net current assets and less long term liabilities.

Interpretation

The net asset turnover indicator shows how well or effectively the net assets of the organisation have been used. It shows how much revenue has been earned for each £1 of net assets.

In the example above this means therefore that for every £1 of net assets £1.04 of turnover has been earned. If management were able to increase the turnover using the same net assets then the profit of the organisation would be likely to increase.

ACTIVITY 16

A summarised balance sheet and profit and loss account for an organisation is given below:

Balance sheet as at 31 May 20X9

	£	£
Fixed assets		142,000
Current assets	16,000	
Current liabilities	14,500	
	———	1,500
		143,500
Long term liabilities		57,500
		———
		86,000
		———

Profit and loss account for the year ended 31 May 20X9

	£
Sales	206,000
Cost of sales	145,000
	———
Gross profit	61,000
Expenses	33,000
	———
Net profit	28,000
	———

Task

What is the net asset turnover for the organisation for this year?

This activity covers performance criterion E in element 7.1.

For a suggested answer, see the 'Answers' section at the end of the book.

11.6 FIXED ASSET TURNOVER

Net asset turnover measures the utilisation of the total net assets employed by a business, by giving a figure for the amount of revenue earned for each £1 of net assets.

The fixed asset turnover similarly measures the amount of revenue earned for every £1 of fixed assets. It is therefore a measure of the efficient utilisation of the fixed assets of the business.

Calculation

Fixed asset turnover is calculated as:

$$\frac{\text{Turnover or sales}}{\text{Fixed assets}}$$

Example

The summarised balance sheet from the previous example is given below. The turnover for the year was £250,000.

Balance sheet as at 31 December 20X4

	£	£
Fixed assets		340,000
Current assets	58,000	
Current liabilities	38,000	
	———	20,000
		———
		360,000
Long term liabilities		120,000
		———
		240,000
		———

Task

What is the fixed asset turnover and what does this figure mean?

Solution

$$\text{Fixed asset turnover} = \frac{\text{Turnover or sales}}{\text{Fixed assets}}$$

$$= \frac{£250,000}{£340,000}$$

$$= 0.74$$

This indicates that for every £1 of fixed assets that the organisation has £0.74 is earned in revenue.

Interpretation of fixed asset turnover

Different types of organisation will tend to have different levels of fixed asset turnover.

Some organisations such as computer software businesses might have high fixed asset turnover figures as they will tend to have fairly low fixed assets as most of their assets are the people that work for them. In contrast a manufacturing organisation that owns its factory and a great deal of plant and machinery is likely to have a much lower fixed asset turnover figure.

CONCLUSION

In this chapter you have learnt how to:

- calculate and interpret the main measures of productivity

- calculate and interpret the main measures of resource utilisation

- calculate and interpret measures of cost per unit

- calculate and interpret measures of profitability, including gross margin, net margin and ROCE

- calculate and interpret a number of balance sheet ratios, which might be used for either internal reporting or in schemes of interfirm comparison.

SELF TEST QUESTIONS

KEY TERMS

Performance reports – are produced by businesses to give the managers information about how well or badly the business, or a part of it, is performing.

Aspects of performance measured – the following aspects of performance are measured: efficiency (productivity measures), capacity utilisation measures, cost measures and return on capital.

Productivity measure – a measure of the efficiency of an operation or the efficiency with which a resource has been used. They relate outputs obtained to input resources consumed.

Production – a quantity of goods or services that are produced in a period.

Productivity – a measure of how efficiently those goods or services have been produced.

Direct costs – costs that can be directly attributed to units of production or sale.

Indirect costs – costs that cannot be directly attributed to units of production or sale.

Fixed cost – cost that should remain the same no matter what the level of production and sales volume.

Variable costs – vary directly with the level of production and sales.

Standard costs – the expected or anticipated costs.

Actual costs – the costs actually incurred in producing the product.

Gross profit – sales revenue minus the cost of goods sold.

Net profit – gross profit minus all other costs.

Gross profit margin (gross profit percentage) – the gross profit figure expressed as a percentage of the sales for the period.

Net profit margin (net profit percentage) – the net profit figure expressed as a percentage of sales.

Return on capital employed (ROCE) – commonly measured as the net profit as a percentage of the capital of the business.

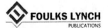

Chapter 8

WRITING REPORTS

This chapter considers the factors that need to be borne in mind when preparing the written elements of a report, and sets out guidelines for good report writing.

CONTENTS

1   Characteristics of good information

2   Types of report: reporting structures

3   Planning a report

4   Key features of a formal report

5   Writing a report - example

KNOWLEDGE AND UNDERSTANDING

		Reference
1	Methods of presenting information: written reports	Item 14
2	The purpose and structure of reporting systems within the organisation	Item 16

PERFORMANCE CRITERIA

		Reference
1	Prepare reports in the appropriate form and present them to management within the required timescales	Item F, element 7.1

LEARNING OUTCOMES

At the end of this chapter, you should be able to:

- Describe reporting structures within an organisation

- Describe the key features of a report

- Understand the rules or guidelines for preparing a report

1   CHARACTERISTICS OF GOOD INFORMATION

A report is intended to provide information to its recipient. No matter what type of report you prepare, the information you give must be:

- **Relevant**. The report should have a purpose. If it doesn't have a purpose, there is no reason for having it at all. You need to be aware what the report is for, and

the information put into it should then be relevant to this purpose. Anything irrelevant should be kept out.

- **Understandable**. The person who reads the report must be able to understand what you have written. This might seem obvious, but in practice, very many reports are difficult to follow, often because they are badly written and often because the information is not presented clearly enough – for example without the use of tables, diagrams or graphs.

- **Reliable**. The reader of the report needs to be able to rely on the accuracy of the information it contains. If there are doubts about the accuracy of any of the information, this should be made clear in the report.

- **In time**. If a report has a purpose, it must be available in time to be put to its intended use. If a report is provided too late for its intended use, it has no value.

The above characteristics of good information should apply to all the reports that you write.

2 TYPES OF REPORT: REPORTING STRUCTURES

Within any organisation, there are reporting structures. Information and reports are generally needed by management, and a system needs to exist whereby managers get all the reports they need.

Within a typical large organisation:

- Many reports are prepared by junior staff for their superiors.

- In addition, some departments or functions are often responsible for providing information to other departments. In particular, accountants are generally expected to provide accounting and financial information to managers throughout the business.

Most reporting is internal, to management or supervisors. However, businesses are also required on occasion to provide reports to external organisations, such as government departments. When reports are produced for an external organisation, they should be:

- written by a person who has been given the responsibility for its preparation

- approved and authorised by an appropriate manager before submission to the outside organisation.

2.1 FORMAL AND INFORMAL REPORTS

Some reports are written as large formal documents. Formal reports are often submitted to a committee or senior manager and used as a basis for discussions and decision-making. However a report could be informal, and written simply as a one-sheet memorandum.

For example a report to the board of directors of a company analysing the potential profitability for a new product might well be in the form of a large formal document, incorporating large amounts of detail such as marketing information and competitor product details. However a report to a manager explaining how a problem customer's complaint was dealt with might simply be in the form of a one- or two-paragraph memo.

2.2 ROUTINE REPORTS AND SPECIAL REPORTS

Some reports will be produced on a regular basis at similar time intervals. These are known as routine reports. As a rule, such reports are required at say monthly, quarterly or yearly intervals. They might be required by management from such units as agencies, units, decentralised areas of the organisation or departments. They are often statistical in nature providing details of trading activities, stocks, profits or losses etc. Regular performance reports are commonly prepared on costs and profitability, and perhaps also

on productivity and resource utilisation. For example, a board of directors might expect to see a monthly or quarterly financial performance report at every regular board meeting.

Other examples of routine reports include weekly sales reports, monthly stock reports or an annual labour turnover report. Due to the statistical nature of many routine reports, they may well include some tables, diagrams or graphs.

In addition to routine reports, one-off or special reports are also produced. For example, reports on possible new products or the effect of computerisation or the level of employee wage rates could be commissioned on an ad hoc basis.

2.3 CONFIDENTIAL REPORTS

Some reports might be confidential and these are usually of a more formal nature and follow a more formal layout than most. Any confidential report must be clearly labelled as such.

Examples of reports

Given below are examples of some of the types of reports that might be produced.

(a) **Production reports**

- idle time reports
- machine downtime reports
- shift reports (e.g. units produced, materials used, hours worked)
- material usage reports
- maintenance reports
- rejection/scrap reports.

These reports would be addressed to the manager of the production function responsible.

(b) **Marketing/sales reports**

- advertising reports (e.g. costs, effectiveness)
- sales orders reports
- customer complaints reports.

These types of reports would be addressed to the marketing and sales managers.

(c) **Accounting reports**

- financial reports (e.g. balance sheets and profit and loss accounts, routine reports on product costs and profits)
- cash reports (ranging from daily to monthly).

3 PLANNING A REPORT

Like any piece of written work, a report should be properly planned. When planning a report there are a number of factors to consider.

3.1 AIM OF THE REPORT

In order to make a report effective, it is obviously important that the purpose of the report is clearly understood by the report writer. One way of ensuring that the aim is clear is to set out the following statement and then complete it:

'As the result of reading this report, the reader will...'

There are a number of possible aims that could be established such as:

- '... agree to authorise the project.'
- '... take the necessary action.'
- '... make a decision.'

3.2 CHECKLIST FOR PLANNING

The following additional points are the sort that should be considered when planning a report:

- Who commissioned the report and who is to use the report? It may be that there are a number of different users of the report with different needs, levels of knowledge and levels of understanding.

- What information does the user of the report require?

- What background information does the user of the report already have?

- What type of report would best suit the subject matter and the user?

- What is required in the report: information only or judgement, opinions and recommendations?

- What is the time scale of the report?

- What format should be used, for example should there be appendices, graphs, diagrams etc?

- What detailed points will need to be made in the body of the report?

- Is the report confidential?

3.3 PRINCIPLES OF REPORT WRITING

Once the bare bones of a report have been sketched in the planning stage, the report will need to be written in detail. When writing any type of report it is worth bearing in mind a few basic stylistic points.

The main purpose of any report is to convey information and this purpose can be advanced by taking care to follow the points considered below.

3.4 LAYOUT OF THE REPORT

Information is not only conveyed by the contents of a report but also by its design and presentation. The layout of the report and the overall impression that is made are therefore important.

Care should be taken to make the report easier to understand by the use of appropriate headings and to make the report pleasing to the eye by the sensible use of spacing and paragraphs. This can all help with the overall impression that the report gives.

More detailed guidance on layout and headings will be given in later paragraphs of this chapter.

3.5 SIZE OF THE REPORT

An early decision in planning a report should be regarding the size of the report. Any diagrammatic, tabulated or graphical illustrations might make the data seem clearer and will emphasise key facts and figures.

However the inclusion of such illustrations will often increase the size of the report. Care should be taken not to waste managers' time by making a report too long.

3.6 LOGIC OF ARGUMENT

In planning the report, the key issues to be covered should be listed. These should form the basic structure of the report. Once the key issues have been identified then they should be arranged into a logical order and appropriate sequence.

It is important to ensure that the points that are to be made in the report are given in a logical order and that they lead to a logical conclusion. The writer of a report should be quite clear whether the purpose of the report is simply to inform or whether a conclusion or recommendations are required.

3.7 LANGUAGE

The language that is used in a formal report should be fairly formal. Abbreviations and colloquialisms should be avoided.

In most reports other than the most informal the first person should be avoided and the third person used. So for example 'you will be able to see that...' would become 'it should now be clear that ...' etc.

If the report is being produced for the layman or non-technical user then jargon or technical language should be avoided.

Informal reports should also use fairly formal language, because it could be shown to someone who does not know you, and who might not be impressed by informal language.

3.8 OBJECTIVITY

Even if the purpose of a report is simply to inform rather than reach any conclusion it is important that the report appears to be written from an objective viewpoint. Therefore any emotive or loaded wording should be avoided at all costs. The report must appear to be unbiased and impartial.

Any bias that exists in the report writer should not be allowed to surface in the report as this could have an adverse effect on the person using the report and his view of any conclusions or recommendations that might have been reached.

4 KEY FEATURES OF A FORMAL REPORT

4.1 USER OF THE REPORT

Before thinking about the actual content of a report, you should first think about who the reader will be. You need to think about the user in order to decide on the amount of detail the report should contain:

- Who is the user?

- How much background information does the user have?

- How much technical or business knowledge does the user have?

- Why does the user want the report?

- What does the user want to get out of the report?

Once these questions have been satisfactorily answered then it is possible to consider the more detailed points of the report.

4.2 ADDRESSEE, AUTHOR AND DATE

A report should state clearly who it is being sent to. It should also state who it is from and be dated.

Addressee, author and date should be the first three items on a report, even an informal memo.

4.3   SUBJECT

The report should be given a title or subject heading that is concise and also gives a clear indication of the subject matter of the report.

So as a matter of routine, always start your reports with:

To:

From:

Date:

Subject

4.4   CONTENTS LIST

Many reports will be quite extensive and will include not only the main report but also appendices (see later in this paragraph). Therefore at the start of such a report there will usually be a summary of contents showing what elements of the report are to be found on what pages or in which paragraph numbers.

4.5   SUMMARY OF THE REPORT

If a report is long and complex, then it is common practice to include a summary of the findings, arguments etc, in the report, as the first element of the report. This ensures that busy executives can find the relevant details easily without having to work through the entire report itself.

4.6   CONCLUSIONS AND RECOMMENDATIONS

It is also common practice in a longer or more formal report to include as the next element of the report the following items:

- any conclusions reached in the report

- any recommendations made in the report regarding further actions.

4.7   MAIN BODY OF THE REPORT

The precise contents and length of the main body of the report will depend upon the type and detailed content of the report. However the following points should be borne in mind when writing this area.

- There will often be an introductory paragraph explaining the **terms of reference** of the report. This might include details of who commissioned the report, why it has been written, its scope and any limitations on the report such as confidentiality limitations or time limitations.

- Many reports involve some sort of investigation or research. There will usually be a paragraph that explains or identifies the **methods of investigation or research used**. If other sources of information have been used in the writing of the report then these will usually also be acknowledged here.

- The results or findings that have come from the commissioning of the report would then be shown.

- These results would then be analysed, discussed and interpreted. This might involve a number of paragraphs in a complex report and these paragraphs should have a logical sequence to them.

Each of the paragraphs of a report may benefit from a heading or perhaps some sort of paragraph numbering. Always remember that it is not only what is written but also how it is produced and structured that is important.

4.8 REPORT CONCLUSION

The main body of the report is then completed with a conclusion of the arguments, findings, recommendations and conclusions of the report.

4.9 APPENDICES

In many reports there are large amounts of information. Some could be very detailed, in particular graphs and tables of figures supporting the arguments, findings or conclusions of the report. However if all this detail were to be included in the main body of the report, the report might become too long and time-consuming for many readers.

Therefore detailed supporting information is usually included in appendices at the end of the report. Readers can look at it if and when they want to. This ensures that the main body of the report is concise, and deals with only the most important areas. The information contained in the appendices of the report should be referred to at appropriate places in the main body of the report.

Conclusion   The possible elements of a report can therefore be listed as follows:

- addressee
- author
- date
- title
- contents
- summary
- main body of the report
- conclusion
- appendices.

Not all reports include all these elements. Most formal, lengthy and complex reports do but other shorter or informal reports may not need all of these elements. Routine reports, such as management accounting reports, might simply be presented as tables of figures with a few introductory words of comment.

5   WRITING A REPORT - EXAMPLE

The process of writing a report will now be considered in detail and step by step, using an illustrative example. The information required for the report will be given and then each of the main elements of the report will be produced.

5.1 EXAMPLE INFORMATION

Given below is a five-year summary of the financial results of a division of your organisation. You are required to write a report explaining, analysing and highlighting these results. The report is to the Employee Representatives Committee of that division and should make particular reference to the part played by wages costs over the period.

Information is also supplied showing the organisation's overall summarised profit and loss account for 20X4.

Five year summary - Division

	20X4 £000	20X3 £000	20X2 £000	20X1 £000	20X0 £000
Turnover	1,000	1,200	900	750	700
Production materials	440	500	400	350	300
Wages	310	300	220	170	150
Selling costs	100	100	80	70	60
Administrative costs	40	50	46	44	20
Profit	110	250	154	116	170

20X4 Summarised profit and loss account - organisation

	£000
Turnover	9,400
Production materials	4,500
Wages	2,000
Selling costs	700
Administration costs	600
Profit	1,600

Step 1   Headings

The first step is to show the addressee of the report, its date, who it is from and its title.

REPORT

To: Employee Representatives Committee

From: Accounts Clerk

Date: 12 March 20X5

Subject: Divisional financial performance 20X0 to 20X4

Step 2   Main body of the report

It is now necessary to write the main body of the report, although this will appear after any summary and conclusion. However the summary and conclusion cannot be written until after the main body of the report.

In order to write the report it will often be necessary to further analyse the data given and prepare tabulations of data. Such analysis and tabulations will eventually appear in an appendix to the report.

(1) **Purpose of report**

This report has been commissioned to provide analysis and explanation of the division's profits from 20X0 to 20X4 for the division's Employee Representatives Committee.

(2) **Information**

The explanation and analysis provided in the report is based upon summarised profit and loss information for the five years from 20X0 to 20X4 together with the overall organisation's results for the year 20X4. This information has been summarised and tabulated in Appendix 1 to this report.

(3) **Annual turnover**

Over the last five years annual turnover has increased from £700,000 to £1,000,000, an increase of 43% over the period. There was however a peak of £1,200,000 in 20X3 but this fell to £1,000,000 in 20X4.

(4) **Annual profit**

The annual profit has decreased over the period both in absolute terms and as a percentage of annual turnover. The 20X4 profit of £110,000 is only 11% as a percentage of turnover. This compares particularly unfavourably to a 21% profit in 20X3 and 24% in 20X0.

(5) **Annual costs**

The percentage of turnover represented by each of the major cost classifications is given in Appendix 1. This illustrates the areas of cost that have altered significantly during the five year period. Most of the costs have remained reasonably constant as a percentage of turnover over the period with the exception of the wages cost that has risen significantly.

(6) **Wages costs**

The wages costs, as a percentage of turnover, have increased from 21% in 20X0 to 31% in 20X4. The increase was fairly steady from 20X0 to 20X3 but then jumped from 25% in 20X3 to 31% in 20X4. This increase seems to have played a major part in the reduced profit percentage over the period discussed above.

(7) **Divisional and organisation wage costs**

The final table in Appendix 1 compares the costs classifications for the division and the organisation as a whole for 20X4 in terms of their percentage of turnover. This shows that all of the cost categories for the division, with the exception of wages, have been reasonably in line with the overall organisational cost. However whereas wages for the organisation as a whole totalled 21% of turnover in 20X4, for the division the relevant percentage was 31%.

APPENDIX 1

Five year summary - division - costs as a percentage of turnover

	20X4 %	20X3 %	20X2 %	20X1 %	20X0 %
Turnover	100	100	100	100	100
Production materials	44	42	44	47	43
Wages	31	25	24	23	21
Selling costs	10	8	9	9	9
Administration costs	4	4	5	6	3

Five year summary - division - profit as a percentage of turnover

	20X4	20X3	20X2	20X1	20X0
Profit £'000	110	250	154	116	170
Profit	11%	21%	17%	15%	24%

20X4 - division and organisation - costs and profits as a percentage of turnover

	Division £'000	Division %	Organisation £'000	Organisation %
Turnover	1,000	100	9,400	100
Production materials	440	44	4,500	48
Wages	310	31	2,000	21
Selling costs	100	10	700	8
Administration costs	40	4	600	6
Profit	110	11	1,600	17

Step 3   **Write the report conclusion**

Conclusion   The conclusion of this explanatory report is that the divisional profits have significantly decreased over the last five years and that this is largely due to a disproportionate increase in wages costs.

Step 4   **Write a report summary**

Summary

This report has summarised, in Appendix 1, the profit and loss account information for the division for the years 20X0 to 20X4. This has shown a significant decrease in divisional profit over the period and the figures indicate that a major cause of this loss of profitability is a disproportionate rise in the level of wage costs. The wage costs for the division, as a percentage of turnover, were also compared to those of the organisation as a whole and again the wage costs for the division seem to be disproportionately high.

Step 5   Prepare any suitable graphs or diagrams

At this stage it is necessary to consider whether there are any alternative ways in which the information in the report might be usefully presented, for example by using graphs or other types of diagrams.

In this instance it might be interesting to plot a graph, for example, showing total turnover, wage costs and profit for each of the five years for the division. Another useful diagram might be pie charts illustrating the differing proportions of cost classifications in the division and organisation as a whole.

This information is shown in Appendix 2.

Step 6   Produce the full report

The final step is to put all of the elements of the report together as one package. This might also include an index to indicate the contents of the report.

REPORT

To: Employee Representatives Committee

From: Accounts Clerk

Date: 12 March 20X5

Subject: Divisional financial performance 20X0 to 20X4

Index

Summary

Conclusion

Report

Appendix 1

Appendix 2

Summary

This report has summarised, in Appendix 1, the profit and loss account information for the division for the years 20X0 to 20X4. This has shown a significant decrease in divisional profit over the period and the figures indicate that a major cause of this loss of profitability is a disproportionate rise in the level of wage costs. The wage costs for the division, as a percentage of turnover, were also compared to those of the organisation as a whole and again the wage costs for the division seem to be disproportionately high.

Conclusion   The conclusion of this explanatory report is that the divisional profits have significantly decreased over the last five years and that this is largely due to a disproportionate increase in wages costs.

REPORT

(1)   **Purpose of report**

      This report has been commissioned to provide analysis and explanation of the division's profits from 20X0 to 20X4 for the division's Employee Representatives Committee.

(2)   **Information**

      The explanation and analysis provided in the report is based upon summarised profit and loss information for the five years from 20X0 to 20X4 together with the overall organisation's results for the year 20X4. This information has been summarised and tabulated in Appendix 1 to this report.

(3)   **Annual turnover**

      Over the last five years annual turnover has increased from £700,000 to £1,000,000, an increase of 43% over the period. There was however a peak of £1,200,000 in 20X3 but this fell to £1,000,000 in 20X4.

(4)   **Annual profit**

The annual profit has however decreased over the period both in absolute terms and as a percentage of annual turnover. The 20X4 profit of £110,000 is only 11% as a percentage of turnover. This compares particularly unfavourably to a 21% profit in 20X3 and 24% in 20X0.

(5)   **Annual costs**

The percentage of turnover represented by each of the major cost classifications is given in Appendix 1. This illustrates the areas of cost that have altered significantly during the five-year period. Most of the costs have remained reasonably constant as a percentage of turnover over the period with the exception of the wages cost that has risen significantly.

(6)   **Wages costs**

The wages costs, as a percentage of turnover, have increased from 21% in 20X0 to 31% in 20X4. The increase was fairly steady from 20X0 to 20X3 but then jumped from 25% in 20X3 to 31% in 20X4. This increase seems to have played a major part in the reduced profit percentage over the period discussed above.

(7)   **Divisional and organisation wage costs**

The final table in Appendix 1 compares the costs classifications for the division and the organisation as a whole for 20X4 in terms of their percentage of turnover. This shows that all of the cost categories for the division, with the exception of wages, have been reasonably in line with the overall organisational cost. However whereas wages for the organisation as a whole totalled 21% of turnover in 20X4, for the division the relevant percentage was 31%.

APPENDIX 1

Five year summary - division - costs as a percentage of turnover

	20X4 %	20X3 %	20X2 %	20X1 %	20X0 %
Turnover	100	100	100	100	100
Production materials	44	42	44	47	43
Wages	31	25	24	23	21
Selling costs	10	8	9	9	9
Administration costs	4	4	5	6	3

Five year summary - division - profit as a percentage of turnover

	20X4	20X3	20X2	20X1	20X0
Profit £'000	110	250	154	116	170
Profit	11%	21%	17%	15%	24%

20X4 - division and organisation - costs and profits as a percentage of turnover

	Division		Organisation	
	£'000	%	£'000	%
Turnover	1,000	100	9,400	100
Production materials	440	44	4,500	48
Wages	310	31	2,000	21
Selling costs	100	10	700	8
Administration costs	40	4	600	6
Profit	110	11	1,600	17

APPENDIX 2

Divisional turnover, wage costs and profit 20X0 to 20X4

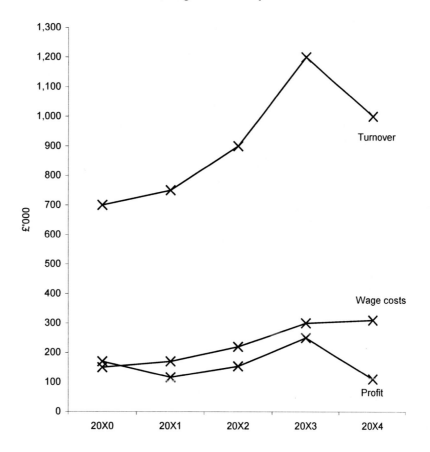

Divisional and organisational costs and profit - 20X4

Division

Organisation

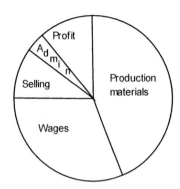

WORKING

Pie chart degrees

	Division		Organisation
Production materials			
$\frac{44}{100} \times 360$	158°	$\frac{48}{100} \times 360$	173°
Wages			
$\frac{31}{100} \times 360$	112°	$\frac{21}{100} \times 360$	75°
Selling costs			
$\frac{10}{100} \times 360$	36°	$\frac{8}{100} \times 360$	29°
Administration costs			
$\frac{4}{100} \times 360$	14°	$\frac{6}{100} \times 360$	22°
Profit			
$\frac{11}{100} \times 360$	40°	$\frac{17}{100} \times 360$	61°

FOULKS LYNCH
PUBLICATIONS

CONCLUSION

In this chapter you have learnt:

- the importance of planning a report

- the key features of a good report

- how to incorporate skills you have learned in previous chapters in your reports, for example the use of diagrams and tables.

The text has looked at a fairly detailed report, but the same guidelines can be applied to the production of shorter memos.

SELF TEST QUESTIONS

		Paragraph
1	What are the characteristics of good information?	1
2	What is the difference between the formal and informal report?	2.1
3	State some examples of routine and special reports.	2.2
4	Give examples of confidential reports.	2.3
5	What points should be borne in mind when planning a report?	3
6	What are the key features of a report?	4
7	What type of information should be included in the appendices to a report?	4.9

KEY TERMS

Good information – needs to be relevant, understandable, reliable and timely.

Formal reports – reports written as large formal documents, often submitted to a committee or senior manager and used as a basis for discussions and decision-making.

Informal report – a report could be written as an informal document, for example as a one-sheet memorandum.

Routine report – report produced on a regular basis at similar time intervals.

Special reports – one-off report, for example an report on possible new products or the effect of computerisation or the level of employee wage rates could be commissioned on an ad hoc basis.

FOULKS LYNCH
PUBLICATIONS

Chapter 9

ORGANISATIONS – STRUCTURE AND PERFORMANCE

The purpose of this chapter is to consider briefly the relevance of the organisation structure to reporting systems. The reports produced by within a business depend on its ownership, its size, its management structure and the nature of its activities.

CONTENTS

KNOWLEDGE AND UNDERSTANDING

		Reference
1	How the accounting systems of an organisation are affected by its organisational structure, its administrative systems and procedures and the nature of its business transactions	Item 15
2	The purpose and structure of reporting systems within the organisation	Item 16
3	Background understanding that recording and accounting practices may vary between organisations and different parts of organisations	Item 17

PERFORMANCE CRITERIA

		Reference
1	Account for transaction between separate units of the organisation in accordance with the organisations procedures	Item D, element 7.1

LEARNING OUTCOMES

At the end of this chapter, you should be able to:

• Discuss how the reports provided within an organisation depend on the nature of the organisation, its structure and what it does.

1 CLASSIFYING ORGANISATIONS

1.1 CLASSIFICATION BY LEGAL STRUCTURE

Some organisations are owned by a single proprietor (a 'sole trader' business). In many sole trader businesses, the owner also runs the business, and keeps an eye on day-to-day business operations. Often, the reporting structure is informal.

Partnerships are owned by a group of individuals. Although most partners also work in the business, they cannot do everything. Partners therefore often require formal reporting so that they can all be kept informed about how the business is progressing.

Companies vary in size from one-man businesses to large global enterprises. In larger companies, there are shareholders who are its owners but not involved in the day-to-day running of the business, and a management team led by the board of directors, who might not own any of the shares in the company. In these organisations, the main reporting systems are the reporting systems for management. After all, managers are responsible for running the business. However, some reports must also be prepared for the shareholders. The main reporting document for shareholders from a company is the annual report and accounts.

Finally some organisations are wholly-owned or partly-owned by government. These are known as public sector organisations. They are usually organisations holding a monopoly position or which have significant social responsibility to provide services that are not commercially profitable. Government-owned organisations are often bedevilled by heavy reporting requirements, both reports for the management and also reports for government. Reporting within the health service and the education service in the UK are two fairly notorious examples.

1.2 CLASSIFICATION BY PROFIT OBJECTIVE

Some organisations have profit as their key objective, whereas others are formed with the intention to provide facilities to their members.

Organisations with a profit motive tend to be sole traders, partnerships and limited companies. 'Not for profit' organisations are either public sector organisations or formed as registered charities.

1.3 CLASSIFICATION BY ACTIVITY

Profit-motivated organisations may be classified by their role in the economy. Typical activity groups are:

(i) manufacturers

(ii) wholesalers

(iii) retailers

(iv) service organisations.

Some larger organisations occupy more than one of these activity positions.

1.4 CLASSIFICATION BY SIZE

Organisations vary in size from those with a single sales outlet (a corner shop or a small plumbing service) to national or even multi-national organisations.

Typically sole traders and partnerships of two or three partners have just a single outlet. Larger partnerships and medium sized limited companies may have more than one outlet within the same local area and large multi-site operations are likely to be formed as limited companies.

Although there is no formal requirement for multi-site organisations to be limited companies, the need for finance for such types of organisation dictates that limited company structures will often be used.

2 THE STRUCTURE OF ORGANISATIONS

In all but the smallest organisations, responsibilities are shared between several senior people. These may be the owners of the organisation or people appointed by them as directors or managers.

2.1 FUNCTIONS IN AN ORGANISATION

Tasks and responsibilities within a business might be organised on the basis of functions. Examples of the functions of a large manufacturing organisation would include:

(i)   production

(ii)   research and development

(iii)   sales and marketing

(iv)   administration.

Each function might be sub-divided into other functions. For example, the administration function might be sub-divided into Human Resources and Finance. The sales and marketing function might be sub-divided into Sales, Marketing and Logistics.

2.2 THE BOARD OF DIRECTORS

The board of directors have the responsibility of agreeing the overall objectives of their company and communicating these throughout the organisation. Individual managers then take actions to implement plans to achieve these objectives. Managers ultimately report to the chief executive officer or managing director.

2.3 MANAGEMENT STRUCTURE

Traditionally management structures have been hierarchical with information and plans being communicated vertically within the organisation. Such structures may be dominated by a functional, product or geographical emphasis (as illustrated in the section below on organisation charts).

3 ORGANISATION CHARTS

An organisation chart is a pictorial representation of the management structure of an organisation. The use of such charts allows lines of responsibility to be clearly indicated and complex organisations to be more easily understood.

Example

BEQ Limited trades in Europe and America. It sells to both retailers and wholesalers, and its activities can be analysed as being concerned with production, selling and administration.

The organisation might be structured by function as follows:

Alternatively, responsibilities might be organised on a geographical basis.

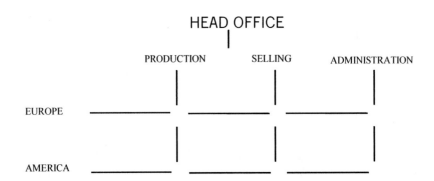

In a matrix management structure, reporting lines are more complex, and individuals might report to different senior managers for different aspects of their work.

The structure chosen will affect how information is collected, summarised and communicated in the organisation.

4 LEVELS OF MANAGEMENT AND INFORMATION NEEDS

In broad terms, within a large organisation, there are three levels of management:

- strategic
- tactical
- operational.

Strategic management is responsible for the long-term plans and objectives of the organisation. The information they need will often be long-term and forward-looking in nature, and much of the information might come from external sources outside the business.

Tactical management is responsible for short-term planning and control (often on a monthly basis). The information they require will be quite detailed and should relate specifically to the recipient's area of responsibility. Monthly management accounting reports are an example of information for management at a tactical level.

Operational managers need information to assist them with the day-to-day operations. This is usually very detailed and concentrates on providing information on specific areas of management responsibility.

5 ACCOUNTING INFORMATION SYSTEMS

An accounting information system collects data from many different parts of the organisation and classifies and summarises it. This is then converted into meaningful information that is communicated to the management of the organisation in the form of formal or informal reports.

Much internal accounting information is information about costs. Costs are collected and charged to cost centres. They are then analysed to provide reports on the costs and profitability of products and services.

- A **cost centre** is an area of the business for which costs are collected. Typically these are departments within an organisation. However, smaller units such as the individual machines or even employees (e.g. individual sales staff) might be a cost centre.

- A **cost unit** is an item of output (typically a product or service) being costed.

The nature of both cost centres and cost units differs between organisations, according to how they are structured and the type of output they produce.

5.1 ACCOUNTING SYSTEMS AND ORGANISATION STRUCTURES

The structure of the organisation affects the type of cost accounting system used. Generally larger organisations require complex accounting systems. An organisation making many products and operating throughout the world needs an accounting system capable of dealing with multi-currency transactions and able to provide detailed reports concerning profitability of individual products, functions and divisions. Legal reporting requirements in different countries must also be considered when designing such systems.

6 RECONCILING INFORMATION

The information provided to managers of an organisation must be reliable and so must be free of material error and it must not be misleading. This means that it must be checked for consistency.

When information comes from different sources within the organisation, it might have to be checked for consistency.

Example - brick manufacturer

Z plc is a manufacturer of building bricks. Many of its employees are paid a rate per unit of work achieved, for example the number of bricks produced from the clay, the number of bricks set on to standard pallets or the number of bricks loaded on to delivery vehicles. When the payroll is computed, the amounts paid to employees will be based on reported production quantities.

There is a risk, however, that the reported production quantities supplied to the accounts department for payroll purposes could be inaccurate. If possible, this should be checked for reliability.

The production figures could possibly be reconciled to other pieces of information produced by other areas of the business. For example all of the above measures of production might be checked by obtaining figures for brick sales and opening and closing stocks of bricks. Production quantities should be equal to sales quantities plus any increase in stock levels or minus any decrease in stocks. Allowing for the stock adjustment, the number of bricks loaded on to vehicles as documented by the employees for wage purposes should equal the number of bricks delivered to customers. These in turn should equal the number of bricks invoiced to customers.

Example - road haulier

The number of miles travelled should reconcile with the speedometer and tachograph readings. The number of deliveries/journeys should reconcile with the invoices raised for customers.

7 TRANSFER PRICING

Transfer pricing is a means of charging for goods and services provided by one part of a business to another part of the same business. Examples of transfer pricing have already been shown earlier in this text.

Transfer pricing is used mainly in large organisations that wish to measure the profitability of each separate area of the business. These may be branches, divisions, or even subsidiary companies within the organisation. If these 'profit centres' do work for each other, or supply goods to each other, a system has to be devised for charging for them, so that the division providing the goods or services makes a reasonable profit on them, and the divisions accepting them pay a fair price.

However, goods or services transferred internally between profit centres do not create a profit for the company as a whole. A profit is only earned for the company when goods or services are eventually sold to outside customers.

7.1 PROFIT CENTRES

A profit centre is similar to a cost centre to the extent that it is an area of the business for which a manager is given responsibility. The difference is that the manager is responsible for both costs and revenues, i.e. profits.

Because divisional performance is measured in relation to profits, inter-divisional transfers have to be charged for. This charge is the transfer price.

The risk of double counting

When producing results for the whole organisation, it is important to eliminate the revenues and costs which relate to transferred goods or services. This is because otherwise the organisation would be double counting.

Example

XYZ has two divisions. Division A produces books. Division B sells paper to Division A and to other customers.

Results for January 20X3:

	Division A	Division B
	£000	£000
Sales	30	50
Cost of sales	15	30
Gross profit	15	20

The gross profit of XYZ is £35,000 (£15,000 + £20,000). However, B sold £10,000 of paper to A at cost. The correct sales figures for Jan 20X3 for XYZ is not £80,000 but £70,000 (30 + 50 −10). This is because sales to external customers were only £70,000. Similarly the cost of sales is £35,000 (15 + 30 −10) because Division A's cost of sales includes £10,000 purchased from Division B.

Total results for XYZ for January 20X3:

	Division A	Division B	Adjustments	XYZ
	£000	£000	£000	£000
Sales	30	50	(10)	70
Cost of sales	15	30	(10)	35
Gross profit	15	20	-	35

This process may be referred to as eliminating interdivisional or inter-company transactions.

7.2 GROUPS OF COMPANIES AND CONSOLIDATION

In the example above, there were two divisions within a single company. Sometimes an organisation is structured as a group of companies, with a 'parent' company and a number of operating subsidiary companies. The subsidiaries are all separate companies, but with the same parent.

To report on the performance of the group as a whole, we need to combine the results of all the companies in the group by adding them together. When their results are added together, the combined results are known as consolidated results, or consolidated accounts.

In the same way that inter-profit centre transactions have to be eliminated from profit reporting, transactions between subsidiaries also need to be eliminated in the consolidated results.

ACTIVITY 1

AB Limited comprises two divisions, Alpha and Beta. Alpha, the sales division, sells its products to various customers in the UK and European Union. Beta is the manufacturing division. It sells most of its products to Alpha at cost. It is the only supplier to Alpha.

Divisional results for Alpha and Beta for the year ending 31 August 20X2

	Alpha £	Beta £
Sales	850,000	600,000
Opening stock	200,000	140,000
Purchases	500,000	300,000
Closing stock	220,000	150,000
Cost of sales	480,000	290,000
Gross profit	370,000	310,000
Production overheads		150,000
Distribution overheads	130,000	10,000
Administration overheads	180,000	30,000
Total overheads	310,000	190,000
Net profit	60,000	120,000

During the year Beta sold £500,000 of product at cost to Alpha.

Prepare the consolidated results for AB Limited for the year ending 31 August 20X2.

For a suggested answer, see the 'Answers' section at the end of the book.

CONCLUSION

This chapter has tried to explain that reporting systems vary according to the nature and structure of the organisation.

When information is gathered from different parts of an organisation and brought together, it is often necessary to re-state it on a common basis. In particular, with transfer pricing for

profit centres and subsidiary companies in a group, double counting should be avoided. For example, internal sales should not be included in the total revenue or total cost figures for the company or group as a whole.

SELF TEST QUESTIONS

Paragraph

1	How can an organisation be classified by legal structure?	1.1
2	Give examples of classifying organisations by profit objective, activity and size.	1
3	What is an organisation chart?	3
4	State the three levels of management that can be found in a large organisation and give examples of their information needs.	4
5	What is a cost centre?	5
6	What is transfer pricing?	7
7	What is a profit centre?	7.1

KEY TERMS

Organisation chart – a pictorial representation of the management structure of an organisation.

Strategic management – management responsible for the long-term plans and objectives of the organisation.

Tactical management – management responsible for short-term planning and control (often on a monthly basis).

Cost centre – an area of the business for which costs are collected. Typically these are departments within an organisation.

Cost unit – an item of output (typically a product or service) being costed.

Transfer pricing – a means of charging for goods and services provided by one part of a business to another part of the same business.

Profit centre – like a cost centre, an area of the business for which a manager is given responsibility. The difference is that the manager is responsible for both costs and revenues, i.e. profits.

Chapter 10

REPORTS AND RETURNS FOR OUTSIDE AGENCIES

This chapter looks at reports and returns that an organisation might prepare for outside agencies, rather than for internal management purposes. In most respects, the nature of the information provided to outside agencies is similar to internal management information, although generally in much less detail.

CONTENTS

1   External reporting

2   The information provided in reports and returns

3   Completing a return for an external agency

4   Filling in returns

KNOWLEDGE AND UNDERSTANDING

		Reference
1	Relevant performance and quality measures	Item 2
2	Main types of outside organisations requiring reports and returns: regulatory; grant awarding; information collecting; trade association	Item 3
3	Ratios: gross profit margin; net profit margin; return on capital employed	Item 12

PERFORMANCE CRITERIA

		Reference
1	Identify, collate and present relevant information in accordance with the conventions and definitions used by outside agencies	Item A, element 7.2
2	Ensure calculations of ratios and performance indicators are accurate	Item B, element 7.2
3	Obtain authorisation of the despatch of completed reports and returns from the appropriate person	Item C, element 7.2
4	Present reports and returns in accordance with outside agencies' requirements and deadlines	Item D, element 7.2

LEARNING OUTCOMES

At the end of this chapter, you should be able to:

- describe the different types of outside agency that might be supplied with reports and returns

- describe the nature of the information that might be supplied, and how it differs from information reported internally to management

- explain the procedures for collating and sending reports and returns to outside agencies

- understand the importance of deadlines for submitting reports and returns to outside agencies.

1 EXTERNAL REPORTING

Most reports and returns prepared within an organisation are for use by supervisors or management. Accounting information is particularly important for managers, because the financial position of any organisation has to be kept under control so that the organisation can survive and prosper.

Some accounting information, however, is also provided to external organisations. These organisations can be grouped into four categories, and the information supplied to each has a different purpose. The four categories are:

- regulatory and government organisations

- grant-awarding bodies

- statistics-gathering organisations

- trade associations.

1.1 REGULATORY BODIES

Regulatory bodies have the power to demand certain information from businesses. They are either government departments, or bodies set up by government. Examples of regulatory bodies and the information they can demand are:

- The Inland Revenue, which obtains information from businesses for tax purposes.

- HM Customs and Excise, which obtains information from VAT-registered businesses for the purposes of collecting value added tax. VAT and VAT returns are described in a later chapter.

- The Registrar of Companies. All UK companies are required by law to submit certain information to the Registrar of Companies. This includes a copy of their annual report and accounts, and also an annual return.

1.2 GRANT-AWARDING BODIES

Some bodies are provided with funds, by the national government or by the European Union, for awarding to businesses. The purpose of the funds is to give financial support to businesses that are planning to make certain types of investment. Often, the funds are available to businesses that invest in a poor region of the country, with a high level of unemployment. Sometimes, funds are available to businesses investing in training or re-training of employees. The purpose of the funds is to encourage the businesses to invest..

Businesses hoping for funds to help finance an investment must apply for a grant of money, and must meet the requirements for being eligible to receive funds. The grant-

awarding body studies the grant application, and decides whether or not to make a grant, and if it makes a grant, how much money should be given.

Having made a grant to a businesses, the grant-awarding body will want to check that the money is spent properly on its intended purpose, and will ask the business to supply evidence of where the money has gone.

A business might therefore submit a report and grant application to a grant-awarding body, and then submit returns with information about spending the grant.

1.3 STATISTICS-GATHERING ORGANISATIONS

Some government departments collect statistical information from businesses. The information is then collated and published as government statistics. These were described at the beginning of this text. Businesses asked to supply statistical information are under a legal obligation to do so.

1.4 TRADE ASSOCIATIONS

Many businesses belong to a trade association. A trade association is a voluntary body, whose members are businesses operating in a particular industry (or 'trade'). Although businesses in an industry compete with each other, they also have many interests in common. For example, they all have a common interest in making sure that the legislation affecting their industry is fair. They might also have a collective interest in promoting industry standards of practice, or in lobbying the government for changes to the law.

Many businesses also have an interest in measuring their own performance against the 'average' for their industry. For example, a wool trader might want to know how its profits compare with those of other wool traders. Some trade associations offer an inter-firm comparison scheme, to supply this information.

Interfirm comparison is not compulsory, and a business will only join in such a scheme if it wants to, and if it thinks it can get useful information from it.

- A business in such a scheme supplies financial information about its business to the trade association.

- This information is kept confidential, and is not disclosed to other businesses.

- The trade association collates the information from all the businesses in the scheme, and calculates average figures for the industry. Each business in the scheme is given the industry average figures, which it can then compare with its own.

Businesses must supply their financial information to the trade association at times specified by the trade association. Unless firms all supply information at the same time, the scheme will be unworkable. The information also has to be supplied according to conventions and definitions specified by the trade association. This is to make sure that all the data received from the scheme members is consistent, and can be collated to provide meaningful and accurate information about the industry averages.

2 THE INFORMATION PROVIDED IN REPORTS AND RETURNS

Information is provided to external organisations in a form that those organisations specify. Typically, the external organisation provides a form or return that the business must fill in.

Many individuals do not like filling in forms, and unless a form is well-designed, there is a high risk that it will not be filled in properly. In practice, great care usually goes into the design of forms, and there are often guidance notes on how to fill in each item on the form.

If you are asked to complete a return for an external agency, the first task is to identify exactly what information is required. A part of this task should be to read carefully any guidance notes supplied with the form, and follow what they tell you to do.

FOULKS LYNCH
PUBLICATIONS

For example, if you are required to supply a financial ratio for your business, such as the net profit ratio or the return on capital employed, look closely at the definition of these ratios, and make sure that you calculate the ratio according to the 'official definition'.

3 COMPLETING A RETURN FOR AN EXTERNAL AGENCY

The procedures for completing a return for an external agency are quite straightforward, but they must be followed properly.

- Work your way through the form, filling in the items of information that are asked for. As stated above, check the guidance notes to make sure what information you are required to supply.

- If you are required to calculate a ratio or performance indicator, make sure that you do so accurately, and in accordance with the definitions specified on the return.

- When you have filled in the return, you should obtain authorisation for sending it to the external agency, from the appropriate person. This could be your supervisor. This person should check what you have written, and be satisfied that you have filled in the return properly, before giving his or her authorisation.

- The return will probably specify a latest date by which the external organisation would like to receive your information. Make sure that you fill in the return, and get it authorised, within the time. Don't miss deadlines!

It is normally a matter of courtesy to submit a return to an external agency with a covering letter. This covering letter could be set out as follows.

Your organisation's name and address [headed notepaper]

Name and address of external body

Date

Dear Sirs

[Name of return]

I enclose a [name of return] from this organisation, which I hope is in order.

Please let me know if there is anything further I can do to assist.

Yours faithfully

[Signature]

[your name and position]

FOULKS LYNCH
PUBLICATIONS

4 FILLING IN RETURNS

A VAT return is described in a later chapter. This is in a set format and there are rules for filling it in.

Returns to trade associations are more variable, and differ from one trade association to another. Here are one or two examples of what they could be like.

Example

You work for NBB Limited, and have gathered the following information relating to performance.

Monthly sales (excluding VAT)	20X4	20X3
	£	£
January	41,250	42,740
February	35,680	37,720
March	51,660	54,700
April	53,210	58,350
May	55,000	53,920
June	58,610	62,260
July	46,970	43,880
August	37,500	39,100
September	51,820	54,680
October	43,690	46,980
November	41,250	47,300
December	48,640	50,590

20X4	£
Production cost of widgets made and sold in the year	202,490
Administration costs	125,660
Selling and distribution costs	186,300
Other costs	18,100
Capital employed	377,400

Your company belongs to the National Widget Makers Association, and subscribes to an interfirm comparison scheme operated by the Association. You have been asked to complete the return on the following page.

National Widget Makers Association
Hill House
Truro
Devon

Dear Member
Please supply the following information in respect of your most recent completed financial accounting period. The figures should be compiled in accordance with the guidance notes below.

1   Turnover for the year

     Percentage change on previous year (+/-)

2   Production costs as a percentage of sales

3   Administration costs as a percentage of sales

4   Selling and distribution costs as a percentage of sales

5   Return on capital employed

Notes

1   Turnover for the year should be stated in £ and excluding VAT

2   Return on capital employed should be calculated as the proportion of net profit to capital employed and expressed as a percentage.

3   Percentages and ratios should be stated to two decimal places.

Solution

To complete the return, you need to gather all the data you need. You have monthly sales figures for 20X3 and 20X4. You can obtain annual sales figures simply by adding up the monthly figures. You need sales figures for 20X3 as well as 20X4, so that you can calculate the percentage change in sales during the year. Remember to calculate this percentage as a percentage of the earlier year figures. Here the percentage change in sales is based on the 20X3 total, not the 20X4 total.

Monthly sales (excluding VAT)	20X4	20X3
	£	£
January	41,250	42,740
February	35,680	37,720
March	51,660	54,700
April	53,210	58,350
May	55,000	53,920
June	58,610	62,260
July	46,970	43,880
August	37,500	39,100
September	51,820	54,680
October	43,690	46,980
November	41,250	47,300
December	48,640	50,590
	565,280	592,220

The increase in sales is £592,220 - £565,280 = £26,940.

As a percentage, this is 100% × (26,940/565,280) = + 4.77% (to 2 decimal places).

We also need to calculate costs as a percentage of sales in 20X4 (to 2 decimal places)

Item	Total cost	Sales	Cost as a percentage of sales
	£	£	%
Production costs	202,490	592,220	34.19
Administration costs	125,660	592,220	21.22
Selling and distribution costs	186,300	592,220	31.46

We need to calculate the net profit, so that we can calculate the return on capital employed. Don't forget the 'other costs'. We don't need to calculate the gross profit for this return, so we can simply deduct total costs from the sales revenue to calculate net profit.

	£	£
Sales		592,220
Production costs	202,490	
Administration costs	125,660	
Selling and distribution costs	186,300	
Other costs	18,100	
Total costs		532,550
Net profit		59,670

$$ROCE = \frac{59,670}{377,400} \times 100\% = 15.81\%$$

Before you complete the return, it is a good idea to check your calculations carefully for mistakes.

Filling in the return is now a simple process. The relevant part of the return is reproduced below.

1	Turnover for the year	£592,220
	Percentage change on previous year (+/-)	+ 4.77%
2	Production costs as a percentage of sales	34.19%
3	Administration costs as a percentage of sales	21.22%
4	Selling and distribution costs as a percentage of sales	31.46%
5	Return on capital employed	15.81%

ACTIVITY 1

You have been asked to prepare a return to the Midlands Microengineering Association for interfirm comparison purposes, on behalf of your company Tractor Limited and its subsidiary Carthorse Limited.

The return you have to complete is shown below.

Task

Complete the return using the data provided.

Midlands Microengineering Association (MMA)

Interfirm comparison

Company _____

	£	% of sales	Industry average *(to be filled in by the MMA)*
Sales			
Gross profit			

Net profit				
Fixed assets				
Current assets				
Current liabilities				
Return on capital employed				

Guidance notes

1   Fixed assets should be stated at net book value.

2   Return on capital employed is net profit before interest charges, divided by the total of fixed assets (stated at net book value) and net current assets.

3   State all ratios and percentages to two decimal places

You have collected the following data.

Tractor Limited and its subsidiary

Consolidated profit and loss account
for the year ended 30 June 20X4

	£
Sales	1,158,630
Cost of sales	436,110
Gross profit	722,520
Wages and salaries	254,800
Distribution costs	123,850
Administration expenses	165,880
Interest payable	25,800
Other expenses	64,740
	635,070
Net profit	87,450

Tractor Limited and its subsidiary
Consolidated balance sheet as at 30 June 20X4

	£	£
Fixed assets at net book value		1,178,640
Current assets		
Stock	48,340	
Trade debtors	249,330	
Cash at bank and in hand	24,700	
	322,370	
Current liabilities		
Trade creditors	127,350	
Other creditors	15,200	
	142,550	
Net current assets		179,820
Total assets less current liabilities		1,358,460
Long term liability		
Bank loan repayable 30 June 20X9		369,400
		989,060
Capital and reserves		
Called up share capital		246,700
Retained profits		742,360
		989,060

For a suggested answer, see the 'Answers' section at the end of the book.

CONCLUSION

Filling in returns for external agencies is largely a process of collecting the data required, and using this to calculate the required ratios or percentages. However, it is easy to make mistakes with the selection of figures and the calculations. You should therefore:

- Be careful when you collate the data, and try to make sure that the figures you select are those that are needed.

- Take note of the guidelines and explanations on the return. These will help you to choose the correct figures.

- Calculate the ratios or percentages carefully. Double-check your computations.

SELF TEST QUESTIONS

Paragraph

1   State four categories of external organisations that need information from businesses.   1

2   Which regulatory bodies can demand information from businesses?   1.1

KEY TERMS

Regulatory bodies – either government departments, or bodies set up by government that have the power to demand certain information from businesses.

The Inland Revenue – regulatory body which obtains information from businesses for tax purposes.

HM Customs and Excise – regulatory body which obtains information from VAT-registered businesses for the purposes of collecting value added tax.

Registrar of Companies – all UK companies are required by law to submit certain information to the Registrar of Companies, for example a copy of their annual report and accounts, and also an annual return.

Grant awarding bodies – bodies provided with funds, by the national government or by the European Union, for awarding to businesses. The purpose of the funds is to give financial support to businesses that are planning to make certain types of investment.

Statistics gathering bodies – government departments that collect statistical information from businesses.

Trade association – a voluntary body whose members are businesses operating in a particular industry (or 'trade').

Chapter 11

VALUE ADDED TAX

The purpose of this chapter is to explain in outline the system of Value Added Tax and how it operates.

CONTENTS

1   Introduction

2   The government department responsible for VAT

3   Types of supply and rates of tax

4   Calculating the VAT

5   Input tax and output tax

6   Registering for VAT

7   The time of supply: the basic tax point

8   The VAT invoice

9   VAT and exports and imports

10   Obtaining guidance about VAT

KNOWLEDGE AND UNDERSTANDING

		Reference
1	The classification of types of supply; registration requirements; the form of VAT invoices; tax points	Item 4
2	Sources of information on VAT: Customs and Excise Guide	Item 5
3	The basis of the relationship between the organisation and the VAT Office	Item 19

PERFORMANCE CRITERIA

		Reference
1	Ensure guidance is sought from the VAT Office when required, in a professional manner	Item D in element 7.3

LEARNING OUTCOMES

At the end of this chapter, you should be able to:

- Explain the basic features of the VAT system, including the different types of supply, different rates of VAT, output tax and input tax, registration requirements for VAT, VAT invoices and tax points.

FOULKS LYNCH
PUBLICATIONS

- Explain the relationship between businesses registered for VAT and their VAT Office.

- Know where information about VAT and assistance with queries can be found.

- Prepare a request for guidance on VAT in a professional manner.

1 INTRODUCTION

VAT is a sales tax or 'tax on consumer expenditure'. It is collected on business transactions in the UK and also on:

- imports from non-European Union countries and

- imports from European Union countries. In VAT terminology, these imports are called 'acquisitions'.

Business transactions involve the supply of goods or services.

VAT is charged within the total selling price when a 'VAT-registered business' sells goods or services, and it is paid by the customer. For example, if a VAT-registered business sells goods to a customer and the sales price is £100 without VAT, the amount payable by the customer is £100 plus the VAT. If VAT is charged at 17.5%, the tax would be £17.50, so the customer would have to pay £117.50. A business collects the tax from its customers, and makes periodic payments to the government (usually every three months).

VAT is payable by the customer, on both cash and credit transactions, if the following conditions exist.

- The supply of the goods or service is made in the UK (or Isle of Man).

- The supply is made by a business that is a 'taxable person'. A **taxable person** is a business that is registered for VAT. Registration is explained later.

- The supply is a business transaction.

- The goods or services supplied are neither exempt from VAT nor zero-rated.

2 THE GOVERNMENT DEPARTMENT RESPONSIBLE FOR VAT

HM Customs and Excise is the government department responsible for the administration of VAT and for collecting the tax from businesses.

There is a head office for VAT administration, the VAT Central Unit, and a central computer centre at Southend. There is also a network of local VAT Offices, with a local office in most major towns.

- VAT Central Office deals with VAT returns and the payments and repayments of the tax.

- The local VAT Offices carry out inspection visits known as 'control visits', to check that businesses are collecting the tax properly.

- Large businesses might be assigned to a special 'Large Trader Team', that provides them with support and information.

Customs and Excise provide extensive information about all aspects of VAT. These are available as information sheets, but businesses are encouraged to visit the Customs and Excise web site to obtain the information they want. The web site address is www.hmce.gov.uk.

The information sheets on the web site are all in PDF format, which means that they can be downloaded on to your computer via the internet, and printed out if required.

The main Customs and Excise Guide on VAT is called 'Notice 700: The VAT Guide'.

If you have access to the internet, we strongly advise you to visit the Customs and Excise web site and look through some of the information sheets ('notices'), particularly the VAT Guide.

If you cannot find the information you are looking for and want some guidance on a point about VAT, you can telephone Customs and Excise. Large businesses can telephone their Large Trader Team, but most businesses should:

- **telephone the National Advice Service** (telephone number 0845 010 9000), or

- **write to your nearest VAT enquiries office** which is the local VAT Office.

3 TYPES OF SUPPLY AND RATES OF TAX

Supplies of goods or services are either:

- exempt supplies, or

- taxable supplies.

3.1 EXEMPT SUPPLIES

Exempt supplies are goods or services that do not come within the VAT system at all. No VAT is charged on these items.

A business selling exempt supplies does not have to submit VAT returns to Customs and Excise.

Exempt supplies include:

- the sale of land and buildings for residential use

- insurance policies

- many financial services, including providing bank loans

- health services

- education services provided by a not-for-profit institution.

Organisations delivering exempt supplies to customers do not have to register for VAT, unless they sell taxable supplies as well.

3.2 TAXABLE SUPPLIES

Taxable supplies are goods and services on which VAT is charged by VAT-registered businesses. There are currently three rates of tax on taxable supplies:

- a standard rate, currently 17.5%

- a reduced rate, currently 5%, and

- a zero rate (0%).

Most taxable items are standard-rated.

Zero-rated items are goods and services on which VAT is charged at a rate of 0%. They include:

- most items of food (but not food supplied by a restaurant or other food caterer)

- books, newspapers and magazines

- transport

- water supply and sewerage services

 FOULKS LYNCH
PUBLICATIONS

- young children's clothing

- drugs and medicines supplied on prescription.

Special zero-rating rules also apply to imports and exports. These are explained later.

It might seem odd that some goods and services should be zero-rated for VAT, rather than treated as exempt supplies. However, there are very important differences between exempt supplies and zero-rated supplies.

- A business selling zero-rated supplies has to register for VAT, if it meets the requirements for registration. As a VAT-registered business, it is accountable to Customs and Excise and has to submit regular VAT returns.

- A VAT-registered business is liable to Customs and Excise for all the VAT it charges its customers. At the same time, it can also claim back from Customs and Excise all (or most) of the VAT it is charged by its suppliers. A business selling zero-rated items is therefore able to obtain a refund from Customs and Excise of all (or most) of the VAT on amounts charged by its suppliers.

- A business not registered for VAT because it sells exempt supplies (for example, a dental surgery) cannot claim back any VAT charged by its suppliers. Its purchase costs are therefore the price paid including the VAT.

This is explained in more detail later.

Reduced-rate items are goods and services on which the rate of tax is 5%. These include the supply of domestic fuel and power. Gas supply companies and electricity supply companies therefore charge VAT at 5% on domestic bills.

ACTIVITY 1

Decide whether the following goods and services are taxable supplies on which VAT should be paid.

1 A meal in a restaurant

2 A ready-to-cook oven meal bought in a supermarket

3 Private medical treatment

4 Theatre tickets

5 The gift of shares in Vodafone by a parent to a son or daughter

6 An inter-city train ticket

7 Annual membership fees charged by a golf club.

For a suggested answer, see the 'Answers' section at the end of the book.

4 CALCULATING THE VAT

Many businesses charging VAT simply add the VAT to the price they want to charge for themselves. For example, suppose that a consultancy firm (registered for VAT) has done some work for a client and wants to charge £2,000 for its services. Consultancy services are standard-rated, so the invoice to the client should be for:

	£
Net price	2,000
VAT at 17.5%	350
Total amount payable	2,350

Whenever the VAT does not come to a whole number of pence, the amount of tax should be rounded down to the nearest penny. For example, VAT at 17.5% on £346.84 is £60.697. The amount of tax charged should be rounded down to £60.97.

You might need to remember that for standard-rated items:

- The total amount payable is the net price multiplied by 117.5/100 (= x 47/40).

- The VAT is 17.5% (= 7/40) of the net price and 17.5/117.5 (= 7/47) of the gross price.

This is important because some businesses charge an all-in price to their customers and then calculate the VAT from the gross price. For example, a restaurant's charges in its menu are prices including VAT.

ACTIVITY 2

1   An electricity supply company charges a customer £124.38 for the quarter, excluding VAT. VAT is chargeable at the reduced. What is the VAT payable and the total amount of the bill?

2   A company installing burglar alarms charges a customer £146.50 excluding VAT for the installation of a new alarm. VAT is chargeable at the standard rate. What is the amount of VAT chargeable, and what must the customer pay in total?

3   A restaurant charges a customer £115.50 for a meal with wine. All the items supplied are taxable at the standard rate. How much VAT has been charged?

4   A supplier of home computers charges £850 for its Model X, inclusive of VAT. What is the amount of VAT within this price?

For a suggested answer, see the 'Answers' section at the end of the book.

5   INPUT TAX AND OUTPUT TAX

A business charges its customers VAT when it sells taxable goods or services. Goods or services sold by a business are called 'outputs' for the purpose of VAT. The VAT charged to customers and collected from them is called **output tax**.

A business must also pay VAT on taxable goods and services that it buys from VAT-registered suppliers. Goods or services purchased by a business are called 'inputs' for the purpose of VAT. The VAT charged by and paid to suppliers and is called **input tax**.

VAT-registered businesses are tax collectors for the government, and hand over tax to Customs and Excise at regular intervals, usually every three months. The amount of tax that a business pays is the **difference between the output tax charged to customers and the input tax charged by suppliers** in the period.

Example 1

A business sells £467,240 of standard-rated supplies in a three-month VAT period, and the VAT on these supplies is £81,767. In the same period, purchases of taxable goods and services totalled £158,000 and the VAT on these was £27,650.

The payment of tax to Customs and Excise for the period will be:

	£
Output tax on sales	81,767.00
Input tax on purchases	27,650.00
Amount payable to Customs and Excise	54,117.00

Sometimes, a business will charge less output tax than it is charged with input tax. This will happen, for example, if a business sells zero-rated goods or services.

_xample 2

A bus company has total revenue of £268,905 in a three-month VAT period. In the same period, purchases of taxable goods and services were £87,432, on which VAT of £15,300.60 was charged.

Transport services are zero-rated, so there is a repayment of tax to the business by Customs and Excise.

	£
Output tax on sales	0.00
Input tax on purchases	15,300.60
Repayment of tax by Customs and Excise	15,300.60

Tutorial note: When a business sells taxable goods or services, it records the sales value in its accounts as the sales excluding VAT. Similarly, when a business buys goods or services, it records the cost of purchases in its accounts as the amount excluding VAT. The output tax and the input tax are recorded separately in a VAT account.

Accounting for VAT in the main ledger of the accounting system is not a feature of this Unit, but it might help your understanding if you can link the accounting aspects of VAT with the tax payments aspects.

ACTIVITY 3

VAT is a sales tax on consumers, but it is collected at different stages in the 'supply chain'. This activity might help to demonstrate this point.

BN Leather Goods sells some leather cases to a customer, charging £799 inclusive of VAT at 17.5%. It purchased these goods from a supplier, Casemaker Ltd, for £300 plus VAT at the standard rate. Casemaker Ltd purchased the leather for the cases from a supplier, T Smith, for £43 plus VAT at the standard rate.

BN Leather Goods, Casemaker Ltd and T Smith are all VAT-registered traders.

Tasks

1   Calculate the VAT payable on the cases by the customer of BN Leather Goods.

2   Calculate the output tax and the input tax on these transactions for each of the three businesses, and the amount of tax payable by each business to Customs and Excise.

3   Demonstrate that the total amount of tax payable by the three businesses equals the total amount of tax paid by the consumer who purchased the cases.

For a suggested answer, see the 'Answers' section at the end of the book.

6   REGISTERING FOR VAT

A business in the UK must register for VAT if it sells more than a certain amount of taxable goods and services in a year. As soon as it is registered, it must start charging VAT on sales to its customers.

The registration limit means that small businesses do not need to register for VAT, although a business can volunteer to be registered, even if its annual sales are below the registration limit.

The registration limit is usually increased each year, but for 2003/2004 the limit is £56,000. This means that any business selling taxable goods or services in the year to the value of £56,000 or more must register for VAT.

A business must apply to register for VAT and it could be fined if it fails to do so at the proper time. (Fines, called 'penalties' for late registration.)

FOULKS LYNCH
PUBLICATIONS

A form for registration (called form VAT 1) must be sent to the Customs and Excise National Registration Service. Copies of the form can be obtained from the Customs and Excise web site or by calling the National Advice Service.

When a business is registered for VAT:

- it is given a unique VAT registration number

- it must start charging VAT on sales of its goods and services

- it must account to Customs and Excise for VAT and submit regular VAT returns.

Deregistration

Sometimes a business might shrink in size, so that its annual sales of taxable items falls below the registration limit. In addition to a registration limit, there is also a deregistration limit. If sales by a business fall below this limit, it is no longer required to be VAT-registered. It can therefore deregister if it wishes to do so. For 2003/2004, the deregistration limit is £54,000. This means that if the sales of taxable items by a business fall below £54,000 a year, the business can apply to be deregistered.

6.1 TESTS TO DECIDE WHETHER A PERSON MUST REGISTER FOR VAT

To decide whether a business must register for VAT (and become a 'taxable person'), we need to look at its annual turnover in taxable goods and services. However, should we look at past sales (historical turnover), or should we be looking at estimated sales in the future?

The answer is that we normally look at historical sales, but we might also need to look at estimated future sales too.

6.2 REGISTRATION BY REFERENCE TO HISTORICAL TURNOVER

Traders are required to monitor their sales of taxable goods and services ('taxable turnover'). At the end of every month they must calculate their taxable turnover for the previous 12 months. A trader is required to register if his taxable turnover for the year then ended exceeds £56,000 (2003/2004).

(A trader liable to registration may claim exemption from registration if his taxable turnover largely comprises zero-rated supplies. Exemption is given if the trader would regularly receive repayments of tax if he were to be registered. However, unless a trader is registered for VAT, he cannot claim back repayments of input tax, and so it is usually in the interests of a trader selling zero-rated goods to register.)

A trader liable to registration must notify Customs and Excise not later than thirty days after the end of the month in which taxable turnover in the previous year exceeds the statutory registration limit. (Notifications are made using on VAT 1).

Example

Harry commenced trading on 1 January 2002. His monthly taxable supplies were as follows:

	2002 £	2003 £
January	2,600	4,490
February	2,700	5,160
March	2,800	5,430
April	2,900	5,200
May	2,940	5,470
June	3,110	5,740

July	3,180	5,810
August	3,150	5,680
September	3,420	5,740
October	3,890	5,810
November	4,150	5,980
December	4,330	5,850

From what date is Harry liable to register for VAT?

Solution

The annual sales of taxable goods and services for the previous 12 months can be calculated. The figures are given in the table below. *Note*: Make sure that you can produce a similar table from the figures given.

End of	*Sales for the previous 12 months*
	£
December 2002	39,170
January 2003	41,060
February 2003	43,520
March 2003	46,150
April 2003	48,450
May 2003	50,980
June 2003	53,610
July 2003	**56,240**
August 2003	58,770
September2003	61,090
October 2003	63,010
November 2003	64,840
December 2003	66,360

At the end of July, his annual sales of taxable goods and services has gone above the registration limit of £56,000 for the first time.

Harry must notify Customs and Excise on Form VAT 1 within 30 days of the end of July, by 30 August.

A trader is normally registered from the start of the following month after notification. In this case, Harry will be registered from 1 September 2003.

6.3 REGISTRATION BY REFERENCE TO FUTURE TURNOVER

A trader must also register if at any time he has reason to believe that sales of taxable goods and services are likely to exceed £56,000 in a future thirty day period. The trader must notify Customs and Excise no later than the end of that period and is normally registered with effect from the start of that period.

If a trader starts a new business, or an established trader expands his business, this rule could require him to register immediately, instead of waiting until taxable turnover for the previous 12 months has reached the registration limit.

Example

Charles leaves his job on 31 December 2003, signs a lease for new business premises on 1 February 2004 and opens for business on 20 June 2004. He estimates, from the outset, that taxable supplies will be in the region of £60,000 per month.

When, if at all, is Charles liable to register?

Solution

Charles is liable to registration because taxable supplies for the thirty days from 20 June 2004 to 19 July 2004 are expected to exceed £56,000. He must notify Customs and Excise of his liability for registration by 19 July 2004 and will be registered with effect from 20 June 2004.

6.4   THE EFFECT OF REGISTRATION ON SALES PRICES AND COSTS

There are some obvious disadvantages in having to register for VAT.

- The trader becomes an unpaid tax collector for the government, and has to spend a lot of time on administration work, such as preparing VAT returns for Customs and Excise.

- If the customers of the trader are not VAT-registered businesses, they will have to pay tax on their purchases. If the goods or services are standard-rated, consumers have to pay tax at 17.5%, which is a lot of money. (Only customers who are not businesses registered for VAT are affected. VAT-registered customers treat the VAT as input tax, which is 'claimed back' by setting it off against their own output tax.)

On the other hand, being registered for VAT means that input VAT can be claimed back. Input tax is set of against output tax in each period, and the business pays just the difference to Customs and Excise. As a consequence, purchases are cheaper for VAT-registered businesses than for businesses that are not registered. Non-registered businesses pay VAT but cannot claim it back.

6.5   VOLUNTARY REGISTRATION

A trader who is not required to register for VAT, because his annual turnover is below the registration limit, can apply to be registered voluntarily.

The reasons for wanting to register voluntarily might be that:

- Input VAT on purchases can be reclaimed from Customs and Excise, so the cost of purchases is reduced by the amount of the VAT.

- Most of the customers of the trader are themselves registered for VAT, so charging VAT on sales would not add to their costs, since they can claim back their input tax.

Voluntary registration is available to both actual traders and persons who are intending to trade but haven't yet started trading.

Example

Sheila decides to set up a business providing bookkeeping services for local businesses and shops, most of which are registered for VAT. Her turnover is not expected to exceed £50,000 per annum.

She has ordered a computer, and has signed two contracts with clients to start next month.

Should Sheila register for VAT?

Solution

If Sheila registers for VAT her customers will be able to claim back their input tax on their VAT returns, so they are unlikely to object to being charged VAT for her services.

She will be able to reclaim the input tax on the computer.

Sheila can apply for voluntary registration, even though she has not yet started trading (and is just an 'intending trader'). She should produce the order for the computer, and the two contracts with customers as evidence of her intention to trade.

6.6 PROCEDURES FOR REGISTRATION

A person who is required to register for VAT, or wishes to register voluntarily, must complete form VAT 1 and send it to the local VAT office (National Registration Service office).

After registration a certificate is issued with a unique VAT number. This VAT registration number must be quoted on all invoices issued by the trader and on all VAT receipts for cash payments by customers.

7 THE TIME OF SUPPLY: THE BASIC TAX POINT

7.1 IMPORTANCE OF THE TIME OF SUPPLY

The time of supply is the date on which the supply of a taxable item is made. This is important, because for each VAT period, a business must account for its input tax and output tax for the period (which is usually three months). Suppose for example that a business sells goods to a customer on 12 May and charges £1,000 plus VAT of £175. The customer eventually pays the invoice on 27 July. Let's suppose that 12 May and 27 July fall into two different VAT periods. Should the output tax be accounted for to Customs and Excise in the period when the invoice is issued, or in the period when the payment – including the tax – is received?

The time of supply might also be important for two other reasons.

• To calculate whether sales by the business have exceeded the registration limit in the past 12 months.

• In the possible event that the government changes the rate of VAT, to establish whether the old rate or the new rate should apply.

7.2 THE TAX POINT: THE BASIC TAX POINT AND THE ACTUAL TAX POINT

Definition   The tax point is the time at which a supply is made.

Either the basic tax point or the actual tax point should be used.

The basic tax point

Definition   The **basic tax point for goods** is the time at which they are collected, delivered or made available to a customer.

Definition   The **basic tax point for a service** is the date on which the service is performed. It is normally taken as the date on which all the work is complete, if it takes more than one day.

Example

Oddments Ltd, a garden centre, did the following work for its customers:

(a)   3 May 2003. Sold some garden furniture to Alf, who took the furniture with him.

(b)   9 June 2003. Delivered a DIY greenhouse to Bert.

(c)   1 July 2003. Delivered a DIY greenhouse to Carol, and erected it for her. The work involved laying concrete and took a few days to complete. It was completed on 11 July 2004.

(d)   7 August 2003. Completed a garden design plan for Doreen. Drawing up the plans had begun on 20 July 2004.

What are the basic tax points of these supplies?

Solution

(a)   3 May 2003. This is the date the goods were removed.

(b)   9 June 2003. This is the date the goods were delivered.

(c)   11 July 2003. This is the date the greenhouse was complete.

(d)   7 August 2003. This is the date the design services were completed.

The actual tax point

The basic tax point is overridden if an actual tax point is created. In other words, the actual tax point is the time of supply, if an actual tax point is created. An actual tax point is created in the following situations:

(a)   **A tax invoice is issued before the basic tax point.** In these circumstances the actual tax point is the date of the invoice.

(b)   **A tax invoice is issued within fourteen days after the basic tax point.** In these circumstances the actual tax point is the invoice date. The fourteen-day period can be extended, for example to accommodate a monthly invoicing system.

(c)   **Payment is received before the basic tax point.** In these circumstances, the actual tax point is the date the payment is received.

An invoice is 'issued' when it is sent or given to a customer.

As a result of these rules, the normal situation that applies is that:

*   for credit sales and purchases, the tax point is the date of the invoice

*   for cash sales and purchases, the tax point is the date of the sale/purchase.

Example

Compositors Ltd sold three printing presses to Alpha Ltd, Beta Ltd, and Gamma Ltd. The presses were each despatched to the customer on 19 September 2003.

(a)   Alpha Ltd had ordered the press on 3 September 2003. A tax invoice was issued on 30 September 2003, and paid by Alpha Ltd on 29 October 2003.

(b)   Beta Ltd had also ordered a press on 3 September 2003. A tax invoice was issued on 30 September 2003, although Beta Ltd had already paid for the press on 20 September 2003.

(c)   Gamma Ltd had also ordered a press on 3 September 2003, and had paid the full price with the order. A tax invoice/receipt was issued on 30 September 2003.

What are the tax points for these supplies?

Solution

In each case the basic tax point is the date of delivery, 19 September 2003. However, in each case an actual tax point is created, which becomes the time of supply.

(a)   Sale to Alpha Ltd. The actual tax point is 30 September 2003, because the tax invoice was issued within 14 days.

(b)   Sale to Beta Ltd. The actual tax point is 30 September 2003, because the tax invoice was issued within 14 days. The payment on 20 September 2003 does not

alter this, since the payment was made after the basic tax point (19 September 2003).

(c)   The actual tax point is 3 September 2003, because payment was received before the basic tax point (19 September 2003).

8   THE VAT INVOICE

A VAT-registered trader must issue invoices as VAT invoices. A VAT invoice is a normal invoice, but contains certain information for VAT purposes.

The information in a VAT invoice includes:

*   the VAT number of the trader issuing the invoice

*   the tax point (invoice date)

*   the amount payable excluding VAT, the VAT and the total amount payable.

VAT invoices provide evidence of the output VAT a business has charged its customers. VAT invoices and VAT receipts from suppliers provide evidence of the input VAT that the business has been charged. They are therefore important documents, which will be needed whenever Customs and Excise carry out a VAT inspection visit.

VAT invoices are described in more detail in the next chapter.

9 VAT AND EXPORTS AND IMPORTS

A business might sell goods or services abroad or might import goods from abroad which would be taxable if sold or purchased in the UK. You need to know how such exports and imports are treated for VAT purposes.

9.1 EXPORTS AND REMOVALS

For VAT purposes, a distinction is made between:

- Goods (or services) exported to a country outside the European Union/Community.

- Goods (or services) exported to another country in the European Union/Community. These are called 'removals' or 'despatches' rather than exports.

Exports to countries outside the UK are **zero-rated for VAT purposes**.

Exports (removals) to countries within the European Community are generally **zero-rated on despatch**.

The zero rating for VAT applies regardless of what the rate of tax on sales of similar goods or services inside the UK.

The exporter should keep evidence of the exports.

If the supplies are to VAT registered traders in other EU member states, they will be zero-rated if the customer's VAT registration number is shown on the invoice. Note it is conventional for VAT purposes to refer to the European Community (EC) and not the European Union (EU) although the terms mean the same.

9.2 EC SALES LIST

If a trader makes supplies to VAT registered traders in other EC member states then he must submit an EC sales list quarterly. This must include each customer's VAT number and the total value of the supplies to each customer.

There is a pre-printed form for the EC sales list, VAT 101, but the list can also be on plain paper or transmitted electronically.

9.3 IMPORTS AND ACQUISITIONS

For VAT purposes, a distinction is made between:

- Goods (or services) imported from a country outside the European Community, and

- Goods (or services) imported from another country in the European Community. These are called 'acquisitions' rather than imports.

Imports from outside the EC

If goods are imported into the UK, the seller will not have charged VAT on them. To bring them into the scope of VAT (and so into line with goods supplied by UK traders), the buyer pays VAT at the point of entry into the UK. In effect, this means that the buyer is paying output tax on items purchased as imports.

As a general rule, this tax is paid when the goods are imported and enter the UK. However, payment can be deferred if your business or your import agent has been approved by Customs and Excise for duty deferment. Duty deferment arrangements allow an importer to pay duty, including VAT on imports, once a month instead of transaction-by-transaction, and so an importer can delay paying VAT on imports by up to one month or so after they arrive in the UK.

The buyer accounts for VAT on imports, at the appropriate rate for the type of goods, on the value of the goods imported at the point of entry into the UK. The value of the goods at the point of entry is the price charged by the supplier plus the packaging, freight, insurance and commission.

The buyer can treat the VAT that he has paid as input tax. In other words, having paid VAT on the imported goods, the VAT can be claimed back again.

Rather than being issued with a VAT invoice, the UK importer receives a monthly certificate from Customs and Excise showing the VAT paid. This is the evidence required to claim back input tax on the VAT return.

Acquisitions from other EC member states

The export of goods from the UK is zero-rated. In the same way, since common rules apply within the EC, goods exported from other EC member states to the UK are also zero-rated. So if a UK importer buys goods from France, then he will not pay VAT on them to the French supplier (and so the French government) because they are zero-rated.

However, in the same way as for imports from outside the EC, the goods must be brought within the scope of UK VAT. The UK importer therefore pays VAT to HM Customs and Excise, at the appropriate rate, on the imported goods ('acquisitions'). This payment is made when the importer completes his VAT return for the period in which the import was made.

There is a separate line on the VAT form for the 'VAT due on acquisitions from other EC member states'. This is added to the traders output tax for that VAT period.

The trader will also be able to include the output tax that he has recorded on the 'acquisition' of the goods as part of his input tax on his purchases. The output tax paid can therefore be recovered because it is also treated as input tax.

These rules might seem rather odd, since an importer pays VAT on imports but then claims it back. However, the end result is that all the VAT paid by the final consumer is paid to the UK government, and no VAT is paid by a business outside the UK to the UK government.

Example

Joblots Ltd buys a consignment of furniture costing £2,000 from France. How will the VAT on this transaction be dealt with?

Joblots then sells the furniture to customers for £5,287.50. How will the VAT on this transaction be dealt with?

Solution

	£
Joblots will pay the French supplier	2,000
Joblots will declare on its VAT return (as output tax) 'VAT due on acquisitions from other EC member states' £2,000 at 17.5%	350
Total outlay	2,350
Joblots will deduct input tax on its VAT return of	350
Net cost of furniture	2,000

When Joblots sells the furniture on, it will be required to charge output tax on the supply. The output VAT is £5,287.50 x 7/47 = £787.50. This is payable to Customs and Excise. The sales price excluding VAT is £4,500 (£5,287.50 - £787.50).

Customs and Excise therefore receives VAT of £787.50, which is 17.5% of the net sales price of the furniture to the final consumer. (17.5% of £4,500 = £787.50.)

ACTIVITY 4

A trader has the following transactions:

(a) Export of wooden furniture to the United States of America.

(b) Import of wood from Malaysia.

(c) Acquisition of cloth from Germany.

What is the VAT treatment of these items?

For a suggested answer, see the 'Answers' section at the end of the book.

ACTIVITY 5

You have gathered the following information relating to a three-month VAT tax period for your business.

	£
Output VAT on sales	96,427.65
VAT on sales returns	2,625.00
VAT on acquisitions from other EC countries	3,605.28
Input VAT on purchases and expenses in the UK	18,295.03
VAT on purchase returns	806.83

Task

From this information, assess the amount of VAT payable to Customs and Excise for the period.

For a suggested answer, see the 'Answers' section at the end of the book.

10 OBTAINING GUIDANCE ABOUT VAT

The rules of VAT are very detailed, and situations might arise where it is not clear what the correct rules or procedures should be.

Customs and Excise provide copies of their notices and copies of many of their forms on the web site www.hmce.gov.uk. Queries can also be referred to the National Advice Service telephone line. Alternatively, queries can be sent in writing to the local VAT Office.

It is important for a business to be aware that it might be required to charge VAT on certain activities, but there are grey areas when it might be unclear whether or not VAT should be charged, and if so at what rate. If in doubt, the business should ask for guidance from Customs and Excise.

When seeking guidance in writing, remember to:

* quote the VAT registration number of the business

* write the date on the letter

* give your own name and position within your business.

FOULKS LYNCH
PUBLICATIONS

ACTIVITY 6

You have been asked about the rules for claiming input VAT on the purchase cost and running costs of company motor vehicles, and on the costs of entertaining clients (the costs of lunches and so on). You are not sure what the rules are.

You are the newly-appointed VAT accountant for TQ Limited, whose VAT number is 430 9248 76.

Task

Write a brief note to your local VAT Office, asking for guidance on these matters.

For a suggested answer, see the 'Answers' section at the end of the book.

CONCLUSION

This chapter has described the main features of VAT. A business registered for VAT must deal with all the administrative requirements, which include accounting for the VAT, submitting VAT returns to Customs and Excise and paying the tax due, and keeping records as evidence that it is accounting for the tax honestly and correctly.

The next chapter looks in more detail at some aspects of VAT including VAT invoices and record-keeping.

SELF TEST QUESTIONS

		Paragraph
1	What is VAT?	1
2	Which government department is responsible for VAT?	2
3	Which are the VAT exempt supplies?	3.1
4	Which supplies are taxable at zero VAT rate, which at reduced VAT rate and which at standard VAT rate?	3.2
5	What is output VAT?	5
6	What is input VAT?	5
7	Who needs to register for VAT?	6
8	What are the advantages and disadvantages of having to register for VAT?	6
9	What is the basic tax point for goods and for services?	7.2
10	How are imports and exports treated for VAT purposes?	9

KEY TERMS

VAT – a sales tax or 'tax on consumer expenditure'. VAT is collected on business transactions in the UK and on acquisitions.

Acquisitions – imports from European Union and non-European Union countries.

HM Customs and Excise – the government department responsible for the administration of VAT and for collecting the tax from businesses.

Notice 700: The VAT Guide – the main Customs and Excise Guide on VAT.

Exempt supplies – goods or services that do not come within the VAT system at all.

Zero-rated items – goods and services on which VAT is charged at a rate of 0%.

Reduced-rate items – goods and services on which the rate of tax is 5%.

Output tax – the VAT charged to customers and collected from them is called.

Input tax – VAT charged by and paid to suppliers.

Tax point – the time at which a supply is made.

Basic tax point for goods – the time at which they are collected, delivered or made available to a customer.

Basic tax point for a service – the date on which the service is performed. It is normally taken as the date on which all the work is complete, if it takes more than one day.

VAT invoice – an invoice that contains certain information for VAT purposes.

FOULKS LYNCH
PUBLICATIONS

Chapter 12

VAT INVOICES, TAX PERIODS, RECORDS AND ENFORCEMENT

The purpose of this chapter is to explain how VAT records originate and how VAT is accounted for. This includes an explanation of VAT tax periods, and the frequency of tax returns. It also explains the records that must be kept relating to VAT that must be kept. Finally, it explains how Customs and Excise enforce the correct administration of VAT by businesses through inspection visits.

CONTENTS

KNOWLEDGE AND UNDERSTANDING

		Reference
1	The classification of types of supply; registration requirements; the form of VAT invoices; tax points	Item 4
2	Administration of VAT: enforcement	Item 6
3	Background understanding that a variety of outside agencies may require reports and returns from organisations and that these requirements must be built into administrative and accounting systems and procedures	Item 17
4	The basis of the relationship between the organisation and the VAT Office	Item 19

LEARNING OUTCOMES

At the end of this chapter, you should be able to:

- prepare a VAT invoice

- explain the treatment of VAT on credit notes

- explain the treatment of VAT on discounts

- define a tax period for the purposes of VAT

- explain what records provide the sources of information for completing a VAT return

- explain what records should be kept and for how long

- explain the nature of VAT enforcement by Customs and Excise.

1 TAX INVOICES

1.1 REQUIREMENT TO ISSUE A TAX INVOICE

If a registered taxable person makes a standard-rated or reduced-rate taxable supply in the UK to a taxable person, he **must** issue a tax invoice.

Tax invoices are not required if all the supplies on the invoice are zero-rated.

(In practice, a business issues similar invoices to all its customers, but in the case of invoices to VAT-registered customers, there is a legal obligation to issue VAT invoices.)

The tax invoice must be issued within 30 days of the tax point.

ACTIVITY 1

What is the latest date on which a tax invoice may be issued in the following cases?

(a) Goods supplied on 11 May 2004, but paid for on 1 May 2004.

(b) Goods supplied on 11 May 2004, but paid for on 15 May 2004.

For a suggested answer, see the 'Answers' section at the end of the book.

1.2 WHAT IS THE TAX INVOICE USED FOR?

A tax invoice issued to a VAT-registered customer is the sales invoice. It provides evidence for the customer of the input tax charged.

A copy must be kept by the supplier to support his calculations of output tax.

There is no requirement to issue tax invoices:

- to customers who are not taxable persons

- for zero-rated supplies.

There is no requirement for a VAT invoice in these cases because a customer who is not a taxable person and a customer paying VAT at 0% do not claim input tax from Customs and Excise.

However, invoices to customers should include VAT information, so that the supplier has evidence of the output tax charged.

FOULKS LYNCH
PUBLICATIONS

1.3 THE INFORMATION REQUIRED ON A TAX INVOICE

A tax invoice is a normal commercial invoice containing the following particulars:

(a) a unique identifying invoice number

(b) the time of supply

(c) the supplier's name, address and VAT registration number

(d) the customer's name and address

(e) the type of supply made, for example: sale, hire purchase, etc.

(f) a description of the goods or services supplied

(g) for each item of goods or services supplied:

- the quantity of goods or extent of the services

- the charge made, excluding VAT (expressed in sterling)

- the rate of VAT.

(h) the total tax-exclusive amount expressed in sterling (with separate totals for zero rated and exempt supplies) of all the goods and services supplied

(i) the rate of any cash discount/settlement discount offered, and

(j) the amount of tax payable (expressed in sterling) at each rate and in total.

Usually a trader uses preprinted invoice forms, with details of his name, address and VAT number already printed. They may already be sequentially numbered. There will be spaces on the form to fill in the other information. Businesses with computerised accounting systems produce most of their invoices automatically.

Example of a tax invoice

Potts and Co
12 Marsh Lane
Cardiff
CF1 1BZ

Invoice number 1023

Date/tax point: 11 April 20X4   VAT number 123 4567 89

Quantity	Description	Rate of VAT	Amount excluding VAT £
6	Size 12 pots at £2 each	17.5%	24.00
12	Size 20 pots at £3 each	17.5%	60.00
			84.00
VAT			14.70
Total amount payable			98.70

ACTIVITY 2

You are required to prepare a VAT invoice on 15th October 20X3 from the following information.

1   Your firm is BVC Limited, address Grand House, Main Way, Stockport, Cheshire SK1 2RW.

2   The firm's VAT registration number is 543 9876 21.

3   The customer is Dorway Limited, Fresh House, 76 John's Walk, Manchester M8 4RG.

4   The invoice is for 25 blue widgets at £4.20 each and 40 green widgets at £5.15 each. Widgets are standard-rated items for VAT.

5   The invoice number is 68682.

For a suggested answer, see the 'Answers' section at the end of the book.

2   VAT AND CREDIT NOTES

When a business issues a credit note to a customer, there is a 'sales return' and total sales for the period are reduced. At the same time there is a reduction in the VAT owed by the customer.

For example, suppose that a customer is supplied with £1,000 of goods plus VAT at £175. The customer returns 20% of these goods. The credit note issued to the customer should be for £200 plus VAT (£35).

VAT on sales returns is treated as a **reduction in the output tax for the tax period**. VAT on credit notes issued is therefore deducted when calculating output VAT for the purpose of filling in a VAT return.

Similarly, when a business receives a credit note from a supplier for purchase returns, the amount owed to the supplier is reduced by the cost of the returned purchases inclusive of VAT.

VAT on purchase returns is treated as a **reduction in the input tax for the tax period**. VAT on credit notes received is therefore deducted when calculating input VAT for the purpose of filling in a VAT return.

To be valid for VAT purposes a credit note must be issued for a genuine reason, such as an overcharge on the original invoice, or on the return of faulty goods. It must include similar information to the information shown on a tax invoice.

3   WHEN IS A DETAILED TAX INVOICE NOT REQUIRED?

Many traders make large volumes of small sales of standard-rated goods to taxable persons

Less detailed invoices

A less-detailed invoice may be issued if the value of supplies in total, including VAT, is less than £100 and the supply is not to another EC country. Zero-rated and exempt supplies must not be included in such an invoice.

This less detailed invoice must still show:

(a)   the supplier's name, address and VAT registration number

(b)   the time of the supply and a description of the goods

(c)   the rate of tax chargeable and the total amount of the invoice including VAT.

VAT receipts for credit cards can be used as less detailed invoices, provided they include all the required details.

Example of a less detailed invoice

All-U-Need
1 High Street
Smalltown
SL1 1FD

12 January 20X4

VAT No 456 7891 23

Cleaning materials   £12.99

(inclusive of VAT at the rate of 17.5%)

4 DISCOUNTS AND VAT

You should be familiar already with the VAT rules for discounts, but here is a reminder.

There are two types of discount that might be offered to a customer.

- Bulk purchase discounts

- Cash discounts or settlement discounts for early payment.

Bulk discounts are discounts given to regular customers. For example, suppose that a regular customer is given a 20% discount on all purchases. If the customer buys goods with a normal price of £200, the price less discount is £160. VAT should be charged on this price less discount. If VAT is at the standard rate, then the VAT payable would be £28.

Cash discounts, also called settlement discounts, are discounts offered to a customer who pays early, instead of taking the usual credit period before paying. For example, a customer might be given standard credit terms of 60 days, meaning that the customer does not have to pay an invoice until 60 days after the invoice date. A cash discount might be offered to encourage the customer to pay earlier. For example, a discount of 1% might be offered for payment within 14 days.

Unlike a bulk purchase discount, a cash discount is not 'certain', in the sense that the customer might take it or leave it. The supplier doesn't know whether the discount will be taken until either payment is received or the discount offer period ends.

This raises the question: should VAT be charged on the sales value ignoring the cash discount, or should VAT be charged on the sales price less the cash discount?

The VAT rules about cash discounts (settlement discounts) are that:

- If a cash discount is offered, the terms of the discount on offer must be shown on the VAT invoice.

- VAT should be charged on the sales price less the cash discount.

- Even if the customer does not take the discount, the VAT payable remains unchanged.

- If more than one rate of cash discount is offered, it is assumed that the highest rate will be taken. For example, a discount of 1.5% might be offered for payment within 7 days and a discount of 1% for payment within 14 days.

Example

A trader sells some goods for £150.00 plus VAT. She offers a 2% cash discount for prompt payment. How much VAT should she charge?

Solution

	£
Price before cash discount	150.00
Cash discount (2%)	3.00
Price net of cash discount	147.00
VAT at 17.5%	£25.72

The VAT invoice will show:

	£
Price excluding VAT	150.00
VAT	25.72
Total amount payable	175.72

If the customer does not take the cash discount, he will pay £175.72. If he does take the cash discount of £3, he will pay £172.72.

ACTIVITY 3

A customer purchases goods costing £5,200 at normal price, but is given a 20% discount on all purchases. The customer is also offered a settlement discount of 1.5% for payment within 7 days of the invoice date.

(a)   What VAT should be charged?

(b)   What will be shown on the invoice as the amount payable?

(c)   What will the customer pay?

For a suggested answer, see the 'Answers' section at the end of the book.

5   PROFORMA INVOICES

A proforma invoice is a document that might be issued by a supplier who does not want to give the customer any credit, but the customer wants an official document stating what the cost of an item will be. For example, a customer in a large organisation might ask for a proforma invoice in order to submit a request to senior management for approval of the purchase.

A proforma invoice sets out how much is to be paid, and usually looks exactly like a normal invoice. However, it must be marked "**This is not a VAT invoice**" and it cannot be used to claim back input tax. When the sale actually takes place a proper VAT invoice is issued.

6   TAX PERIODS

A trader registered for VAT is required to complete VAT returns. A VAT return is prepared for each period, setting out the total output tax and the total input tax for the period, and the amount of tax payable to (or recoverable from) Customs and Excise.

The period covered by a VAT return is decided by Customs and Excise according to standard rules.

Definition The **tax period** is the period for which the trader must prepare his VAT return. It is also known as the **prescribed accounting period**.

- The standard length of a prescribed accounting period is 3 months.

- It ends on the final day of the calendar month.

- The next tax period starts on the first day of the next calendar month.

The first three-month period starts from the date that the business is first registered for VAT. For example, if a business was first registered for VAT on 1st June 2002, its tax periods will be June – August, September – November, December – February and March – June.

A business must include in its VAT return all the output and input tax relating to transactions with tax points during that period.

The amount of VAT payable for a tax period (or the amount refundable by Customs and Excise)

7 KEEPING RECORDS

Records and accounts of all goods and services received and supplied in the course of business must be kept so that VAT returns can be completed and also so that Customs and Excise can carry out inspection visits and check the figures that have been included on the VAT returns. Records and accounts can be kept on paper, microfiche, microfilm or computer.

7.1 RECORDS REQUIRED

The records that must be kept include:

(a) Copies of all tax invoices issued

(b) Copies of all credit notes issued (and debit notes received, if any).

(c) All tax invoices received

(d) All credit notes received (and copies of all debit notes issued, if any).

(e) A record of goods sent to other EC member countries, and copies of completed EC sales lists.

(f) A record of goods sent received from other EC member countries.

(g) Documents recording imports of goods from countries that are not EC members.

(h) Documents recording services received from abroad.

(i) Documents recording exports to countries that are not EC members.

(j) A record of all outputs and inputs. In other words a record of the VAT on all individual transactions. This is kept within an accounting system in the sales day book and purchase day book for credit transactions, and the cash book for cash transactions.

(k) A VAT account (in the main ledger)

(l) Records of zero-rated and exempt items.

7.2 PERIOD OF RETENTION

The records required by Customs and Excise must be kept for **six years**.

If keeping records for this length of time causes the trader undue difficulty, expense, or storage problems, he may ask the local VAT office for permission to keep some of the records for a shorter time. HM Customs and Excise must agree before any of the records can be destroyed within the six-year period.

7.3 FORM OF RECORDS REQUIRED FOR OUTPUTS

A trader must keep records of all his outputs, whether standard rated, zero-rated or exempt. The records must include all the details that must be included on a tax invoice.

If the trader issues a tax invoice in respect of **all** his supplies (i.e. all his sales), it is sufficient to keep a summary of the invoices, in addition to the copy invoices.

The summary must be in the same order as the copy invoices, and must show:

(a)   the VAT chargeable on the supplies

(b)   the value of standard-rated and zero-rated supplies excluding the VAT

(c)   the value of any exempt supplies

(d)   credits allowed to customers.

Many businesses keep these records as books of prime entry, in the sales day book, sales returns day book and cash receipts book.

7.4 FORM OF RECORDS REQUIRED FOR INPUTS

A trader must also keep similar records of all his taxable inputs. The records must show the details of the transactions and the VAT.

If the trader has received invoices in respect of all his inputs, and they are filed in such a way that they can easily be referred to, it will be sufficient to keep a summary of the invoices.

The summary must show:

(a)   the VAT charged on inputs, including imports

(b)   VAT due on services received from abroad

(c)   the value of all supplies received excluding the VAT

(d)   credits received from suppliers.

A record must also be kept of inputs where the input tax is non-deductible on the VAT return.

Many businesses keep these records in books of prime entry, i.e. the purchases day book, the purchases returns day book, the cash payments book, and the petty cash book.

7.5 EC DOCUMENTATION

Where a trader buys goods from, or sells goods to, other EU member states, additional records must be kept.

- The trader must keep records of acquisitions (imports) from other EC member states so that both the amount of the purchases excluding VAT and the VAT relating to the purchases can be shown on the VAT return.

- He must also keep copies of his EC sales list, which is the list of all goods he has despatched to other EC member states (see earlier chapter).

The tax invoices that a trader issues for goods despatched to other EC member states should to be amended to show the customer's VAT registration number. The trader's own VAT registration number on the invoice should be prefixed with the letters 'GB'.

7.6 VAT CONTROL ACCOUNT

The VAT control account is a summary of the totals of output tax and input tax for the tax period. At the end of the tax period the balance on the account will represent the amount due to Customs and Excise (if it is a credit balance), or the amount repayable by Customs and Excise (if it is a debit balance).

The entries in the VAT control account for a tax period will be:

(a)   Credits:

*   output tax charged on sales, less VAT on credit notes issued to customers

*   VAT on acquisitions from other EU member states

*   any under-statement of output tax on previous VAT returns or any over-statement of input tax

*   any other adjustments.

(b)   Debits:

*   input tax charged on purchases less VAT on credits received from suppliers

*   input tax on acquisitions from other EU member states

*   any under-statements of output tax on previous VAT returns or any under-statement of input tax

*   bad debt relief (described later)

*   any other adjustments.

The VAT control account may be kept independently, or it may form part of the trader's accounting system.

7.7   OTHER ENTRIES IN THE VAT CONTROL ACCOUNT

1   Errors on previous VAT returns

A trader may discover that he has made errors on his VAT return in an earlier tax period, either by understating or by overstating his input or output tax. These entries should be corrected through the VAT control account, and should be debited or credited to the account. An appropriate double entry should be made in another main ledger account (usually the sales account or purchases account).

2   Bad debt relief

If a trader claims bad debt relief, this will be shown as a debit in the VAT control account. (Bad debt relief is explained in a later chapter).

Example

During the three months to 30 June 20X4, Bangles Ltd had the following transactions involving VAT:

		£
Sales (all standard rated)		
April (VAT exclusive)		2,400
May "		2,280
June "		1,840
Purchases (all standard rated)		
April (VAT inclusive)		1,880
May "		1,645
June "		1,833

The accountant discovered that the input tax for March 20X4 had been understated by £58, and the output tax had been overstated by £44.

Bad debt relief of £75 was claimed.

Construct the VAT control account for the quarter to 30 June 20X4, showing the closing balance on the account.

Solution

In this example, input tax is calculated as (x 7/47) of the VAT-inclusive cost. Output tax is calculated as 17.5% of the VAT-exclusive value of sales.

VAT Control Account

	£		£
Purchases (input tax)		Sales (output tax)	
April	280	April	420
May	245	May	399
June	273	June	322
Under-stated input tax	58		
Over-stated output tax	44		
Bad debt relief	75		
Balance c/d	166		
	1,141		1,141
		Balance b/d	166

The VAT control account shows a credit balance of £166 at the end of the quarter to 30 June 20X4. Bangles Ltd must remit this amount to HM Customs and Excise with the VAT return for the quarter.

ACTIVITY 4

During the three months to 30 April 20X4, Gruff Hairdressing had the following transactions involving VAT:

	£
Sales (all standard-rated)	
February (VAT inclusive)	5,328.66
March "	7,021.50
April "	8,456.25
Purchases (all standard rated)	
February (VAT exclusive)	1,680.00
March "	1,734.40
April "	1,566.33

The accountant discovered that the output tax for January 20X4 had been understated by £16.50, and the input tax had also been understated by £23.00.

Bad debt relief of £17.50 was claimed.

Task

Construct the VAT control account for the quarter to 30 April 20X4, showing the closing balance on the account.

For a suggested answer, see the 'Answers' section at the end of the book.

8 ADMINISTRATION OF VAT: ENFORCEMENT

8.1 ADMINISTRATION

In the VAT system, businesses act as tax collectors for the government, and the administration of the VAT system is designed:

- to make it as simple as possible for businesses to calculate how much VAT they should pay
- to make the procedures for payment as free from error or delay as possible
- to enforce the procedures, to make sure that businesses do what they are required to.

The system for collecting VAT payments from businesses (and making VAT repayments to some businesses) is mainly the responsibility of VAT Central Units.

VAT-registered businesses are required to submit a VAT return, usually every three months, giving details of their output and input tax for the tax period. A payment should accompany the VAT return.

VAT returns can be submitted either on a paper form or electronically through the Customs and Excise web site. Most businesses still use paper forms. A form is sent out to each business by Customs and Excise for each tax period, containing some pre-printed information:

- The tax period (for example, 'for the period 30 04 04 to 30 06 04')
- The name and address of the VAT-registered trader
- The VAT registration number of the trader
- The due date for payment, which is usually one month after the end of the tax period. For example, if a tax period ends on 28 February 2004, the VAT return and payment of tax must be submitted by 31 March 2004. A trader submitting a return and payment after the due date could be liable to a fine (a 'financial penalty').

Another box is also pre-printed, showing the tax period in coded form. The code consists of the digits 01, 02, 03 or 04, depending on whether it is the trader's first, second, third or fourth tax return for the calendar year, followed by two digits for the year. For example, tax period 03 04 would be the trader's third VAT return in 2004.

VAT returns are described in the next chapter. At this stage however, you should understand that VAT forms are issued for individual tax periods and individual VAT-registered traders. There are no blank VAT return forms. Traders receive forms with the pre-printed information and are required to enter information for the tax period, which will show how much VAT is payable (or refundable).

If a business needs help or guidance, it can go to the Customs and Excise web site, or contact the National Advice Service by telephone, or write to the local VAT Office. However, the administration of VAT is intended to operate smoothly and extensive guidance is available in the form of Notices to assist businesses with carrying out the procedures and keeping the records correctly.

8.2 ENFORCEMENT

Customs and Excise need to make sure that businesses are collecting and accounting for VAT properly, and to enforce the VAT rules and procedures. The main method of checking and enforcement is to carry out control visits to traders to inspect their VAT records. Control visits are carried out by local VAT Offices.

8.3 WHY AND WHEN CONTROL VISITS ARE MADE

Control visits are made by a VAT officer to ensure that the full amount of VAT due is correctly recorded by the trader, and accounted for to Customs and Excise. The trader's VAT records will also be examined to ensure that full and accurate records are kept.

Customs and Excise describe their control visits in Notice 700 (The VAT Guide) as follows: 'The officer will examine your business records, methods and premises and give you guidance. The reason for this is to ensure that the correct tax is accounted for at the right time. We want you to pay no more and no less than is due.'

Visits are usually arranged by appointment, although Customs and Excise occasionally makes unexpected visits without an appointment (which it has the right to do).

The first control visit will normally be made within three years of registration. This is to put right any teething problems as soon as possible.

The **frequency of subsequent visits** will depend on the nature and complexity of the business. Other points will trigger more frequent visits:

(a)   If a trader consistently submits his VAT returns late

(b)   If a trader does not submit a VAT return, a visit will be arranged even if he pays all the tax demanded by Customs and Excise when it issues an assessment.

(c)   If the VAT return is submitted on time, but is inconsistent with previous returns submitted.

8.4 THE CONTROL VISIT

The VAT officer (Customs and Excise official) has the power to enter the trader's premises for the purposes of a control visit at any reasonable time, but will normally prefer to arrange the time of the visit either by letter or phone. It will be during working hours, and will usually be at the trader's main place of business.

For a small business, a visit might last a few hours. For a larger business, the visit could last two or more days.

The VAT officer will wish to speak to the trader, or person dealing with the VAT, to understand the nature of the business, and will then wish to examine the records. At that stage the trader can arrange for a member of his staff to look after the VAT officer, and answer queries.

The trader may arrange for his accountant to be present if he wishes, but this is not compulsory.

Examining the records

The VAT officer will wish to examine all relevant records. This will include not only tax invoices, summaries of inputs and outputs, and the VAT account in the main ledger, but also bank statements, accounts and relevant business correspondence.

It is an offence not to make the records available to the VAT officer.

The VAT officer has the power to remove documents to examine them at the VAT office. If so, he must, if asked by the trader, provide copies of the documents removed to the trader.

Queries and errors

Most of the queries raised by the VAT officer will be dealt with at the time of the visit. Some of the more complicated ones may need to be dealt with after the visit.

If errors are found, the VAT officer will discuss it with the trader so that they will not happen again. If as a result of any error, the trader owes some VAT, a notice of assessment will be sent to the trader after the visit. Payments of interest and/or penalties might also be due. If VAT has been overpaid, it will either be repaid, or set against the VAT due on the next return.

Errors discovered by the trader should be notified to Customs and Excise immediately, rather than waiting for a control visit, because penalties and/or interest payments might be charged.

It should not be assumed that a control visit guarantees that everything is in order. The VAT officer does have time to carry out a complete audit of the trader's records.

Complaints

If a trader is dissatisfied with any actions or decisions by Customs and Excise during a control visit, he should complain and try to resolve the issue on the spot during the visit itself. However, if this is not possible, complaints can be referred to a Regional Complaint Unit.

If a trader is dissatisfied with a decision by the Regional complaints Unit, it can ask an Adjudicator to look into the case. The Adjudicator is an independent referee.

CONCLUSION

In this chapter you have learned:

- the details that have to be shown on a VAT invoice or credit note

- how a VAT period is decided

- the form of records to be kept and for what length of time

- the administration system for VAT and the system of enforcement through control visits.

You should now know enough about VAT to understand how to fill in a VAT return. This is described in the next chapter.

SELF TEST QUESTIONS

		Paragraph
1	What is a VAT invoice used for?	1.2
2	What information is shown on a VAT invoice?	1.3
3	When is a detailed tax invoice not required?	3
4	What are the VAT rules about cash discount?	4
5	When would a proforma invoice be issued?	5
6	What is a tax period?	6
7	How long must VAT records be kept for?	7
8	Why and when are control visits made?	8.3

KEY TERMS

Cash discounts (settlement discounts) - discounts offered to a customer who pays early, instead of taking the usual credit period before paying.

Bulk discounts - discounts given to regular customers.

Tax period or (prescribed accounting period) - the period for which the trader must prepare his VAT return.

VAT control account - a summary of the totals of output tax and input tax for the tax period.

Bad debt - a debt which is considered to be uncollectable.

Chapter 13

COMPLETING THE VAT RETURN

The purpose of this chapter is to explain how a VAT return is completed. However, bad debt relief and the cash accounting and annual accounting schemes are explained in the next chapter.

CONTENTS

1   The VAT Return

2   The boxes on the form

3   Making a mistake and correcting it

4   Completing the form

5   Submitting the return to Customs and Excise

6   Correcting errors on earlier returns

PERFORMANCE CRITERIA

		Reference
1	Complete and submit VAT returns correctly, using data from the appropriate recording systems, within the statutory time limits	Item A in element 7.3
2	Correctly identify and calculate relevant inputs and outputs	Item B in element 7.3
3	Ensure submissions are made in accordance with current legislation	Item C in element 7.3

LEARNING OUTCOMES

At the end of this chapter, you should be able to:

*   be able to complete a VAT return

*   explain when a VAT return must be submitted

*   identify and calculate relevant inputs and outputs for completing a VAT return

*   submit VAT returns in accordance with current legislation.

1 THE VAT RETURN

Under the normal VAT rules, a business must submit a VAT return every three months. The return can be submitted either electronically (via the internet and the Customs and Excise web site) or on paper. The main focus of this chapter is on how to fill in the paper VAT return.

As explained in the previous chapter, the VAT Central Unit sends out a VAT return to each VAT-registered trader. A VAT return contains, as pre-printed information, the three-month period covered by the return, the name and address of the business and its VAT registration number

- When a VAT return is in paper form, it must be filled in and submitted to the VAT Central Unit, to arrive at the latest by a the due date shown on the form. The return should be accompanies by the amount of tax payable for the period. The form must be accompanied by a payment by cheque or crossed postal order.

- When a VAT return is in electronic form, it must be submitted at the latest by the due date shown on the electronic return form. Payment of the tax must be made into the bank account of Customs and Excise by the same due date. An electronic method of payment should be used (BACS, CHAPS or Bank Giro transfer).

1.1 PRESCRIBED ACCOUNTING PERIOD

The VAT return form, VAT 100, is issued by the VAT Central Unit shortly before the end of the tax period for which it is due. The front of the form shows the period it covers, the prescribed accounting period.

If the trader considers that the form should cover a period other than the prescribed accounting period recorded on the form, he should write to the local VAT office requesting it to be changed.

An example of a VAT return form is shown overleaf.

1.2   THE FORM VAT 100 – THE VAT RETURN

Value Added Tax Return

For the period

HM Customs
and Excise

01 02 04   **to**   30 04 04

For Official Use

ZORRO LIMITED

MASK HOUSE

23 FARADAY STREET

LONDON   EC2 6YH

Registration Number	Period
123 4567 89	02 04

**You could be liable to a financial penalty
if your completed return and all the VAT payable
are not received by the due date.**

Due date: 31 05 04

For official use

Fold │ Here

Before you fill in this form please read the notes on the back and the VAT leaflet *"Filling in your VAT return"*. Fill in all boxes clearly in ink, and write 'none' where necessary. Don't put a dash or leave any box blank. If there are no pence write '**00**' in the pence columns. Do not enter more than one amount in any box.

For official use		£	p
VAT due in this period on **sales** and other outputs	**1**		
VAT due in this period on **acquisitions** from other **EC Member States**	**2**		
Total VAT due (the sum of 1 and 2)	**3**		
VAT reclaimed in this period on **purchases** and other inputs (including acquisitions from the EC)	**4**		
Net VAT to be paid to Customs or reclaimed by you **(Difference between boxes 3 and 4)**	**5**		
Total value of **sales** and all other outputs excluding any VAT. **Including your box 8 figure**	**6**		00
Total value of **purchases** and all other inputs excluding any VAT. **Including your box 9 figure**	**7**		00
Total value of all **supplies** of goods and related services, excluding any VAT, to other **EC Member States**	**8**		00
Total value of all **acquisitions** of goods and related services, excluding any VAT, from other **EC Member States**	**9**		00

If you are enclosing a payment please tick the box.	DECLARATION: You, or someone on your behalf, must sign below.

I, ...declare that the

(Full name of signatory in BLOCK LETTERS)

information given above is true and complete.

Signature .... Date ....

A false declaration can result in prosecution.

VAT 100 (Full)   IB (October 2000)

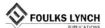

1.3 INFORMATION REQUIRED

The VAT return requires the trader to complete details of output tax and input tax.

The net output tax due to HM Customs and Excise, or the net input tax repayable, is calculated and entered on the form.

The return also requires details of outputs and inputs, including sales to and purchases from other EC member states.

If there are no details to enter in any particular box on the form, the box should not be left blank. Instead the word 'NONE' should be entered. For example, if there is no VAT due in the period from purchases and other inputs from other EC member states, NONE should be entered in box 2.

1.4 RETURNING THE FORM

The form must be completed and returned to the VAT Central Unit within one month of the end of the prescribed accounting period. The due date is shown on the form.

2 THE BOXES ON THE FORM

You need to be able to fill in a VAT return form, and so you have to understand what figures go into each box. To complete the form, there are just nine boxes to fill in, together with a declaration and a tick box to indicate whether a tax payment is accompanying the return.

Each box is explained below.

2.1 BOX 1: VAT DUE ON SALES AND OTHER OUTPUTS

This box is for entering the output VAT on sales and other outputs for the tax period.

However, there are some adjustments that you might have to make.

(a)   If there have been some credit notes issued to customers in the period for sales returns, the VAT on the sales returns should be deducted.

(b)   Output VAT should be charged on disposal sales of fixed assets, such as office furniture, machinery and equipment and vans or trucks.

(c)   There are also some detailed rules about when to charge VAT. For example, VAT should be charged when the business makes a gift of goods costing more than £50, and VAT should also be charged on goods taken out of the business for personal use by the business owner. In each case, VAT should be charged at the appropriate rate on the market value of the item or items. The output VAT on these items should also be included in the box 1 total.

(d)   Occasionally, an error might be discovered in a previous VAT return. Errors are explained in more detail below. However, if the error is for £2,000 or less and as a result, more tax should be paid to Customs and Excise, the extra amount payable to correct the error should be added to the box 1 total.

2.2 BOX 2: VAT ON ACQUISITIONS FROM OTHER EC MEMBER STATES

This box is for entering the total VAT due on all acquisitions of **goods** from other EC member states in the period. The supplier from the other EC member state charges VAT at a zero rate, but the UK business must then account for VAT at the appropriate UK rate to Customs and Excise.

For example, suppose that a UK business has imported goods from Germany with a sterling value of £1,000. The VAT on the invoice from the supplier will be 0%. However, if the goods are standard-rated in the UK, the business account to Customs and Excise for £175 as VAT payable. This £175 would be included in the box 2 total.

However, the business will also be able to reclaim this VAT payable as input tax, so it will also be included in the box 4 total.

If there is no VAT due on acquisitions, the word NONE should be written in box 2 (paper form).

2.3 BOX 3: TOTAL VAT DUE

The amount to be entered in box 3 is the total of the figures entered in boxes 1 and 2. It is the trader's total output tax for the tax period.

2.4 BOX 4: VAT RECLAIMED ON PURCHASES AND OTHER INPUTS

The entry for box 4 is the total input tax that the trader can deduct for the tax period.

This box is for entering the input VAT on purchases and other inputs for the tax period.

However, there are some adjustments that you might have to make.

(a)　The total must include any VAT paid by the business to Customs and Excise on imports from outside the UK. VAT is payable on imports to clear them through Customs.

(b)　The total must also include VAT on acquisitions from other EC member states (as explained above).

(c)　If some credit notes have been received in the period for purchases returns, the VAT on the purchases returns should be deducted from the total.

(d)　The total input VAT should exclude amounts that the business has been charged by suppliers, but which cannot be claimed back from Customs and Excise, under the VAT rules. Non-reclaimable VAT includes the VAT on business entertainment expenses and cars.

(e)　Occasionally, an error might be discovered in a previous VAT return. Errors are explained in more detail below. However, if the error is for £2,000 or less and as a result, more less tax should be paid to Customs and Excise, the reduction in the amount payable to correct the error should be added to the box 4 total.

(f)　If bad debt relief is claimed, the amount of the relief claimed should also be included in this box 4 total. Bad debt relief is explained in the next chapter.

2.5 BOX 5: NET VAT TO BE PAID TO CUSTOMS AND EXCISE

The figure to be entered in box 5 is the difference between the output tax in box 3 and the input tax in box 4.

If box 3 is greater than box 4, a payment of VAT should be sent with the form. The box for this purpose to the left of the declaration must be ticked.

If box 4 is greater than box 3, a repayment of VAT is due. This will be made shortly after the return is received by the VAT Central Unit. The figure in box 5 should be written in brackets, to indicate that the box 4 total exceeds the box 3 total and that VAT is being reclaimed.

2.6   BOX 6: TOTAL VALUE EXCLUDING VAT OF SALES AND OTHER OUTPUTS

The figure to be entered in box 6 is the total VAT exclusive amount of the trader's outputs for the period.

The total should include:

(a)   the VAT-exclusive amount of standard-rated supplies

(b)   supplies of goods and services to registered traders in other EC member states

(c)   zero-rated supplies, including exports

(d)   exempt supplies.

The figures should be entered after deducting credits for sales returns, but before deduction of any cash discounts/settlement discounts.

2.7   BOX 7: VALUE EXCLUDING VAT OF PURCHASES AND OTHER INPUTS

The figure to be entered in box 7 is the total VAT-exclusive amount of the trader's inputs.

The total should include:

(a)   purchases made by the business within the UK and expenses incurred within the UK

(b)   acquisitions from other EC member states

(c)   imports.

The figures should be entered after deducting credits for purchase returns, but before deducting any cash discounts/settlement discounts.

Some expenses should be excluded from the total for box 7. These items to exclude include:

*   wages and salary payments

*   payments of other taxation: specifically, PAYE income tax and National Insurance contributions, MOT certificate costs, costs of motor vehicle licence duty and local authority rates

*   drawings from the business by its owner.

2.8   BOX 8: TOTAL VALUE EXCLUDING VAT OF SUPPLIES TO OTHER EC MEMBER STATES

This box must be completed if goods or services are supplied to another EC member state. (This includes goods despatched to an EC member state, even if the invoice goes to a person outside the EC.)

The amount of the supply **excluding VAT** must be entered.

The figure entered in box 8 should also be included within the total figure entered in box 6.

If there have been no supplies to other EC member states, the word 'NONE' should be entered in the box (for a paper VAT return).

2.9 BOX 9: TOTAL VALUE EXCLUDING VAT OF ACQUISITIONS FROM OTHER EC MEMBER STATES

This box must be completed if goods have been acquired from another EC member state. This applies even if there has been no purchase of the goods, or if the invoice is rendered to a person outside the EC.

The amount of the acquisitions **excluding VAT** must be entered.

The figure entered in box 9 should also be included within the total figure entered in box 7.

If there have been no acquisitions (imports) from other EC member states, the word 'NONE' should be entered in the box (for a paper VAT return).

2.10 RETAIL SCHEMES

There are some special retail schemes available to retail traders. If a retailer uses one of these schemes there are special rules for filling in the VAT return.

2.11 DECLARATION

The form must be signed and dated by the trader, or by a company official or one of the partners. The declaration is that the information given on the form is true and complete.

3 MAKING A MISTAKE AND CORRECTING IT

A trader should try to avoid making a mistake, but mistakes can happen. The most significant mistakes are when the amount of output tax for the period or the amount of input tax is calculated or stated incorrectly. For example, a VAT invoice show the wrong amount of VAT, or a credit note might exclude the VAT.

3.1 CORRECTING ERRORS BEFORE A VAT RETURN

When an error is found before the VAT return is made, it is sufficient to correct the error.

If an error is discovered on a tax sales invoice, the trader should adjust for it:

(a)   If the VAT charged is too high, the trader should either:

    (i)   account in the VAT return for the full amount of tax shown on the invoice, or

    (ii)   issue a credit note to the customer and account for the correct amount of VAT.

(b)   If the VAT charged is too low, the trader should either:

    (i)   account for the correct amount of tax, which should be 7/47 of the total invoice amount, or

    (ii)   issue an additional invoice to the customer and account for the correct amount of tax.

For example, suppose that an invoice is issued to a customer for a standard-rated item but the amount charged on the invoice is £1,000 plus £150 VAT. The total invoice is for £1,150. If the business does not want to issue a new invoice to the customer to demand the extra £25 of VAT, it can account for VAT on the total invoice of £1,150 on the next VAT return (and adjust the accounting records accordingly). The correct VAT in this example would be £171.27 (£1,150 $\times$ 7/47).

3.2   CORRECTING ERRORS IN A PREVIOUS VAT RETURN

An error on a VAT return might not be identified until after the return has been submitted. If so, the error must be corrected in one of the following ways.

- If the error is for £2,000 or less, the error can be corrected by including an adjustment in the next VAT return.

- If the error is for more than £2,000, the error should not be corrected by including it on the next VAT return. Instead, the trader should inform its local Business Advice Centre (Customs and Excise VAT office) by letter or on a standard form.

When an error for £2,000 or less is corrected:

- If the adjustment is for an amount of money is payable to Customs and Excise, it should be included in the total amount in box 1 or (in the case of acquisitions from another EC member state) box 2.

- If the adjustment is for an amount repayable from Customs and Excise (input VAT), it should be included in box 4.

In other words, the figures for boxes 1 or 2 will be increased if VAT has been understated in a previous return and the figure in box 4 will be increased if VAT has been overstated in a previous return.

There might be several errors to correct. For example, the output tax and the input tax might both have been over-stated on the previous VAT return. The errors should then be calculated as a **net amount**. If the net amount is payable to Customs and Excise, it should be included in box 1. If the net amount is repayable by Customs and Excise it should be entered in box 4.

4   COMPLETING THE FORM

4.1   COMPLETING THE FORM FROM THE BOOKS OF PRIME ENTRY

The VAT control account provides a record of the VAT on transactions in the period, as well as the correction of previous errors and bad debt relief claimed. This account could therefore be used to prepare a VAT return, with the accounting records in the books of prime entry and the VAT invoices and other documents providing supporting evidence.

However, you should also be able to prepare a VAT return from information taken from the books of prime entry.

- The figures in the books of prime entry form the basis of the entries in boxes 1, 4, 6 and 7 of the VAT return

- If the business makes acquisitions from, or sales to, other EC member states, the details must be extracted from the records of those transactions to complete boxes 2, 8 and 9.

Completing box 3 and box 5 is a question of simple arithmetic.

Example

The books of prime entry for Zenith for the quarter to 31 March 20X4 give the following totals.

Sales day book

Total	VAT	Sales
£	£	£
24,675	3,675	21,000

Sales returns day book

Total	VAT	Sales returns
£	£	£
1,175	175	1,000

Purchases day book

Total	VAT	Purchases	Expenses
£	£	£	£
21,000	2,950	15,000	3,050

Cash receipts book

Total	VAT	Sales	Debtors	Discounts allowed
£	£	£	£	£
24,580	350	2,000	22,230	300

Cash payments book

Total	VAT	Purchases	Creditors	Expenses	Discounts received
£	£	£	£	£	£
20,320	525	3,525	14,660	1,610	200

Zenith Ltd has no trade with other EC member countries.

Show the amounts that would appear in boxes 1 to 9 of Zenith Ltd's VAT return for the quarter to 31 March 20X4.

Solution

Workings:

Output tax = 3,675 + 350 – 175 = 3,850

Input tax = 2,950 + 525 = 3,475

Value of sales excluding VAT = 21,000 – 1,000 + 2,000 = 22,000

Value of purchases excluding VAT = 15,000 + 3,050 +3,525 + 1,610 = 23,185

Value Added Tax Return

		For Official Use

For the period

HM Customs and Excise   01 01 04 **to** 31 03 04

Registration Number	Period
345 6789 01	01 04

ZENITH LTD

HYTE HOUSE

PARK SQUARE

BIRMINGHAM   B3 5MF

You could be liable to a financial penalty if your completed return and all the VAT payable are not received by the due date.

Due date: 30 04 04

Fold | Here

	For official use

Before you fill in this form please read the notes on the back and the VAT leaflet *"Filling in your VAT return"*. Fill in all boxes clearly in ink, and write 'none' where necessary. Don't put a dash or leave any box blank. If there are no pence write '**00**' in the pence columns. Do not enter more than one amount in any box.

For official use			£	p
	VAT due in this period on **sales** and other outputs	**1**	3,850	00
	VAT due in this period on **acquisitions** from other **EC Member States**	**2**	NONE	
	Total VAT due (the sum of 1 and 2)	**3**	3,850	00
	VAT reclaimed in this period on **purchases** and other inputs (including acquisitions from the EC)	**4**	3,475	00
	Net VAT to be paid to Customs or reclaimed by you **(Difference between boxes 3 and 4)**	**5**	375	00
	Total value of **sales** and all other outputs excluding any VAT. **Including your box 8 figure**	**6**	22,000	**00**
	Total value of **purchases** and all other inputs excluding any VAT. **Including your box 9 figure**	**7**	23,185	**00**
	Total value of all **supplies** of goods and related services, excluding any VAT, to other **EC Member States**	**8**	NONE	**00**
	Total value of all **acquisitions** of goods and related services, excluding any VAT, from other **EC Member States**	**9**	NONE	**00**

If you are enclosing a payment please tick the box.	DECLARATION: You, or someone on your behalf, must sign below.
	I,...declare that the
	(Full name of signatory in BLOCK LETTERS)
	information given above is true and complete.
	Signature .... Date ....
	A false declaration can result in prosecution.

VAT 100 (Full)   IB (October 2000)

 **FOULKS LYNCH** PUBLICATIONS

4.2 COMPLETING THE FORM FROM GIVEN SALES AND PURCHASE INVOICES

If the sales and purchase day books have not been written up, but the underlying sales and purchase invoices are available, the VAT return should be prepared in stages.

(a)   List:

- the sales invoices and

- the purchase invoices

showing in each list the VAT and the VAT exclusive amounts. (The sales invoices summary should show separate totals of exempt inputs to comply with the VAT record keeping requirements).

If there are credit notes for either sales returns or purchases returns, these should be listed too.

(b)   Extract:

- the outputs (sales less returns)

- the output tax

- the inputs (purchases and expenses less returns) and

- the input tax from the summaries.

(c)   Enter the figures on the form.

If any of the transactions included acquisitions from or sales to other EC member states, the analyses should disclose these details so that the appropriate figures can be transferred on to the return form.

ACTIVITY 1

The books of prime entry for ZAX for the quarter to 30 November 20X3 give the following totals.

Sales day book

Total	VAT	Sales
£	£	£
63,802	9,502	54,300

Sales returns day book

Total	VAT	Sales returns
£	£	£
2,585	385	2,200

Purchases day book

Total	VAT	Purchases	Expenses
£	£	£	£
26,314	3,786	17,400	5,128

Purchases returns day book

Total	VAT	Purchases returns
£	£	£
1,022	152	870

Cash receipts book

Total	VAT	Sales	Debtors	Discounts allowed
£	£	£	£	£
66,774	245	1,400	65,129	200

Cash payments book

Total	VAT	Purchases	Creditors	Expenses	Discounts received
£	£	£	£	£	£
23,874	1,172	3,525	15,933	3,244	100

ZAX has no trade with other EC member countries.

An error has been discovered in the VAT return for the three months to 31 August 20X3. Input tax on this form was overstated by £107.

Show the amounts that would appear in boxes 1 to 9 of ZAX's VAT return for the quarter to 30 November 20X3.

For a suggested answer, see the 'Answers' section at the end of the book.

5 SUBMITTING THE RETURN TO CUSTOMS AND EXCISE

The VAT return must normally be submitted to the VAT Central Unit within one month of the end of the return period. The due date is shown on the return.

A trader can choose to submit VAT returns electronically. Information about doing this is on the Customs and Excise web site, www.hmce.gov.uk.

(If the trader has applied for annual accounting, two months are allowed from the end of the year within which to submit the return. The annual accounting scheme is explained in the next chapter.)

5.1 WHAT IF THE TRADER HAS A PROBLEM?

If the trader does not receive his form or spoils it, he may obtain a replacement form from his local VAT office.

If he is unable to complete his form because not all the information is available before the due date, the trader should contact his local VAT office. He might be allowed to use estimated figures.

5.2 PAYING THE VAT

Normally the VAT is paid by enclosing a cheque with the VAT return form, payable to HM Customs and Excise, but it is also possible to pay by credit transfer or electronically electronic payment is a requirement when the VAT return is submitted in electronic form.

5.3 REPAYMENTS OF VAT

If a VAT repayment is due, the VAT return should be sent to the VAT Central Unit in the normal way. The repayment due will normally be processed within two or three weeks. It will usually be credited to the trader's bank account.

5.4 PENALTIES FOR LATE SUBMISSION OF RETURNS

A default occurs if a return is not submitted on time or a payment is made late. On the first default, Customs and Excise serve a surcharge liability notice on the VAT trader. The notice specifies a one year surcharge period.

If a trader defaults again during the surcharge period, there are two consequences:

(a)   the surcharge period is extended, and

(b)   the VAT trader is subject to a surcharge penalty.

To escape a surcharge liability notice, the trader must submit four consecutive quarterly returns on time accompanied by the full amounts of VAT due.

6   CORRECTING ERRORS ON EARLIER RETURNS

If HM Customs and Excise discover that a trader has made errors on his VAT return, they may impose a serious misdeclaration penalty. To avoid this, the trader should make **voluntary disclosure** of any errors that he discovers.

It is important to disclose errors as soon as they are discovered, and certainly before HM Customs and Excise make enquiries into a trader's affairs.

*   Where a trader discovers that he has made net errors (VAT payable less VAT deductible) of less than £2,000, he is not required to notify them to HM Customs and Excise. Instead, he can simply correct them on the next VAT return.

*   Where the trader discovers net errors in excess of £2,000 he must notify them to the local VAT office separately, either by letter, or on form VAT 652. If an additional amount of VAT is due, payment should be enclosed with the letter.

CONCLUSION

This chapter has explained the rules for filling in a VAT return when the normal method of accounting for VAT is used.

The next chapter explains refunds for bad debts and also alternative schemes of accounting for VAT, the cash accounting scheme and the annual accounting scheme.

These all have implications for filling in a VAT return.

SELF TEST QUESTIONS

Paragraph

1	What is a VAT prescribed accounting period?	1.1
2	By what date must the VAT return be submitted?	5.1
3	What is a default by a trader?	5.4
4	If a trader discovers an error on a VAT invoice, what action should be taken?	6

FOULKS LYNCH
PUBLICATIONS

Chapter 14

BAD DEBT RELIEF, CASH ACCOUNTING AND ANNUAL ACCOUNTING

The purpose of this chapter is to explain three special schemes for VAT: the bad debt relief scheme, the cash accounting scheme and the annual accounting system

CONTENTS

KNOWLEDGE AND UNDERSTANDING

		Reference
1	Special schemes: annual accounting; cash accounting; bad debt relief	Item 7
2	The basis of the relationship between the organisation and the VAT Office	Item 19

PERFORMANCE CRITERIA

		Reference
1	Complete and submit VAT returns correctly, using data from the appropriate recording systems, within the statutory time limits	Item A in element 7.3
2	Correctly identify and calculate relevant inputs and outputs	Item B in element 7.3
3	Ensure submissions are made in accordance with current legislation	Item C in element 7.3

LEARNING OUTCOMES

At the end of this chapter, you should be able to:

- describe the system for bad debt relief with VAT

- complete a VAT return where bad debt relief is claimed

- explain the cash accounting scheme and how it differs from the normal scheme of accounting to Customs and Excise for VAT

- explain the annual accounting system for VAT

1 BAD DEBT RELIEF

When a trader supplies goods or services on credit but is not paid by the customer, he might be able to claim bad debt relief.

- When the invoice is sent to the customer, the VAT on the invoice is treated as output VAT for the tax period.

- If the customer fails to pay, the trader will have paid output VAT to Customs and Excise, but will not receive payment of the VAT from the customer .

- The supplier cannot simply issue a credit note in an attempt to reclaim the VAT, since a credit note can only be issued for a genuine commercial reason (such as the goods being faulty or returned).

- The trader might therefore be able to claim back the VAT on the bad debt. This will be in a later tax period, after it is recognised that the debt will not be paid. Customs and Excise imposes a condition about the timing of a bad debt relief claim (see below).

Bad debt relief is available if certain conditions are met.

1.1 CONDITIONS FOR BAD DEBT RELIEF

Bad debt relief will be given by Customs and Excise only if the following conditions are satisfied:

(a) The trader must already have accounted for the output VAT to Customs and Excise on an earlier VAT return.

(b) The debt must have been written off as bad in the trader's accounting system, with a transfer of the debt to the bad debt account in the main ledger.

(c) The value of the item sold must not be more than its usual selling price.

(d) The debt must have remained unpaid for at least six months after either the date the payment was due or the date of the supply - whichever is the *later* date.

If only part of the debt has been written off, for example where a payment on account was received, then bad debt relief is available only on the VAT for the part of the debt written off.

1.2 HOW IS RELIEF GIVEN?

Where bad debt relief is claimed, it is simply included as input tax on the VAT return form. In other words, the bad debt relief is included in the total for box 4 of the return.

There is no need to advise HM Customs and Excise separately.

1.3 KEEPING RECORDS

Records must be kept to provide evidence supporting bad debt relief claims. Customs and Excise can then check the claims during their next control visit. The records to be kept are:

* A copy of the VAT invoice or invoices for which a bad debt refund is being claimed.

* A bad debt account (in the accounting system) which must show:

    – the total amount written off as a bad debt

    – the total amount of VAT charged on the sale (remember, only a part of the debt might be written off, if some has been paid already)

    – the payment received on the debt (if any)

    – the amount of VAT being claimed as bad debt relief

    – the date of the invoice to which the bad debt relates

    – the VAT period in which the output tax was originally accounted for

    – the VAT period in which the refund is claimed

    – the name of the customer.

Example

B Harris is a trader registered for VAT. In May 2003, he issued the following invoices:

(a) An invoice for £2,000 plus VAT of £350 to A Allen, payable on 30 June

(b) An invoice for £5,000 plus VAT of £875 to B Brown, also payable on 30 June.

A Allen paid nothing, and B Brown paid £1,500 on 30 June as a part-payment.

By the end of 2003, six months after the payments were due, neither customer has paid anything further. On 2 January 2004, B Harris decides to write off the outstanding debts as bad, and prepares the bad debt account records in accordance with Customs and Excise requirements.

He also decides to claim bad debt relief on his next VAT return.

(a) The amount that can be claimed on the A Allen debt is the full amount of VAT, £350.

(b) B Brown paid £1,500, leaving £4,375 (£5,875 - £1,500) still unpaid. In this example, it should be assumed that the £1,500 paid by B Brown includes some VAT. The VAT in the amount paid is £223.40 (£1,500 × 7/47). The VAT in the outstanding debt is £651.59 (£4,375 × 7/47). The bad debt relief that can be claimed is therefore £651.59.

(c) The total bad debt relief that can be claimed is £350 + £651.59 = £1,001.59.

(d) This amount should be included in the total for VAT reclaimed in box 4 of the VAT return.

ACTIVITY 1

The books of prime entry for Sam Costain for the quarter to 30 November 2003 give the following totals.

Sales day book

Total	VAT	Sales
£	£	£
102,460	15,260	87,200

Sales returns day book

Total	VAT	Sales returns
£	£	£
2,585	385	3,150

Purchases day book

Total	VAT	Purchases	Expenses
£	£	£	£
37,134	5,530	25,104	6,500

Purchases returns day book

Total	VAT	Purchases returns
£	£	£
1,175	175	1,000

Cash receipts book

Total	VAT	Sales	Debtors
£	£	£	£
87,073	736	4,210	82,127

Cash payments book

Total	VAT	Purchases	Creditors	Expenses
£	£	£	£	£
35,619	997	4,000	28,922	1,700

Sam Costain has no trade with other EC member countries.

An error has been discovered in the VAT return for the three months to 31 August 2003. Output tax on this form was understated by £35.

Sam Costain would also like to claim bad debt relief. There are three debts he is writing off as bad in his accounts.

(a)   A debt of £440 plus VAT of £77. This was dated 23 April 2003 and payment was due on 30 April.

(b)   A debt of £320 plus VAT of £56. This was dated 1 March 2003 and payment was due on 31 March

(c)   A debt of £520 plus £91 VAT. This was dated 15 May 2003 and payment was due on 30 June.

FOULKS LYNCH
PUBLICATIONS

Task

Show the amounts that would appear in boxes 1 to 9 of ZAX's VAT return for the quarter to 30 November 2003.

For a suggested answer, see the 'Answers' section at the end of the book.

2 CASH ACCOUNTING

Under cash accounting the trader accounts for VAT on the basis of the **cash payments made and received** in the tax period, rather than on the basis of the tax invoices issued and received.

In other words, output tax is not shown on the VAT return until the payment is received from the customer, which is later than the date of the invoice. On the other hand, input tax cannot be reclaimed until the supplier has been paid, which is later than the date the purchase invoice is received.

The VAT due for each tax period under the cash accounting scheme is:

(a)   the output tax on all amounts of cash received from sales in the tax period, less

(b)   the input tax on all cash payments to suppliers in the same tax period.

2.1 WHAT ARE THE ADVANTAGES OF CASH ACCOUNTING?

Cash accounting for VAT will help the cash flow of a business if most of its sales are made on credit, since VAT is not paid to Customs and Excise until the cash is actually received for the sale.

The cash accounting scheme is therefore likely to benefit most businesses. It will not benefit businesses that make most of their sales for cash, or businesses that usually reclaim VAT from Customs and Excise because their sales are mainly of zero-rated items.

2.2 WHO MAY USE CASH ACCOUNTING?

A trader may join the cash accounting scheme if the following conditions are met.

(a)   He is registered for VAT.

(b)   He does not expect the value of his taxable supplies (standard-rate, lower-rate and zero-rate sales, but excluding exempt supplies) to exceed £600,000 in the next 12 months. (This total should exclude any expected sale of capital assets of the business.)

(c)   His VAT affairs are in order and up to date. For example, all VAT returns due up to date have been sent in to Customs and Excise when the trader starts to use the cash accounting scheme.

2.3 THE RULES OF THE CASH ACCOUNTING SCHEME

The cash accounting scheme cannot be applied retrospectively.

If the trader operates the cash accounting scheme, bad debt relief will not be available. customs and Excise makes this point as follows: 'One advantage of the cash accounting scheme is that you do not have to account for VAT on bad debts.'

The reason for this is that the VAT is only accounted for when payment is received from the customer, so the trader will not have accounted for the VAT on the debt to Customs and Excise in the first place. Since the VAT on the sale has never been paid, it cannot be claimed back!

The cash accounting scheme is not available for acquisitions (imports) from other EC member states. The normal rules for accounting for VAT should apply to acquisitions.

When must the trader account for VAT on sales?

Method of receiving payment	*The date you receive payment, for cash accounting purposes*
Notes and coins (cash)	The date the money is received
Cheque	Either the date on the cheque or the date you receive the cheque, whichever is the **later.** (If the cheque is subsequently dishonoured, there is no need to account for the VAT.)
Giro transfer, direct debit, standing order	The date the bank account is credited with the payment.
Credit card or debit card	The date the card voucher is made out.

When can a trader reclaim VAT on purchases and expenses?

Method payment	*The date you make the payment, for cash accounting purposes*
Notes and coins (cash)	The date the money is paid
Cheque	Either the date on the cheque or the date you send the cheque, whichever is the **later.**
Giro transfer, direct debit, standing order	The date the bank account is debited with the payment.
Credit card or debit card	The date the card voucher is made out.

3 ANNUAL ACCOUNTING SCHEME

Most businesses complete and submit four VAT returns every year. The annual accounting scheme allows the trader to submit just one VAT return every year, two months after the end of the year. (The 12 month period selected will usually coincide with the trader's accounting year.)

Traders who have an annual taxable turnover of less than £600,000, and have been registered for VAT for at least a year, can apply to use the annual accounting scheme and have an annual tax period. The calculation of estimated turnover should include standard-rate, reduced-rate and zero-rated items.

A business that registers for VAT for the first time can apply to use the annual accounting scheme only if its annual turnover of taxable supplies is expected to be less than £150,000.

Instead of making quarterly payments of VAT, the trader makes nine payments on account ('interim instalments') are made. These are based on the trader's total VAT liability to Customs and Excise for the year. The nine instalments are paid at the end of months 4-12 inclusive during the year.

- If the trader has been registered for more than 12 months before joining the annual accounting scheme, the nine interim payments are each 10% of the previous year's VAT liability.

- If the trader has been registered for less than 12 months, each instalment is 10% of the trader's estimated total VAT liability for the year.

A final payment will be made on submission of the return, within two months of the year end.

The potential advantages of the annual accounting scheme are that:

- only one VAT return has to be filled in each year, not four

- a business can plan its VAT payments with more certainty, as regular monthly payments over nine months and a balancing payment of VAT two months later (two months after the end of the 12 month period)

- the trader has an extra month after the end of the year to complete and send in the VAT return and make the balancing payment.

Example

Graham Cowan has been a VAT-registered trader for over two years. He has just arranged to join the annual accounting scheme for VAT, because his annual turnover is about £400,000 each year. The annual period will begin on 1st April. Last year, his VAT liability in the year to 31 March was £56,000.

If the annual accounting scheme starts on 1 April Year 1, he will make nine interim payments of £5,600 at the end of months 4 – 12 (end of July Year 1 to end February Year 2 inclusive). The final balancing payment will be made two months after the year end, at the end May/beginning June Year 2. This balancing payment will accompany his annual VAT return.

ACTIVITY 2

Caroline Redding started in business some years ago, and has now become registered for VAT. She expects her turnover of taxable supplies to be £110,000 in the next twelve months from 1 September, when she will have been registered for six months. She expects her VAT liability for the 12 months to be £14,900. She would like to join the annual accounting scheme for VAT from this date.

Task

What payments of VAT will she be required to make under the scheme, and when will the payments be made?

For a suggested answer, see the 'Answers' section at the end of the book.

3.1 DETAILS OF THE ANNUAL ACCOUNTING SCHEME

There are a number of details about the annual accounting scheme for VAT that it might be helpful to know.

Cash accounting scheme and the annual accounting scheme

A business can use both the cash accounting scheme and the annual accounting scheme at the same time, provided that it meets the conditions for each scheme.

Does the first period have to be 12 months long?

A business can arrange for the year in its VAT annual accounting scheme to coincide with its financial year. (This is often convenient, so that the business can do all its accounting and tax 'paper work' at the same time.) If it wants to join the scheme this at a time other than the end of its financial year, the first period in the scheme need not be exactly 12 months. It can be made longer or shorter than 12 months, so that the first period ends on the same date as the financial year end of the business.

For example, suppose that a business wants to join the annual accounting scheme from 1 August, but would also like its VAT annual accounting year to coincide with its financial year, which ends on 31 December. To arrange this, the first period in the annual accounting scheme will run from 1 August to 31 December. After that the VAT annual accounting year and the financial year of the business will coincide.

If the first period in the annual accounting scheme is for less than five months, the business will not be required to make any interim VAT payments for the first period.

What happens if the annual VAT liability works out much higher or lower than expected?

A problem with the annual accounting scheme is that the interim payments are based on what the annual VAT liability is expected to be. This expectation could turn out wrong, and the actual VAT liability could be much high or much lower. This could affect cash planning by the business. For example, suppose that a business in the VAT annual accounting scheme expects its VAT liability to be £30,000, and so it agrees with Customs and Excise to make nine interim payments of £3,000. However, suppose the business grows much faster than expected, and that as a result its VAT liability for the year will be £60,000. If the business makes nine interim payments of £3,000 or £27,000 in total, it will face a balancing payment of £33,000 after the end of the year. It might struggle to find this amount of cash.

When the expected VAT liability looks like being much higher or lower than expected, the business is encouraged to contact its local VAT Office for advice. If appropriate, the amount of each monthly instalment will be adjusted.

How do you apply to join the annual accounting scheme?

A business should apply to join the annual accounting scheme by filling in an application form available from Customs and Excise, most easily from its web site. The business is required to state the month when it wants its annual return to finish, so if it wants the annual period to end on 30 June and start on 1 July, it must state JUNE on the application form.

If the application is approved, Customs and Excise will write to the business to let it know, and will state the amount of the interim payments. The business will be required to make the payments by an electronic method, not by cheque, and so Customs and Excise will confirm chosen method (and provide a bank mandate for the business to fill in and send to its bank, if the chosen method of payment is direct debit or standing order).

3.2 FILLING IN AN ANNUAL VAT RETURN

Under the annual accounting scheme, the same rules apply to filling in the VAT return as for quarterly returns, except that the period covered is one year, not one quarter.

The figures entered on the form, for example for output VAT and input VAT, should be the figures for the year as a whole. The interim payments that have been made already should not be deducted on the form itself.

The business should send the balancing payment together with the annual return. The balancing payment should be the total VAT liability for the year as a whole, less the interim payments already made. If a refund is due from Customs and Excise, no balancing payment is required. however, the annual return must still be submitted within two months of the year end.

ACTIVITY 3

FRW Traders is registered for VAT, and is in the annual accounting scheme and the cash accounting scheme. Its year end is 31 December.

Relevant data for the year ended 31 December 20X3 is as follows:

Cash receipts	Receipts net of VAT	VAT	Total cash receipts
	£	£	£
	500,460.00	87,580.50	588,040.50

Cash payments	Payments net of VAT	VAT	Total cash payments for VAT
	£	£	£
Salaries			224,809.76
Other payments	174,005.25	30,450.91	204,456.16

Bad debt relief is to be claimed on a debt written off at the end of March. the debt was for 3200 plus VAT of £35.

An adjustment is to be made for an overstatement of input VAT in the previous annual return. This amounts to £45.50.

The business has made nine interim payments of £5,400 each.

The business had no acquisitions from other member states of the EC.

Tasks

1   Specify what figures should go into each of the nine boxes, 1 to 9, on the VAT return.

2   By what date must the annual VAT return be submitted, and what is the amount of the payment to accompany the return?

Value Added Tax Return

For the period

HM Customs
and Excise

01 01 X3 **to** 31 12 X3

FRW TRADERS

12 HIGH STREET

KENSINGTON

LONDON   W8 8XX

For Official Use

Registration Number	Period
312 7564 97	

**You could be liable to a financial penalty
if your completed return and all the VAT payable
are not received by the due date.**

Due date: ?????

For official use	

Fold Here

Before you fill in this form please read the notes on the back and the VAT leaflet *"Filling in your VAT return"*. Fill in all boxes clearly in ink, and write 'none' where necessary. Don't put a dash or leave any box blank. If there are no pence write '**00**' in the pence columns. Do not enter more than one amount in any box.

For official use			£	p
	VAT due in this period on **sales** and other outputs	**1**		
	VAT due in this period on **acquisitions** from other **EC Member States**	**2**		
	Total VAT due (the sum of 1 and 2)	**3**		
	VAT reclaimed in this period on **purchases** and other inputs (including acquisitions from the EC)	**4**		
	Net VAT to be paid to Customs or reclaimed by you **(Difference between boxes 3 and 4)**	**5**		
	Total value of **sales** and all other outputs excluding any VAT. **Including your box 8 figure**	**6**		00
	Total value of **purchases** and all other inputs excluding any VAT. **Including your box 9 figure**	**7**		00
	Total value of all **supplies** of goods and related services, excluding any VAT, to other **EC Member States**	**8**		00
	Total value of all **acquisitions** of goods and related services, excluding any VAT, from other **EC Member States**	**9**		00

If you are enclosing a payment please tick the box.	DECLARATION: You, or someone on your behalf, must sign below.

I,..declare that the

(Full name of signatory in BLOCK LETTERS)

information given above is true and complete.

Signature .... Date ....

A false declaration can result in prosecution.

VAT 100 (Full)   IB (October 2000)

246

4 FURTHER POINTS TO NOTE ABOUT VAT AND VAT RETURNS

VAT is quite a complex tax, and whenever an individual is uncertain about the rules and what to do in practice, he or she should ask Customs and Excise.

The administration of the tax has now been described in as much detail as you should require, but one or two closing points might be worth noting.

- You have been shown how to complete a VAT return on paper. Customs and Excise encourages businesses to submit their returns in electronic form. This can be arranged through the Customs and Excise web site.

- A business cannot claim back all the input VAT that it incurs. The ability to claim back input VAT is restricted or prohibited for certain kinds of expenditure. These include input VAT on the purchase cost of motor cars for use in the business (although VAT on vans and trucks can be reclaimed) and VAT on business entertainment expenses for clients. As a result of the detailed rules on VAT, the calculation of the input VAT figure to go into box 4 on the VAT return can be rather complicated.

CONCLUSION

This chapter has explained bad debt relief for VAT and the cash accounting scheme and the annual accounting scheme. This brings us to the end of the study materials for Preparing Reports and Returns.

SELF TEST QUESTIONS

		Paragraph
1	What is bad debt relief?	1
2	What are the conditions for bad debt relief?	1.1
3	How is relief given?	1.2
4	What is the VAT due for each tax period under the cash accounting scheme?	2
5	What is allowed by the annual accounting scheme?	3
6	State the details of annual accounting scheme.	3.1

KEY TERMS

Bad debt relief - when a trader supplies goods or services on credit but is not paid by the customer, he might be able to claim bad debt relief.

Cash payments made and received - under cash accounting the trader accounts for VAT on the basis of the cash payments made and received in the tax period, rather than on the basis of the tax invoices issued and received.

Annual accounting scheme - allows the trader to submit just one VAT return every year, two months after the end of the year.

FOULKS LYNCH
PUBLICATIONS

ANSWERS TO ACTIVITIES

CHAPTER 1

ACTIVITY 1

		20X4 £		20X3 £
External sales				
X	(1/3 of 300)	200,000	(1/4 of 320)	80,000
Y	(1/4 of 560)	140,000	(20% of 500)	100,000
Z		800,000		780,000
Total		1,140,000		960,000
Costs (excluding transfers)				
X		275,000		280,000
Y	(490 – 2/3 of 300)	290,000	(470 – ¾ of 320)	230,000
Z	(750 – ¾ of 560)	430,000	(738 – 80% of 500)	338,000
Total		995,000		848,000
Profit		145,000		112,000

Tutorial note. The revenue for the company as a whole excludes the transfer value of the units transferred internally. This value is excluded from both the sales figure and the costs figure for the company as a whole.

Total profit has increased by £33,000 (£145,000 - £112,000). This represents an increase above the 20X3 profit figure of [33,000/112,000] × 100% = 29.46%.

Total revenue from external sales has increased by £180,000 (£1,140,000 - £960,000). This represents an increase above the 20X3 revenue figure of [180,000/960,000] × 100% = 18.75%.

CHAPTER 2

ACTIVITY 1

	Widgets £	Fidgets £
Direct material costs	24,510	31,402
Direct labour costs	32,791	18,934
Overhead costs	47,567	27,454
Total cost	104,868	77,790
Units produced	12,450	31,550
Average cost per unit	£8.42	£2.47

ACTIVITY 2

Model	Quantity bought	Price per unit	Quantity x Price £
QS102	34	£9.50	323.00
QS105	24	£12.70	304.80
QS110	15	£16.90	253.50
QS114	<u>11</u>	£21.00	<u>231.00</u>
	<u>84</u>		<u>1,112.30</u>

$$\text{Average} = \frac{£1,112.30}{84} = £13.24$$

ACTIVITY 3

Here we calculate a moving total of sales over a 12-month period. The first moving total is for sales for quarters 1 to 4 in year 1. The mid point is half way between quarter 2 and quarter 3, but in the table below, the moving total and moving average are shown against quarter 3.

The moving average of sales per quarter is the annual moving total divided by 4.

Quarter	Sales	Moving annual total	Moving quarterly average (Total/4)
	£000	£000	£000
Year 1			
Quarter 1	435		
Quarter 2	427		
Quarter 3	449	1,763	441
Quarter 4	452	1,783	446
Year 2			
Quarter 1	455	1,802	451
Quarter 2	446	1,803	451
Quarter 3	450	1,810	453
Quarter 4	459	1,819	455
Year 3			
Quarter 1	464	1,843	461
Quarter 2	470	1,856	464
Quarter 3	463	1,875	469
Quarter 4	478		

The trend in the quarterly moving average is upwards.

ACTIVITY 4

(a) Increase in price = £225 – £206 = £19.

Increase as a percentage of last year's price = $\dfrac{£19}{£206} \times 100$

= 9.2%.

(b) Increase claimed = $£240 \times \dfrac{5}{100}$

= £12 per week.

ACTIVITY 5

Total of ratio numbers = 2 + 4 + 9 + 5

= 20

North = $£400,000 \times \dfrac{2}{20}$

= £40,000

South = $£400,000 \times \dfrac{4}{20}$

= £80,000

East = $£400,000 \times \dfrac{9}{20}$

= £180,000

West = $£400,000 \times \dfrac{5}{20}$

= £100,000

ACTIVITY 6

(a) Export sales = 82,000

Domestic (UK) sales = 574,000 – 82,000

= 492,000

Ratio = 82,000 : 574,000 or 82 : 574.

Dividing 492,000 by 82,000 gives a whole number answer, 6. This means that the ratio can be simplified still further, to 1 : 6

(b) Percentage of sales that were export sales = $\dfrac{82,000}{574,000} \times 100\%$

= 14.3%

(c) Proportion of sales that were export sales = $\dfrac{82,000}{574,000}$

$$= \frac{82}{574} \text{ or } = \frac{41}{287} \text{ or}$$

$$= \quad ^1/_7 \text{ or } 0.143.$$

ACTIVITY 7

The columns could be for the regions and the rows for the types of worker, or the columns could be for the type of worker and the rows for the regions. In the answer shown here, the columns are used for the regions.

Be careful when you fill in the figures in the table, to make sure you put the right figures in each box.

Cater Professional Services Staff numbers				
	North Region	Central Region	South Region	Total
Accountants	16	15	18	49
Solicitors	12	6	11	29
IT specialists	8	20	15	43
Support staff	14	19	17	50
Total	50	60	61	171

ACTIVITY 8

In this situation the key fact is that figures to be highlighted are the percentages of total turnover for each division that each category of sales makes up. Therefore the optimal layout would be to show the sales for each division and the percentages as the columns and the categories of sales as the rows.

Again if you are not convinced by this choice of layout then try it the other way around and you will see that it is not so informative.

Reptar Ltd - Division sales turnover by category for 20X2

	North		East		South		West		Total	
	£000	%	£000	%	£000	%	£000	%	£000	%
Security systems	200	55.9	140	46.4	269	59.1	200	68.5	809	57.5
Contract main'ce	110	30.7	130	43.0	165	36.3	80	27.4	485	34.5
General electrical	48	13.4	32	10.6	21	4.6	12	4.1	113	8.0
	358	100.0	302	100.0	455	100.0	292	100.0	1,407	100.0

ACTIVITY 9

In this solution, the goods in transit have to be included in closing stock. They are missing from the closing stock of both Division X and division Y, so remember to add £500 to the closing stock total value.

FOULKS LYNCH
PUBLICATIONS

Check your calculations of percentages carefully. Take the difference between the two years, and calculate this as a percentage of the figure for 20X2.

Trading, profit and loss account
for the year ended 31 December

	20X3	20X2	% change
	£	£	
Sales	273,450	268,700	+ 1.8%
Opening stock	11,850	22,450	- 47.2%
Purchases	158,400	157,300	+ 0.7%
	170,250	179,750	
Closing stock	(12,250)	(11,850)	+ 3.4%
Cost of sales	158,000	167,900	- 5.9%
Gross profit	115,450	100,800	+ 14.5%
Other expenses	103,250	92,100	+ 12.1%
Net profit	12,200	8,700	+ 40.2

ACTIVITY 10

Frequency distribution – new clients won by sales representatives.

Number of clients	Number of times
0	I
1	III
2	III
3	II
4	IIII
5	HHI II
6	III
7	II
8	HHI

The table to record the frequency distribution can now be prepared as follows:

Frequency distribution –new clients won by sales representatives

New clients	Number of times
0	1
1	3
2	3
3	2
4	4

FOULKS LYNCH
PUBLICATIONS

5	7
6	3
7	2
8	<u>5</u>
	<u>30</u>

ACTIVITY 11

Step 1   Find the highest and lowest figures from the data.

Highest 639

Lowest 551

Step 2   Determine the range of values between the highest and lowest.

Range = 639 – 551 = 88

Step 3   Decide on the class intervals to be used. Here, bands or class intervals of 10 are used.

550 - 559

560 - 569

570 - 579

580 - 589

590 - 599

600 - 609

610 - 619

620 - 639

In order to cover the one result that is above 630 the final class interval has been made twice the size of the other class intervals.

Step 4   Work through the raw data inserting a tally mark in each class interval whenever a score falls within the class interval.

550 - 559	II
560 - 569	III
570 - 579	H̶H̶
580 - 589	H̶H̶
590 - 599	II
600 - 609	II
610 - 619	III
620 - 639	III

FOULKS LYNCH
PUBLICATIONS

Step 5 Total the tally marks in order to find the class or group frequencies.

Daily output   Number of times

Daily output	Number of times
550 - 559	2
560 - 569	3
570 - 579	5
580 - 589	5
590 - 599	2
600 - 609	2
610 - 619	3
620 - 639	3

CHAPTER 3

ACTIVITY 1

Employee numbers 20X1 to 20X3

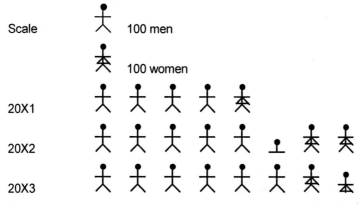

Scale — 100 men

100 women

20X1

20X2

20X3

Tutorial note: The main problem of pictograms is that it is difficult to present and interpret data accurately. For example in order to represent 550 men in 20X2, half a man has to be drawn. To represent 170 women in 20X3, we need to draw about 70% of the woman diagram to show the 70. This is both difficult to draw and to interpret. For example does the picture for the 20X3 number of women employees show 160, 170 or 180 or any other number in between?

It might make more sense to round the figures to the nearest 100, and use just complete diagrams.

ACTIVITY 2

The grand total is the amount of sales revenue, £420,000. The segment sizes are calculated as follows:

	£	Conversion factor	Segment size (degrees)
Production costs	160,000	(160,000/420,000) × 360	137
Administration costs	75,000	(76,000/420,000) × 360	65
Selling and distribution costs	104,000	(104,000/420,000) × 360	89

Research and development costs	63,000	(63,000/420,000) × 360	54
Profit	18,000	(17,000/420,000) × 360	15
	420,000		360

ACTIVITY 3

Step 1   Calculate the size of each segment in degrees.

Division	Profit		Degrees	Percentage of total profit
	£000			
A	240	$360 \times \dfrac{240}{1,400}$	61°	17%
B	380	$360 \times \dfrac{300}{1,400}$	97°	27%
C	140	$360 \times \dfrac{140}{1,400}$	36°	10%
D	170	$360 \times \dfrac{170}{1,400}$	43°	12%
E	290	$360 \times \dfrac{290}{1,400}$	76°	21%
F	180	$360 \times \dfrac{180}{1,400}$	47°	13%
Total	1,400		360°	100%

Step 2   Draw the pie chart.

Remember to give the pie chart a title, to label each segment clearly and to indicate the size of each segment. Here, the profit earned by each division is shown as a percentage of the total profit. However, you could also shown the actual profit figures for each division instead of percentage figures.

Pie chart to illustrate profitability of different divisions in 20X4

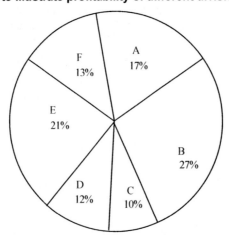

ACTIVITY 4

Akia Ltd – Sales 20X4 to 20X9

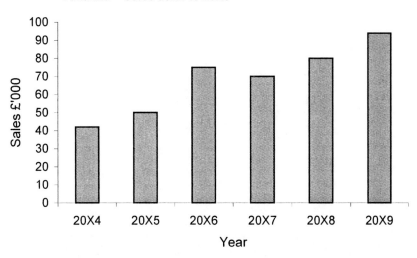

Tutorial note: From this bar chart it can be seen that the amount of sales has been increasing each year, with the exception of 20X7. If more detailed information were required then the actual amount of sales for each year could be read off from the chart.

ACTIVITY 5

Akia Ltd – sales 20X4 to 20X9

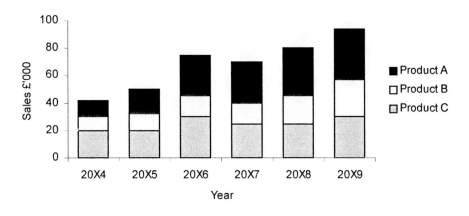

Tutorial note: In this solution the component elements of each bar are shown as product C at the bottom, product B above product C and product A above product B. The component elements could be shown in any order, for example with product A at the bottom and product C on top.

ACTIVITY 6

Step 1   Convert the absolute numbers into percentages of the total.

Year	Total sales	Product group						
		A			B		C	
	£000	£000	%		£000	%	£000	%
20X4	42	12	28		10	24	20	48
20X5	50	18	36		12	24	20	40
20X6	75	30	40		15	20	30	40
20X7	70	30	43		15	21	25	36
20X8	80	35	44		20	25	25	31
20X9	94	37	39		27	29	30	32

Step 2   Draw the percentage component bar chart with the scale on the vertical axis running from 0% to 100%. Here product C sales are shown at the bottom of the bar, product B in the middle and product A on top, but you could arrange them in a different order within the bars, for example with product A sales at the bottom and product C sales on top.

Akia Ltd sales – 20X4 to 20X9

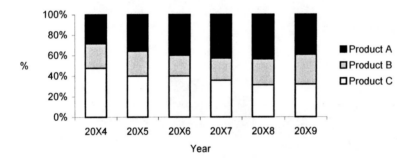

ACTIVITY 7

For each year, there should be one bar for each product. The maximum annual sales of any individual product in any year is £37,000 (product A sales in 20X9) so the vertical scale is taken up to 40,000 in the chart shown overleaf.

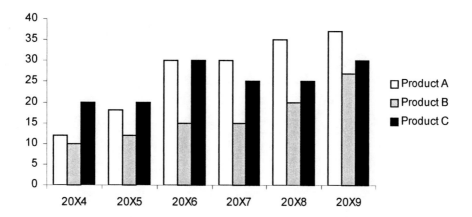

The chart shows the annual sales for each product. It is clear from the chart that:

- Sales of product A and product B have been growing fairly steadily over the period, whereas sales of product C have not increased since 20X6.

- Whereas the top-selling product in 20X4 was product C, it has been product A since 20X7.

ACTIVITY 8

Step 1   Decide the standard class interval. In this case the standard class interval selected is the most common, which is 10 units.

Step 2   Prepare a table of the heights of the bars to be shown on the histogram, bearing in mind the class intervals.

Class	Range of class	Frequency	Height of bar
550 - 559	10	2	2
560 - 569	10	3	3
570 - 579	10	5	5
580 - 589	10	5	5
590 - 599	10	2	2
600 - 609	10	2	2
610 - 619	10	3	3
620 - 639	20	$3 \times \frac{1}{2}$	1.5

Step 3   Draw the histogram.

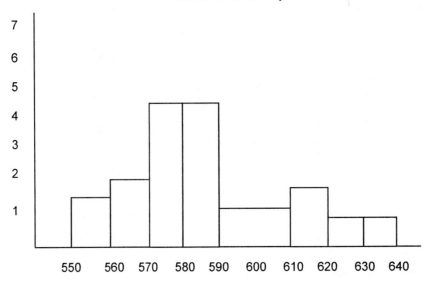

Record of units output

CHAPTER 4

ACTIVITY 1

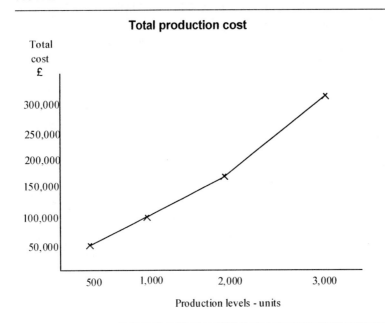

ACTIVITY 2

Year 20X4	Sales revenue
	£
January	18,400
February	17,200

March	24,900
April	35,200
May	38,800
June	24,700
July	19,600
August	17,100
September	29,500
October	35,500
November	39,400
December	21,000

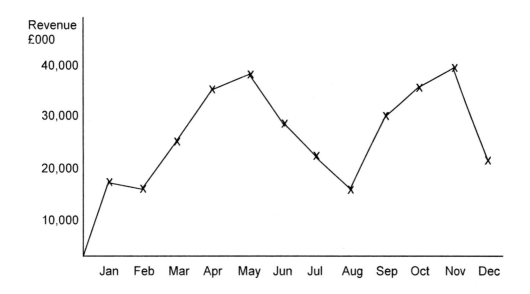

ACTIVITY 3

Week	Output in £000
1	120
2	100
3	150
4	200
5	140
6	190
7	150
8	210
9	200
10	160
11	170
12	200

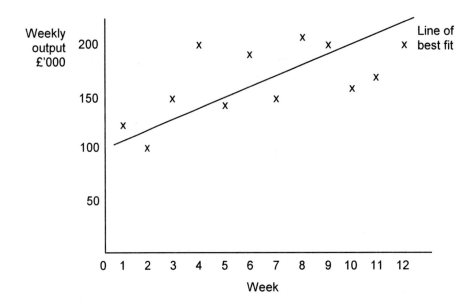

A line of best fit is drawn by eye. You should use your own judgement and common sense. There is no correct or incorrect line, because the judgement of different individuals will not be the same. However, make sure that the points n your scatter graph have been plotted correctly. as each individual will draw the line slightly differently.

ACTIVITY 4

Step 1   Calculate the cumulative frequency for each class.

Units of output	Frequency	Cumulative frequency
550 - 559	2	2
560 - 569	3	5
570 - 579	5	10
580 - 589	5	15
590 - 599	2	17
600 - 609	2	19
610 - 619	3	22
620 - 639	3	25

Step 2   Plot the cumulative frequencies on a graph using the upper class limit to plot each frequency.

Step 3   Join the points you have plotted to produce the cumulative frequency distribution.

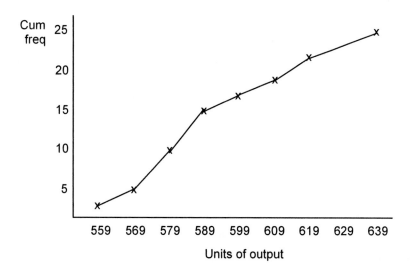

Output was less than 605 units on approximately 18 days out of the 25 day period.

50% of 25 days is say 12.5 days. The corresponding value on the ogive is about 584 or 585 units.

ACTIVITY 5

Step 1   Produce a table showing the monthly sales, cumulative monthly sales and moving annual sales.

Month (20X9)	Sales in month	Cumulative sales for the year		Sales for the previous 12 months (Moving annual total)
	£000		£000	£000
January	90		90 (note 1)	1,330
February	80	(80 + 90)	170 (note 1)	1,330
March	80	(80 + 170)	250 (note 1)	1,340
April	90	(90 + 250)	340 (note 1)	1,330
May	120	(120 + 340)	460 (note 1)	1,340
June	120	(120 + 460)	580 (note 1)	1,340
July	130	(130 + 580)	710 (note 1)	1,350
August	150	(150 +710)	860 (note 1)	1,360
September	140	(140+ 860)	1,000 (note 1)	1,350
October	120	(120 + 1,000)	1,120 (note 1)	1,340
November	120	(120 + 1,120)	1,240 (note 1)	1,340
December	90	(90 + 1,240)	1,330 (note 1)	1,330

Note 1: moving annual totals

Moving annual total of sales for January = Sales in Feb 20X8 to Jan 20X9 = (80 + 70 + 100 + 110 + 120 + 120 + 140 + 150 + 130 + 120 + 100 + 90) = 1,330.

February   =   1,330 - 80 + 80   =   1,330

March	=	1,330 - 70 + 80	=	1,340
April	=	1,340 - 100 + 90	=	1,330
May	=	1,330 - 110 + 120	=	1,340
June	=	1,340 - 120 + 120	=	1,340
July	=	1,340 - 120 + 130	=	1,350
August	=	1,350 - 140 + 150	=	1,360
September	=	1,360 - 150 + 140	=	1,350
October	=	1,350 - 130 + 120	=	1,340
November	=	1,340 - 120 + 120	=	1,340
December	=	1,340 - 100 + 90	=	1,330

Step 2   Decide the scales to be used on the graph. Here the y axis has to go up to at least 1,360 (£1,360,000).

Step 3   Plot the three sets of figures from the table on to the graph.

Step 4   Join each of the points for each of the graph lines to produce the Z chart.

George Ltd - monthly sales 20X9 - Z-chart

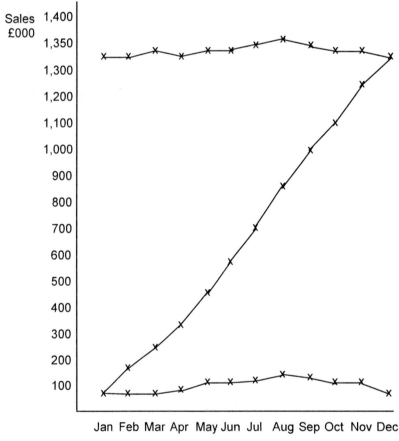

Interpretation

The graph of the monthly sales shows a clear trend of higher sales in the summer months reducing again as the winter approaches. This is also indicated by the increasing steepness of the cumulative total sales during the summer months.

The moving annual sales line is very similar throughout the year indicating little change over last year's performance. There is however some increase in the middle months of the year showing a performance that is better than last year at this time but then a decrease towards the end of the year indicating that this increased performance has not been kept up.

ACTIVITY 6

(a)   Produce a break even chart.

Step 1   Draw up a graph so that the scale of the y axis is big enough to include total revenue as well as total costs.

The x axis must run from 1,000 units to 10,000 units.

The maximum sales value on the y axis must be £250,000 (10,000 units × £25).

Step 2   Plot the total cost line on the graph.

When   x = 0, y = 50,000

When   x = 10,000, y = (£50,000 fixed costs plus

(£12.50 x 10,000) variable costs)

= 175,000

Step 3   Plot the total sales revenue line on the graph.

When   x = 0, y = 0

x   = 10,000, y = 250,000 (£25 x £10,000)

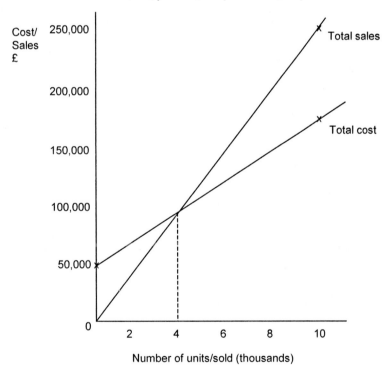

(b)

Step 4 Indicate the break even point as the point where the costs and sales lines intersect.

From the graph the break even point would appear to be 4,000 units.

This can be proved as follows:

	£
Sales (4,000 units × £25)	100,000
Costs (£50,000 + (£12.50 × 4,000 units))	100,000
	———
Profit	-
	———

This means that at any level of production and sales below 4,000 units a loss will be made on the product but that if production and sales rise above 4,000 units then the organisation will be in profit from splodgets.

ACTIVITY 7

Step 1 Set out the profits for each year. Calculate these from the information given in the narrative.

Year	Profit
	£
20X1	100,000
20X2	100,000
20X3 (100,000 × 1.1)	110,000
20X4 (110,000 × 1.15)	126,500
20X5 (126,500 × 1.2)	151,800
20X6 (151,800 × 0.75)	113,850
20X7 (113,850 - 4,600)	109,250
20X8 (109,250 - 3,800)	105,450

Step 2 Draw a graph to show these profits for the years from 20X1 to 20X8. It is a time series, so the years are shown on the x axis and the profits on the y axis.

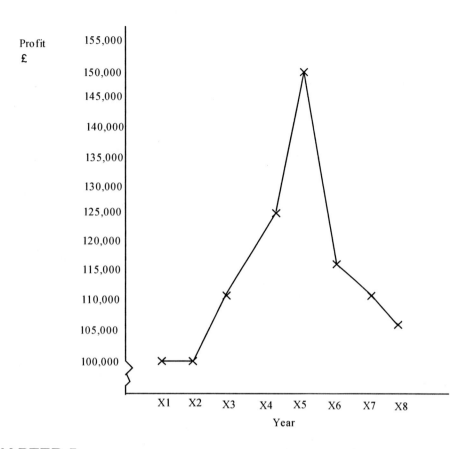

CHAPTER 5

ACTIVITY 1

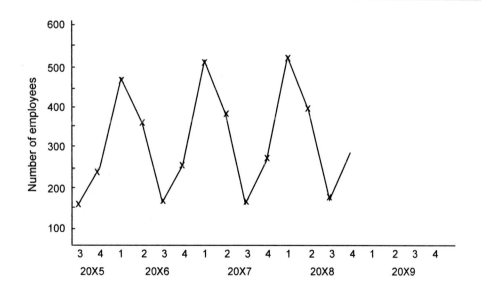

ACTIVITY 2

Month	Trend line sales	Seasonal variation Above (+) or below (-) trend	Forecast sales
	£	£	£
January	300,000	- 30,000	270,000
February	310,000	- 10,000	300,000
March	320,000	+ 5,000	325,000
April	330,000	+ 15,000	345,000
May	340,000	+ 35,000	375,000
June	350,000	0	350,000
July	360,000	- 8,000	352,000
August	370,000	- 12,000	358,000
September	380,000	- 5,000	375,000
October	390,000	+ 14,000	404,000
November	400,000	- 6,000	394,000
December	410,000	+ 2,000	412,000

ACTIVITY 3

Day	Temperature	3 day moving total	3 day moving average
Monday	68	-	-
Tuesday	74	212	71
Wednesday	70	215	72
Thursday	71	219	73
Friday	78	222	74
Saturday	73	231	77
Sunday	80	-	-

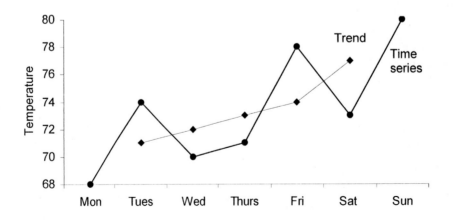

ACTIVITY 4

	Sales	Seven-day moving total	Seven-day moving average
Week 1	£	£	£
Sunday	250		
Monday	266		
Tuesday	248		
Wednesday	270	2,177	311
Thursday	290	2,189	313
Friday	364	2,216	317
Saturday	489	2,248	321
Week 2			
Sunday	262	2,318	331
Monday	293	2,398	343
Tuesday	280	2,412	345
Wednesday	340	2,425	346
Thursday	370		
Friday	378		
Saturday	502		

You might notice that the upward trend in the moving average has started to 'flatten out' over the most recent two days.

ACTIVITY 5

Quarter	Numbers	Four period moving total	Four period moving average	Trend
20X5 - Q3	92			
20X5 - Q4	195			
		1,044	261	
20X6 – Q1	433			262
		1,047	262	
20X6 – Q2	324			263
		1,054	264	
20X6 – Q3	95			271
		1,107	277	
20X6 – Q4	202			280
		1,130	283	
20X7 – Q1	486			283
		1,133	283	
20X7 – Q2	347			285
		1,149	287	
20X7 – Q3	98			289

		1,162	291	
20X7 – Q4	218			293
		1,175	294	
20X8 – Q1	499			295
		1,181	295	
20X8 – Q2	360			298
		1,199	300	
20X8 – Q3	104			
20X8 – Q4	236			

These trend figures can now be plotted on the time series graph.

Ski Fun Ltd – Quarterly chalet occupancy

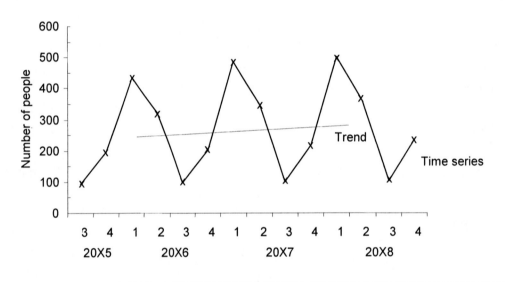

ACTIVITY 6

Week	Sales	5-week moving total	5-week moving average	Difference
	£	£	£	£
1	10,200			
2	11,300			
3	7,800	45,400	9,080	+ 1,280
4	6,200	47,500	9,500	+ 3,300
5	9,900	47,300	9,460	- 440
6	12,300	51,200	10,240	- 2,060
7	11,100	55,800	11,160	+ 60
8	11,700	57,900	11,580	- 120
9	10,800	59,100	11,820	+ 1,020
10	12,000	60,900	12,180	+ 180
11	13,500			
12	12,900			
				+ 3,220

The average weekly difference between the moving average and actual sales is +3,220/8 = + 403.

We might use these figures to assume that the weekly increase in the trend line will be about 403. If so, the estimates of future sales will be based on the week 10 trend value, as follows:

Week 13: 12,180 + (3 x 403) = 13,389

Week 14: 12,180 + (4 x 403) = 13,792.

ACTIVITY 7

		Seasonally-adjusted figures	Trend
Quarter 1	486 – 196	290	283
Quarter 2	347 – 62	285	285
Quarter 3	98 – (-181)	279	289
Quarter 4	218 – (-77)	295	293

The seasonally-adjusted figures for the year show that only quarter 2 and quarter 4 are approximately in line with the trend. Quarter 1 is significantly above the trend and quarter 3 significantly below it.

ACTIVITY 8

Step 1   Extend the trend line on the graph in order to estimate the future trend numbers.

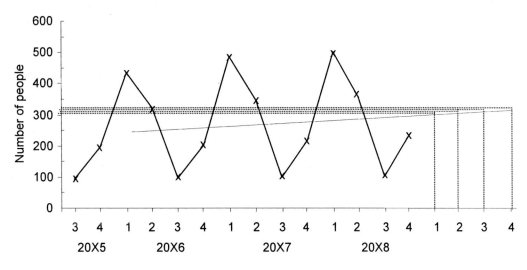

Reading off from the graph the appropriate figures for the trend for 20X9 are as follows:

	Number of people
Quarter 1	310
Quarter 2	315
Quarter 3	320
Quarter 4	325

Step 2   Adjust the appropriate trend figures for the seasonal variation.

Quarter 1   -   Trend 310, seasonal variation 196

        Forecast   310 + 196   =   506 people

Quarter 2   -   Trend 315, seasonal variation 62

        Forecast   315 + 62   =   377 people

Quarter 3   -   Trend 320, seasonal variation -181

        Forecast   320 + (-181)   =   139 people

Quarter 4   -   Trend 325, seasonal variation -77

        Forecast   325 + (-77)   =   248 people

CHAPTER 6

ACTIVITY 1

Year 1 costs: £460,000 (1.03) = £473,800

Year 2 costs: £460,000 (1.03)(1.04) = £492,752

Year 3 costs: £460,000 (1.07)(1.03)(1.04)(1.04) = £548,334

The year 3 estimate allows for the growth in the size of the work force as well as for the inflationary increase in salaries.

If the estimates are rounded to the nearest £1,000, they would be £474,000, £493,000 and £548,000.

ACTIVITY 2

The calculation of the index for each year is as follows:

20X2 $\dfrac{232}{200} \times 100$ = 116

20X3 $\dfrac{256}{200} \times 100$ = 128

20X4 $\dfrac{250}{200} \times 100$ = 125

20X5 $\dfrac{280}{200} \times 100$ = 140

The completed table will appear as follows:

Year	Selling price £	Index
20X1	200	100
20X2	232	116
20X3	256	128
20X4	250	125
20X5	280	140

ACTIVITY 3

Simple price index $\qquad = \dfrac{13.65}{12.50} \times 100$

$\qquad\qquad\qquad\qquad = 1.092 \times 100$

$\qquad\qquad\qquad\qquad = 109.2$

This means that the price has increased by 9.2% on its base year price of £12.50.

ACTIVITY 4

The increase in the index is (306 – 267) 39 index points.

The increase in the index is 39 points from its 20X5 level of 267. This can be calculated as a percentage as follows:

$\dfrac{39}{267} \times 100\% = 14.6\%$ (to one decimal place)

ACTIVITY 5

Reduction or deflation of sales figures

The sales figures for each year are deflated or reduced by dividing by the price index for the year being considered and multiplying by the index for the earliest year.

Year	Sales	Adjustment factor	Sales at 20X4 prices
20X4	£500,000	$\times \dfrac{131}{131}$	£500,000
20X5	£510,000	$\times \dfrac{131}{139}$	£480,647
20X6	£540,000	$\times \dfrac{131}{149}$	£474,765
20X7	£580,000	$\times \dfrac{131}{154}$	£493,377
20X8	£650,000	$\times \dfrac{131}{164}$	£519,207

Adjust all amounts to current year prices

Year	Sales	Adjustment factor	Sales at current (20X8) prices
20X4	£500,000	$\times \dfrac{164}{131}$	£625,954
20X5	£510,000	$\times \dfrac{164}{139}$	£601,727
20X6	£540,000	$\times \dfrac{164}{149}$	£594,362
20X7	£580,000	$\times \dfrac{164}{154}$	£617,662
20X8	£650,000	$\times \dfrac{164}{164}$	£650,000

Comparisons

Both sets of figures show that in real terms sales values decreased in 20X5 and 20X6 and increased again in 20X7 and 20X8. By 20X8, in real terms, sales were higher than in 20X4, by 3.8%.

(Workings: at 20X8 prices)

$$\frac{650,000 - 625,954}{581625,954} \times 100\% = 3.8\%$$

ACTIVITY 6

20X2 costs		Adjustment factor	Sales at current (20X5) prices
Fixed costs	£176,000	$\times \dfrac{687}{635}$	£190,413
Variable costs	£118,000	$\times \dfrac{687}{635}$	£127,663

Fixed costs should be the same regardless of the volume of activity, and the figures suggest that total fixed costs have risen by less than the general level of cost rises. The decrease is (£184,900 - £190,413) £5,513 at 20X3 prices, which represents a 'real' decrease of 2.9% (100% × 5,513/190,413).

Variable costs go up or down with the volume of activity, and in 20X3, sales were 206,000 units compared with 214,000 units in 20X2.

Taking 20X2 costs as a base point, we would expect total variable costs in 20X3 to be:

$$£127,668 \times \frac{206,000}{214,000} = £122,891$$

Actual variable costs were just £121,700 in 20X3, suggesting that control over variable costs has improved since 20X2.

Another way of making the analysis of variable costs is to say that at 20X3 price levels, the variable cost per unit was £0.60 in 20X2 (£127,663/214,000 units) but slightly less at £0.59 (£121,700/206,000 units) in 20X3.

CHAPTER 7

ACTIVITY 1

Production per labour hour:

January	$\dfrac{24,000 \text{ units}}{12,000 \text{ hours}}$	=	2 units per hour
February	$\dfrac{20,000 \text{ units}}{9,100 \text{ hours}}$	=	2.2 units per hour
March	$\dfrac{28,000 \text{ units}}{15,000 \text{ hours}}$	=	1.9 units per hour

In February the volume of production fell compared with January, but productivity increased. In March there was an increase in production volume, but productivity fell to only 1.9 units per hour, the worst level in the period.

ACTIVITY 2

Production per employee per month:

June $\dfrac{168{,}000 \text{ units}}{50 \text{ employees}}$ = 3,360 units per employee

July $\dfrac{180{,}000 \text{ units}}{54 \text{ employees}}$ = 3,333 units per employee

Production levels for July were higher than for June but **productivity was marginally lower** at 3,333 units per employee.

ACTIVITY 3

Chargeable hours per architect:

May $\dfrac{495 \text{ hours}}{3 \text{ architects}}$ = 165 hours per architect

June $\dfrac{340 \text{ hours}}{2 \text{ architects}}$ = 170 hours per architect

The productivity, or hours worked per architect, increased in June compared with May.

ACTIVITY 4

	Process 1		Process 2		Total
	Standard hours per unit	Standard hours produced	Standard hours per unit	Standard hours produced	Standard hours produced
6,200 widgets	0.75	4,650	0.25	1,550	6,200
5,500 grommits	0.50	2,750	1.25	6,875	9,625
		7,400		8,425	15,825

Efficiency ratio, Process 1 $= \dfrac{7{,}400}{7{,}500} \times 100\% = 98.7\%$

Efficiency ratio, Process 2 $= \dfrac{8{,}425}{8{,}100} \times 100\% = 104.0\%$

Efficiency ratio, overall $= \dfrac{15{,}825}{15{,}600} \times 100\% = 101.4\%$

ACTIVITY 5

Production per machine hour:

Week 27 $\dfrac{3{,}000 \text{ units}}{480 \text{ hours}}$ = 6.25 units per machine hour

Week 28 $\dfrac{2{,}800 \text{ units}}{440 \text{ hours}}$ = 6.36 units per machine hour

Productivity in week 28 is slightly better than in week 27.

ACTIVITY 6

Dustbins emptied per dustcart:

Week 31 $\dfrac{22,500 \text{ dustbins}}{45 \text{ dustcarts}}$ = 500 bins per cart

Week 32 $\dfrac{21,000 \text{ dustbins}}{40 \text{ dustcarts}}$ = 525 bins per cart

ACTIVITY 7

Capacity each week = 8 taxi cabs × 9 hours each day × 5 days each week = 360 hours.

Capacity utilisation was therefore:

$$\frac{211\,\text{hours}}{360\,\text{hours}} \times 100\% = 58.6$$

ACTIVITY 8

To calculate the production cost per unit, you need to adjust for the change in stock level during the month.

Product T costs: October

Units sold: 21,800

	Total costs		Cost per unit sold
	£	£	£
Opening stock	14,000		
Direct materials	57,100		
Direct labour	43,700		
Production overhead	68,900		
	183,700		
Less: Closing stock	(19,000)		
Production cost of sales		164,700	7.56
Administration overhead		31,500	1.44
Selling and distribution overhead		68,200	3.13
Total costs of sale		264,400	12.13

ACTIVITY 9

Month 6: unit costs

Quantity produced = 12,000 units

	Total cost	Cost per unit
	£	£
Direct costs:		
Direct materials	68,000	5.67
Direct labour	72,000	6.00
Direct expenses	15,000	1.25
Total direct cost	155,000	12.92
Production overhead	54,000	4.50
Total production costs	209,000	17.42

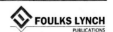

ACTIVITY 10

Standard direct cost per unit

	£
Direct materials 10kg × £4.50	45.00
Direct labour 3 hours × £5	15.00
Direct expenses	2.00
	62.00

Actual direct cost per unit

$$= \frac{\text{Actual total direct costs}}{\text{Number of units produced}}$$

$$= \frac{£1,200,000 + £480,000 + £80,000}{30,000 \text{ units}}$$

$$= \frac{£1,760,000}{30,000 \text{ units}}$$

$$= £58.67$$

The standard direct cost per unit was £62.00 and the actual direct cost per unit for March was £58.67.

ACTIVITY 11

The paper sent from Basildon to Walton is not shown as closing stock for either print shop, but should not be ignored.

The most logical way of dealing with it would be to account for it as if the transfer has been made, which means that the £2,500 of paper should be included in both:

- the closing stock of paper at Walton, and
- the cost of transfers received from Walton.

The closing stock at Walton is therefore increased from £3,400 to £5,900, and the transfers from Basildon are increased from £3,800 to £6,300.

It would be equally acceptable to add it to the closing stock of Basildon instead, but the transfers to Walton would also have to be reduced by £2,500.

	Basildon £	Walton £	Total £
Sales	68,100	95,000	163,100
Opening stock	3,800	4,100	7,900
Purchases of paper	21,000	17,500	38,500
Purchases of ink	2,600	3,900	6,500
Transfers	(6,300)	6,300	
Closing stock	(5,100)	(5,900)	(11,000)
Cost of goods sold	16,000	25,900	41,900

FOULKS LYNCH
PUBLICATIONS

Gross profit	52,100	69,100	121,200
Salaries	25,400	31,800	57,200
Building rental	1,700	1,900	3,600
Printing machine rental	3,300	3,700	7,000
Sundry expenses	18,500	26,600	45,100
Net profit	3,200	5,100	8,300

ACTIVITY 12

Gross profit margin

$$= \frac{\text{Gross profit}}{\text{Sales}} \times 100\%$$

$$= \frac{425}{2,000} \times 100\%$$

$$= 21.25\%$$

Net profit margin

$$= \frac{\text{Net profit}}{\text{Sales}} \times 100\%$$

$$= \frac{175}{2,000} \times 100\%$$

$$= 8.75\%$$

ACTIVITY 13

Cost of sales

$$= \frac{1,575}{2,000} \times 100$$

$$= 78.75\%$$

Total expenses

$$= \frac{250}{2,000} \times 100$$

$$= 12.5\%$$

Selling and distribution expenses

$$= \frac{110}{2,000} \times 100$$

$$= 5.5\%$$

Administrative expenses

$$= \frac{126}{2,000} \times 100$$

$$= 6.3\%$$

Finance expenses

$$= \frac{14}{2,000} \times 100$$

$$= 0.7\%$$

Profit and loss account

	£000	£000	%
Sales		2,000	100.00
Cost of sales		1,575	78.75
		——	
Gross profit		425	21.25
Less: Expenses			
Selling and distribution expenses	110		5.50
Administrative	126		6.30
Finance	14		0.70
	——	250	12.50
		——	
Net profit		175	8.75
		——	

ACTIVITY 14

Average stock level $\quad = \dfrac{3,600 + 4,100}{2}$

$\qquad\qquad\qquad\qquad = \text{£}3,850$

Stock turnover $\quad = \dfrac{\text{Cost of sales}}{\text{Average stock level during the period}}$

$\qquad\qquad\qquad = \dfrac{\text{£}43,500}{\text{£}3,850}$

$\qquad\qquad\qquad = 11.3 \text{ times per annum}$

Alternatively this could be shown as:

$\dfrac{\text{Average stock level during the period}}{\text{Cost of sales}} \times 365$

$= \dfrac{\text{£}3,850}{\text{£}43,500} \times 365$

$= 32.3 \text{ days}$

ACTIVITY 15

Debtors turnover $\quad = \dfrac{\text{Closing trade debtors}}{\text{Credit sales for the year}} \times 365$

$\qquad\qquad\qquad = \dfrac{\text{£}460,000}{\text{£}3,000,000} \times 365$

$\qquad\qquad\qquad = 56 \text{ days}$

ACTIVITY 16

Net asset turnover	=	$\dfrac{\text{Turnover or sales}}{\text{Net assets}}$
	=	$\dfrac{\text{£206,000}}{\text{£86,000}}$
	=	2.40 times

CHAPTER 9

ACTIVITY 1

Beta's sales must be eliminated from the consolidated results so that transactions are not counted twice. This is best done by using a table showing the results of the two divisions, an adjustment column and a total column.

Divisional results for Alpha and Beta for the year ending 31st August 20X2

	Alpha	Beta	Adjustments	AB Limited
	£	£	£	£
Sales	850,000	600,000	-500,000	950,000
Opening stock	200,000	140,000		340,000
Purchases	500,000	300,000	-500,000	300,000
Closing stock	220,000	150,000		370,000
Cost of sales	480,000	290,000		770,000
Gross profit	370,000	310,000		680,000
Production overheads		150,000		150,000
Distribution overheads	130,000	10,000		140,000
Administration	180,000	30,000		210,000
Total overheads	310,000	190,000		500,000
Net profit	60,000	120,000		180,000

The profit is unaffected by the adjustment, but notice that the overall size of the company was measured by sales, is smaller than it would appear if the adjustment was not made. (£950,000 compared with £1,450,000). This is one of the reasons why eliminating inter-company transfers is important.

CHAPTER 10

ACTIVITY 1

Workings

Gross profit margin =	$\dfrac{722,520}{1,158,630}$	x 100%	= 62.36%

Net profit margin = $\dfrac{87,450}{1,158,630}$ x 100% = 7.55%

Net profit before interest charges: This is the net profit but with interest charges added back. £87,450 + £25,800 = £113,250.

Return on capital employed = $\dfrac{113,250}{1,358,460}$ x 100% = 8.34%

The return can now be completed.

Midlands Microengineering Association (MMA)

Interfirm comparison

Company   Tractor Limited and its subsidiary

	£	% of sales	Industry average (to be filled in by the MMA)
Sales	1,158,630		
Gross profit	722,520	62.36	
Net profit	87,450	7.55	
Fixed assets	1,178,640		
Current assets	322,370		
Current liabilities	142,550		
Return on capital employed		8.34	

Guidance notes

1   Fixed assets should be stated at net book value.

2   Return on capital employed is net profit before interest charges, divided by the total of fixed assets (stated at net book value) and net current assets.

3   State all ratios and percentages to two decimal places

CHAPTER 11

ACTIVITY 1

1 Taxable at the standard rate

2 A taxable item, but zero-rated (food)

3 Exempt

4 Taxable at the standard rate

5 Not a business transaction, so outside the scope of VAT

6 A taxable item, but zero-rated (travel)

7 Taxable at the standard rate. This might surprise you, but membership fees for clubs are taxable supplies. Whenever an organisation is in doubt about whether an item is taxable or not, it should contact Customs and Excise (initially, by telephoning the National Advice Service) to find out.

ACTIVITY 2

1

	£
Net price	124.38
VAT at 5%	6.21
Total amount payable	130.59

2

	£
Net price	146.50
VAT at 17.5%	25.63
Total amount payable	172.13

3

VAT = £115.50 x 7/47 = £17.12. The price excluding VAT is therefore (£146.50 - £17.12) = £129.38.

You could use the fraction 17.5/117.5 instead of 7/47. They are the same value.

4

VAT = £850 x 7/47 = £126.59. The price excluding VAT is therefore (£850 - £126.59) = £723.41.

ACTIVITY 3

1 Total sales price, including VAT = £799.00.

VAT at standard rate = £799 x 7/47 = £119.00.

2 The VAT on the cases sold by Casemaker to BN Leather Goods was 17.5% x £300 = £52.50. The VAT on the leather sold by T Smith to Casemaker was 17.5% of £43 = £7.52.

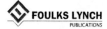

	T Smith	Casemaker	BN Leather	Total
	£	£	£	£
Output tax	7.52	52.50	119.00	
Input tax	0.00	7.52	52.50	
Net tax payable	7.52	44.98	66.50	119.00

3   As the table above shows, the total VAT payable to Customs and Excise is £119, which is the amount of tax paid by the consumer buying the cases from BN Leather Goods. However, the tax of £119 is collected at different stages of the supply chain, from T Smith, Casemaker Ltd and BN Leather Goods.

ACTIVITY 4

(a)   The export of wooden furniture to the United States of America is zero-rated.

(b)   VAT must be accounted for at the point of entry on the import of wood from Malaysia. The importer therefore pays VAT at the appropriate rate. The importer can also claim the VAT as input tax on its VAT return for the period.

(c)   Output tax on the acquisition of the cloth from Germany should be included on the VAT return as 'VAT due on acquisition of goods from another EC member state'. Input tax will also be claimed on the same VAT return.

ACTIVITY 5

There are two important points to note.

(a)   VAT on sales returns is deducted from the output tax for the period, and VAT on purchase returns is deducted from the input tax.

(b)   VAT on acquisitions from other EC Member States (in other words, VAT relating to imports from other EC countries) should be both added to the VAT payable and included in the input VAT reclaimable. Here, it is assumed that the same figure should be used in the totals for output and input VAT.

	£	£
Output VAT on sales		96,427.65
Less: VAT on sales returns		(2,625.00)
		93,802.65
VAT on acquisitions from other EC countries		3,605.28
Total output VAT due		97,407.93
Input VAT on purchases and expenses in the UK	18,295.03	
Less: VAT on purchase returns	(806.83)	
	17,488.20	
VAT on acquisitions from other EC countries	3,605.28	
Total input tax reclaimed		21,093.48
VAT payable to Customs and Excise		76,314.45

ACTIVITY 6

To: VAT Office

[Address]

Date

Dear Sirs

Request for guidance

I have recently been appointed to a position in my company giving me responsibility for VAT returns.

I should be grateful if you would send me information about the rules for claiming input VAT on the purchase costs and running costs of company cars, and on the costs of entertaining clients.

My company's VAT number is 430 9248 76.

Yours faithfully

[Name]

VAT accountant

CHAPTER 12

ACTIVITY 1

In each case, you have to start by identifying the tax point. This is either the basic tax point or the actual tax point, if an actual tax point is created.

(a)   The basic tax point is 11 May, but an actual tax point is created because payment is made before the basic tax point. The actual tax point is the date of payment, 1 May 2004. The invoice must therefore be issued within 30 days of this date, by 31 May 2004.

(b)   The basic tax point is the time of supply, 11 May 2004. An actual tax point is not created by the payment, because payment occurs after the basic tax point. The invoice must be issued within 30 days of the basic tax point, date by 10 June 2004. (Note May 11 + 30 days = May 41. May 41 = June 10.)

Note. If the tax invoice in (b) is issued within 14 days of the basic tax point, i.e. by 25 May 2004, an actual tax point will be created. This would be the date of issue of the invoice.

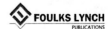

ACTIVITY 2

BVC Limited
Grand House,
Main Way,
Stockport,
Cheshire SK1 2RW

Invoice number 68682

Date/tax point: 15 October 20X3

VAT number 123 4567 89

To: Dorway Limited
Fresh House
76 John's Walk
Manchester M8 4RG

Quantity	Description	Rate of VAT	Amount excluding VAT
			£
25	blue widgets at £4.20 each	17.5%	105.00
40	green widgets at £5.15each	17.5%	206.00
			311.00
VAT			54.42
Total amount payable			365.42

ACTIVITY 3

	£
Full price	5,200.00
Less regular discount (20%)	1,040.00
Price before cash discount	4,160.00
Cash discount (1.5%)	62.40
Price net of cash discount	4,097.60
VAT at 17.5%	£721.17

The VAT invoice will show:

	£
Price excluding VAT	4,160.00
VAT	721.17
Total amount payable	4,881.17

If the customer does not take the cash discount, he will pay £4,881.17. If he does take the cash discount of £62.40, he will pay £4,818.77.

ACTIVITY 4

In this example, output tax is calculated as (x 7/47) of the VAT-inclusive sales revenue. Output tax is calculated as 17.5% of the VAT-exclusive cost of inputs (purchases). Remember that the amount of VAT is always rounded down to the nearest £0.01 below.

Output tax was understated in the previous tax period to 31 January, and the understated amount should therefore be added to the VAT liability. This is done by entering the output tax under-statement as a credit in the VAT account. Input tax was also understated in the previous period, which means that not enough tax was reclaimed. The correction in the current period is therefore to reduce the VAT payable. This is done by entering a debit entry in the VAT account. (The corresponding double entries are likely to be to the sales account and the purchases account or other expense account.)

VAT Control Account

	£		£
Purchases (input tax)		Sales (output tax)	
February	294.00	February	793.63
March	303.52	March	1,045.75
April	274.10	April	1,259.40
Under-stated input tax	23.00	Under-stated output tax	16.50
Bad debt relief	17.50		
Balance c/d	2,203.16		
	3,115.28		3,115.28
		Balance b/d	2,203.16

The VAT control account shows a credit balance of £2,203.16 at the end of the quarter to 30 April 20X4. The trader must remit this amount to HM Customs and Excise with the VAT return for the quarter.

CHAPTER 13

ACTIVITY 1

Workings:

Output tax = 9,502 − 385 + 245 + error correction 107 = 9,469

Input tax = 3,786 − 152 + 1,172 = 4,806

Value of sales excluding VAT = 54,300 − 2,200 = 52,100

Value of purchases excluding VAT = 17,400 + 5,128 – 870 + 3,525 + 3,244 = 28,427.

Note: The correction of the error adds to the amount payable to Customs and Excise, so it is included in the box 1 total.

The form would be completed as follows.

Value Added Tax Return

For Official Use

For the period

HM Customs
and Excise

01 09 03 **to** 30 11 03

Registration Number	Period
454 6767 23	04 03

ZAX

3 HIGH DRIVE

CANTERBURY

KENT   CT5 6EW

**You could be liable to a financial penalty
if your completed return and all the VAT payable
are not received by the due date.**

Due date: 31 12 03

Fold Here

For official use

Before you fill in this form please read the notes on the back and the VAT leaflet *"Filling in your VAT return"*. Fill in all boxes clearly in ink, and write 'none' where necessary. Don't put a dash or leave any box blank. If there are no pence write '**00**' in the pence columns. Do not enter more than one amount in any box.

			£	p
For official use	VAT due in this period on **sales** and other outputs	**1**	9,469	00
	VAT due in this period on **acquisitions** from other **EC Member States**	**2**	NONE	
	Total VAT due (the sum of 1 and 2)	**3**	9,469	00
	VAT reclaimed in this period on **purchases** and other inputs (including acquisitions from the EC)	**4**	4,806	00
	Net VAT to be paid to Customs or reclaimed by you **(Difference between boxes 3 and 4)**	**5**	4,663	00
	Total value of **sales** and all other outputs excluding any VAT. **Including your box 8 figure**	**6**	52,100	00
	Total value of **purchases** and all other inputs excluding any VAT. **Including your box 9 figure**	**7**	28,427	00
	Total value of all **supplies** of goods and related services, excluding any VAT, to other **EC Member States**	**8**	NONE	00
	Total value of all **acquisitions** of goods and related services, excluding any VAT, from other **EC Member States**	**9**	NONE	00

If you are enclosing a payment please tick the box.

DECLARATION: You, or someone on your behalf, must sign below.

I, ...declare that the

(Full name of signatory in BLOCK LETTERS)

information given above is true and complete.

Signature .... Date ....

A false declaration can result in prosecution.

VAT 100 (Full)   IB (October 2000)

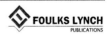
FOULKS LYNCH
PUBLICATIONS

CHAPTER 14

ACTIVITY 1

Workings:

Output tax = 15,260 – 385 + 736 + correction of error 35 = 15,646

Input tax = 5,530 – 175 + 997 + bad debt relief (77 + 56) = 6,485

Value of sales excluding VAT = 87,200 – 3,150 + 4,210 = 88,260

Value of purchases excluding VAT = 25,104 + 6,500 – 1,000 + 4,000 + 1,700 = 36,304.

The error correction is added to the box 1 total because it increases the total amount of VAT payable.

Bad debt relief is not yet available on the debt due on 30 June, because the minimum six month period has not yet expired by 30 November.

The form would be completed as follows.

Note: The declaration should be signed and dated, and the box indicating that a payment is enclosed with the VAT return should be ticked. These items are not shown here.

Value Added Tax Return

For Official Use

For the period

HM Customs
and Excise

01 09 03 **to** 30 11 03

SAM COSTAIN

4 THE YARD

BEECH WAY

IPSWICH   IP3 5XZ

Registration Number	Period
712 7393 88	04 03

**You could be liable to a financial penalty
if your completed return and all the VAT payable
are not received by the due date.**

Due date: 31 12 03

Fold | Here

| For
official
use | |

Before you fill in this form please read the notes on the back and the VAT leaflet "Filling in your VAT return". Fill in all boxes clearly in
ink, and write 'none' where necessary. Don't put a dash or leave any box blank. If there are no pence write '**00**' in the pence columns. Do not
enter more than one amount in any box.

For official use				£	p
	VAT due in this period on **sales** and other outputs	**1**		15,646	00
	VAT due in this period on **acquisitions** from other **EC Member States**	**2**		NONE	
	Total VAT due (the sum of 1 and 2)	**3**		15,646	00
	VAT reclaimed in this period on **purchases** and other inputs (including acquisitions from the EC)	**4**		6,485	00
	Net VAT to be paid to Customs or reclaimed by you **(Difference between boxes 3 and 4)**	**5**		9,161	00
	Total value of **sales** and all other outputs excluding any VAT. **Including your box 8 figure**	**6**		88,260	**00**
	Total value of **purchases** and all other inputs excluding any VAT. **Including your box 9 figure**	**7**		36,304	**00**
	Total value of all **supplies** of goods and related services, excluding any VAT, to other **EC Member States**	**8**		NONE	**00**
	Total value of all **acquisitions** of goods and related services, excluding any VAT, from other **EC Member States**	**9**		NONE	**00**

If you are enclosing
a payment please
tick the box.

DECLARATION: You, or someone on your behalf, must sign below.

I,...declare that the

(Full name of signatory in BLOCK LETTERS)

information given above is true and complete.

Signature .... Date ....

A false declaration can result in prosecution.

VAT 100 (Full)   IB (October 2000)

FOULKS LYNCH
PUBLICATIONS

ACTIVITY 2

She will make nine interim payments of VAT, each of £1,490 (10% of the estimated annual liability) and then a final balancing payment (or possibly will receive a balancing repayment of tax). The interim payments will be at the end of months 4 to 12 inclusive, which in this case will be from the end of December to the end of August inclusive. The balancing payment will be two months after the end of the 12-month period, which in this case is at the end of October. The payment should accompany her annual VAT return.

ACTIVITY 3

The output tax for box 1 consists of:

The input tax for box 4 consists of:

	£
VAT on expenditures	30,450.91
Bad debt relief	35.00
Overstatement of input tax from previous year	45.50
	30,531.41

The balancing payment is:

	£
Total VAT due	87,580.50
VAT reclaimed	30,531.41
	57,049.09
Instalments paid (9 x £5,400)	48,600.00
Balancing payment due	8,449.09

This payment, together with the VAT annual return, should be submitted no later than 28 February 20X4, two months after the year end.

Value Added Tax Return

For the period

HM Customs
and Excise

01 01 X3 **to** 31 12 X3

For Official Use

FRW TRADERS

12 HIGH STREET

KENSINGTON

LONDON   W8 8XX

Registration Number

312 7564 97

Period

**You could be liable to a financial penalty
if your completed return and all the VAT payable
are not received by the due date.**

Due date: 28 02 X4

Fold | Here

**For
official
use**

Before you fill in this form please read the notes on the back and the VAT leaflet *"Filling in your VAT return".* Fill in all boxes clearly in ink, and write 'none' where necessary. Don't put a dash or leave any box blank. If there are no pence write '**00**' in the pence columns. Do not enter more than one amount in any box.

For official use			£	p
VAT due in this period on **sales** and other outputs	**1**		87,580	50
VAT due in this period on **acquisitions** from other **EC Member States**	**2**		NONE	
Total VAT due (the sum of 1 and 2)	**3**		87,580	50
VAT reclaimed in this period on **purchases** and other inputs (including acquisitions from the EC)	**4**		30,531	41
Net VAT to be paid to Customs or reclaimed by you **(Difference between boxes 3 and 4)**	**5**		57,049	09
Total value of **sales** and all other outputs excluding any VAT. **Including your box 8 figure**	**6**		500,460	00
Total value of **purchases** and all other inputs excluding any VAT. **Including your box 9 figure**	**7**		174,005	00
Total value of all **supplies** of goods and related services, excluding any VAT, to other **EC Member States**	**8**		NONE	00
Total value of all **acquisitions** of goods and related services, excluding any VAT, from other **EC Member States**	**9**		NONE	00

If you are enclosing a payment please tick the box.

DECLARATION: You, or someone on your behalf, must sign below.

I,..declare that the

(Full name of signatory in BLOCK LETTERS)

information given above is true and complete.

Signature .... Date ....

A false declaration can result in prosecution.

VAT 100 (Full)   IB (October 2000)

FOULKS LYNCH
PUBLICATIONS

INDEX

FOULKS LYNCH
PUBLICATIONS

FOULKS LYNCH
PUBLICATIONS

FOULKS LYNCH
PUBLICATIONS

TEXTBOOK REVIEW FORM

Thank you for choosing a Foulks Lynch Textbook for the AAT NVQ/SVQ in Accounting. As we are constantly striving to improve our products, we would be grateful if you could provide us with feedback about how useful you found this textbook.

Name: ....

Address: ....

....

Email: ....

Why did you decide to purchase this textbook?

Have used them in the past	☐
Recommended by lecturer	☐
Recommended by friend	☐
Saw advertising	☐
Other (please specify)	☐

Have you used the Foulks Lynch workbooks?

Yes	☐
No	☐

How do you study?

At a college	☐
On a distance learning course	☐
Home study	☐
Other	☐

Please specify...

Overall opinion of this textbook

	Excellent	Adequate	Poor
Introductory pages	☐	☐	☐
Coverage of standards	☐	☐	☐
Clarity of explanations	☐	☐	☐
Diagrams	☐	☐	☐
Activities	☐	☐	☐
Self-test questions	☐	☐	☐
Layout	☐	☐	☐
Index	☐	☐	☐

If you have further comments/suggestions or have spotted any errors, please write them on the next page.

Please return this form to: Veronica Wastell, Publisher, Foulks Lynch, FREEPOST 2254, Feltham TW14 0BR

Other comments/suggestions and errors

AAT Order Form

4 The Griffin Centre, Staines Road, Feltham, Middlesex, TW14 0HS, UK.
Tel: +44 (0) 20 8831 9990 Fax: + 44 (0) 20 8831 9991
Order online: www.foulkslynch.com Email: sales@ewfl-global.com

For assessments in 2003/2004		Textbooks		Workbooks		Combined Textbooks/ Workbooks	
Foundation stage – NVQ/SVQ 2							
1 & 2	Receipts and Payments	£10.95	☐	£10.95	☐		
3	Preparing Ledger Balances and an Initial Trial Balance	£10.95	☐	£10.95	☐		
4	Supplying Information for Management Control					£10.95	☐
21*	Working with Computers					£10.95	☐
23#	Achieving Personal Effectiveness and Health & Safety					£10.95	☐
Intermediate stage – NVQ/SVQ 3							
5	Maintaining Financial Records and Preparing Accounts	£10.95	☐	£10.95	☐		
6	Recording and Evaluating Cost and Revenue	£10.95	☐	£10.95	☐		
7	Preparing Reports and Returns	£10.95	☐	£10.95	☐		
8 & 9	Performance Management, Value Enhancement and Resource Planning and Control	£10.95	☐	£10.95	☐		
Technician stage – NVQ/SVQ 4							
10	Managing Systems and People in the Accounting Environment	£10.95	☐	£10.95	☐		
11	Preparing Financial Statements	£10.95	☐	£10.95	☐		
15	Cash Management and Credit Control	£10.95	☐	£10.95	☐		
17	Implementing Auditing Procedures	£10.95	☐	£10.95	☐		
18	Business Taxation FA 2003	£10.95	☐	£10.95	☐		
19	Personal Taxation FA 2003	£10.95	☐	£10.95	☐		

* Unit 21 can be taken at Foundation Level or Intermediate Level
\# Unit 23 can be taken at any level

Postage, Packaging and Delivery (Per Item):

	First	Each Extra
UK	£5.00	£2.00
Europe (incl ROI and CI)	£7.00	£4.00
Rest of World	£22.00	£8.00

Product Sub Total £..................	Post & Packaging £.................	Order Total £....................	(Payments in UK £ Sterling)

Customer Details

☐ Mr ☐ Mrs ☐ Ms ☐ Miss Other ....

Initials:................................... Surname: ....

Address: ....

....

....

Postcode: ....

Telephone: ....

Email: ....

Fax: ....

Delivery Address – if different from above

Address: ....

....

Postcode: ....

Telephone: ....

Payment

1 I enclose Cheque/PO/Bankers Draft for £.....................................
Please make cheques payable to '**Foulks Lynch**'.

2 Charge MasterCard/Visa/Switch a/c no:

⊔⊔⊔⊔ ⊔⊔⊔⊔ ⊔⊔⊔⊔ ⊔⊔⊔⊔

Valid from: ⊔⊔⊔   Expiry date: ⊔⊔⊔

Issue No: (Switch only) ⊔⊔

Signature: .... Date: ....

Declaration
I agree to pay as indicated on this form and understand that
Foulks Lynch Terms and Conditions apply (available on request).
Signature: .... Date: ....

Notes: Prices are correct at time of going to print but are subject to change

Delivery please allow:	United Kingdom	– 5 working days
	Eire & EU Countries	– 10 working days
	Rest of World	– 10 working days

Notes: All orders over 1kg will be fully tracked & insured.
Signature required on receipt of order. Delivery times
subject to stock availability.